QMW Library

23 1103556 5

DATE DUE FOR RETURN

01. DEC		2 0 MAR 2000
	- 6 JAN 1998	
04. FEB 93	16 JAN 1998	- 5 MAY 2000
		8 JUN 2001
04. FEB 93	- 9 FEB 1998	1 2 MAR 2002
04. FEB 93	1 MAY 1998	2 2 MAY 2006
17. JUN. 1994	- 2 OCT 1998	
03. DEC 93	02 OCT 1998	
2 5 NOV 1994	19 OCT 1998	
16 JUN 1995	9/11/98	
12 FEB 1996	- 8 DEC 1998	
7 May 96	- 9 NOV 1	

W
FR
QMUL LIBRARY

D1380518

WITHDRAWN FROM STOCK
UNIVERSITY LIBRARY

0165186
29.7.91

CONFLICTS OF DISCOURSE

PETER W. EVANS *editor*

Conflicts of discourse: Spanish literature in the Golden Age

MANCHESTER UNIVERSITY PRESS
Manchester and New York

distributed exclusively in the USA and Canada
. by ST. MARTIN'S PRESS

UNIV.
LONDON
COLLEGE

Copyright © Manchester University Press 1990

Whilst copyright in the volume as a whole is vested in Manchester University Press, copyright in individual chapters belongs to their respective authors, and no chapter may be reproduced wholly or in part without express permission in writing of both author and publisher.

Published by Manchester University Press
Oxford Road, Manchester M13 9PL, UK
and Room 400, 175 Fifth Avenue, New York, NY 10010, USA

Distributed exclusively in the USA and Canada
by St. Martin's Press, Inc.,
175 Fifth Avenue, New York, NY 10010, USA

British Library cataloguing in publication data
Conflicts of discourse: Spanish literature in the Golden Age.
   1. Spanish literature, 1516–1700 – Critical studies
   I. Evans, Peter W.
   860.9003

Library of Congress cataloging in publication data
Conflicts of discourse: Spanish literature in the Golden Age / edited by
   Peter W. Evans.
       p.   cm.
     ISBN 0-7190-3192-3
     1. Spanish literature – Classical period, 1500–1700 – History and
   criticism.   I. Evans, Peter William.
   PQ6064.C66   1990
   860.9'003 – dc20   90-31458

ISBN 0 7190 3192 3 *hardback*

Printed in Great Britain
by Billings of Worcester

CONTENTS

PREFACE

University modern languages departments are entering another period of crisis. In the UK at least, as the enterprise culture spreads its wings over a civilising but hybrid discipline — all too shy in the past of theorising its own *raison d'être* — utilitarian, pragmatic initiatives are in vogue, the *prima facie* but not primarily cost-effective benefits of the old 'content-based' courses out of favour. In some ways, of course, we have only ourselves to blame, for we have made it easy for the Philistines. Where any contact existed at all in the past between departments and the foreign countries whose culture we were supposed to be teaching, complacent indifference towards stressing the vital importance of the spoken modern language, tortured but elitist justifications of research and publication on arcane specialisms of all too often marginal significance to the core discipline, stodgy diets of traditional courses, theoretical and critical practice increasingly out of step with new approaches being introduced in sister disciplines, have all taken their toll of the place of literature in modern language departments, making it easy for the Philistines to stake their claim.

All of this, plus disenchantment with literature by schoolteachers coping with a non-reading culture, falling numbers in high grade A level applicants, has created a perfect climate for market-forces gurus of government and higher education to interfere in the working lives of modern language departments. So it's no Calderón today boys, just clapping on the headphones and mastering the syntax of Swiss cheese-buying supermarket French, the chronomorphs of Costa-packet travel-agent Spanish, or how do I develop my communicative skills and say 'car-phones' in all those EEC languages we're frantically learning for the 1992 bonanza of free-marketeering initiatives of Europe's latest and in some ways tattiest Golden Age?

Once again, it's time to live by bread alone. But what few seem to realise, of course, is that even car-phone salesmen actually want to talk about something other than car-phones over dinner with their Anglo-Saxon equivalents. Even there, at the up-town wine bar and in the *soignée brasserie* it's Calderón as well as car-phone talk that will be at a premium. When everyone's exhausted the conversational potential of the Dow Jones Index, there will still be a desire and a desperate need, for the benefit of wine-bar patrons as well as the rest, to understand the roots of foreign cultures, partly so as to know how the continental mind works, but partly also so as to become informed about the shared assumptions of interrelated European civilisations, and not least so as to be able to know how it has all come to this: the necessity of defending scholarly enquiry into philosophy, art and history in a Mammon-crazed generation.

This volume takes two things for granted: first, the primary importance of culture-based courses in modern languages departments; second, the need to become familiar with and to absorb, though not necessarily to accept either wholly or in part, developments in poststructuralism. The new critical approaches are used here as a way of opening up mummified texts. There is no dominant theoretical position uniformly adopted by all the contributors. In one chapter, moreover, after much careful argument, deconstruction is eventually considered unhelpful as a way of talking about Cervantes. But even in such an instance thinking about new premises, testing the old against the new is a healthy exercise, at the very least offering the possibility of more persuasive justification of the old.

The three broad aims of the volume are: first, to argue the case for standing by literature courses in modern language departments; second, to continue the vital but largely restricted work of applying to Golden Age texts the theories and practice of post-structuralism (we very much regret not being able to find space for the Celestina, Garcilaso, Tirso and Quevedo); third, to reaffirm the historical and cultural importance of a period of Spanish civilisation seriously in danger of being eclipsed by obsession with the ultra-modern or the ultra-practical. Attempts to understand fully the minds of those hyper-modern symbols of the New Spain, Pedro Almodóvar and the car-phone salesman, can only be heightened by familiarity with the work, for instance, of that great seventeenth-century Jesuit stylist and moralist, Gracián. Literature in general, and Spanish Golden Age literature in particular, is in dire need not of yet more re-evaluation but of theoretical and critical revitalisation, of subjection to processes aiming to discover not only how those texts mirrored or sabotaged the cultural, sociological and historical clichés of the age, but also in what ways it seems necessary now in the last decade of the twentieth century and beyond to continue to explicate them and to allow them an integral, front-rank place in the curriculum of civilised establishments of education.

What from the 40s to the 60s the Mays, Woodwards, Wilsons and Parkers did for Golden Age literature, insisting – like the authors they wrote about — on the centrality of literature in the workings of the whole culture, the inheritors of the post-structuralist legacy, using different methodologies, must do in the 90s. We must take this simultaneously marvellous and conventional, consistent and contradictory, challenging and subservient literature out of its moribund academic contexts — and the uninhabited wastes to which the Philistines would condemn it — and into the hearts and minds of anyone unenthusiastic about spending an entire university career adjusting the volume of sound and fury flooding out of those over-heated headphones.

ACKNOWLEDGEMENTS

I am deeply grateful to John Banks for his support and encouragement throughout all stages of this project; to Juanita Bullough, also of MUP, for help and advice. Sue Davidson, Secretary in the Department of Spanish and Latin American Studies, typed parts of the manuscript. The section on *El mayor encanto, amor* in Margaret Greer's chapter is a reworking of part of an article published as 'Art and power in the spectacle plays of Calderón de la Barca', *Publications of the Modern Language Association*, CIV, 1989: 329–39.

I would like to record my gratitude to the University of Newcastle upon Tyne for granting me leave of absence from April to October 1989 partly in order to put together this volume of essays.

P.W.E.
University of Newcastle upon Tyne

LIST OF CONTRIBUTORS

PETER W. EVANS
is Senior Lecturer in Spanish and Latin American Studies at the University of Newcastle upon Tyne.

ANTHONY CLOSE
is Lecturer in Spanish at the University of Cambridge.

LORNA CLOSE
is Lecturer in Spanish at the University of Cambridge.

NINA COX DAVIS
is Professor of Spanish at the University of Washington, St Louis, Missouri.

MARGARET R. GREER
is Professor of Spanish at the University of Princeton.

KAREN HOLLIS
is a Graduate Student at the University of California, San Diego.

GEORGE MARISCAL
is Professor of Spanish at the University of California, San Diego.

PAUL JULIAN SMITH
is Reader in Spanish at Queen Mary College, University of London.

HENRY W. SULLIVAN
is Professor of Spanish at the University of Missouri-Columbia.

COLIN P. THOMPSON
is Lecturer in Spanish at the University of Oxford.

1 GEORGE MARISCAL

An introduction to the ideology of Hispanism in the US and Britain

One of the most pressing issues confronting those of us who write about early modern Spanish literature has to do with the theoretical revolution of the last twenty-five years. Given the emergence of new reading strategies within an institutional context still dominated by traditional interpretive models, to what extent will we be able to productively rethink the fundamental categories of our discipline? As we begin to answer this question and thus reconstitute the field of Spanish Golden Age studies, we will need to understand how the critical practices that preceded us were made possible and, more importantly, the ways in which we continue to be implicated in them. In my account of several key moments in the genealogy of Anglophone Hispanism, however, I will avoid positing simple origins. The discipline marked as 'Spanish studies' was less the creation of great men than it was the intersection of multiple and often contradictory practices. Thus I want to employ another approach to historiography, itself a product of contemporary theory, that seeks to problematise all origins and subvert conventional narratives. The desire for sources and beginnings that motivates traditional criticism will not be easily fulfilled by a genealogical account such as mine that is not written as a continuous process but as a series of complex transformations within a sociocultural field.

What is at stake in refusing to accept that Hispanism emerged from the mind of individual critics or that its history is one of the progressive revelation of truth is nothing less than what the relationship of our own writing will be to literature, academic institutions, and contemporary social problems. Although I will necessarily speak about the patriarchs of Spanish studies, my concern is to dismantle the names Ticknor, Fitzmaurice-Kelly and others so that we can begin to map the ideological terrain that produced each of these critics and their work. The protagonists of my essay, therefore, are

1

not the founding fathers and their descendants nor even the critical projects with which they attempted to represent Spanish literature to Anglo-American culture.[1] I am more interested in the wider field of discourses and practices that made these projects possible. Who or what, then, will be the principal actors in my account? The powerful and persistent tropes: Nationality, Man, the Individual, the Literary Work.

I

It may indeed seem the height of presumption for any foreigner to inquire into the qualities of the cryptic and elusive genius of Spain.
A. F. G. Bell, 1938

It is not an insignificant irony of history that to a great extent Anglophone Hispanism took shape at the crossroads of German Romanticism, New England Federalism and an American scholar who in 1818 made his only journey to Spain. It would be difficult to find in the cultural history of the West a more striking example of the ways in which the founding gestures of an institutional discourse were less the actions of individuals than they were the products of multiple practices and interests. If the wealthy Boston merchant Abiel Smith had not made a contribution to Harvard in 1814 for the establishment of a chair of French and Spanish, the emergence of modern Hispanism as a disciplinary field might have been deferred and realised elsewhere. But when George Ticknor accepted the position in 1819 for an annual salary of $1,000 (with the stipulation that he not be required to teach language), the formidable disciplinary tools of classical and German philology, which Ticknor had acquired at Göttingen, were directed at peninsular culture.[2] Thus the encounter between northern European high culture and southern European literature was concretised in the work of one of the first cultural prophets of the newly-invented American nation. Using his lecture notes as a foundation, Ticknor published his *History of Spanish Literature* in 1849. Previous manuals of Spanish literature such as that of Bouterwek were soon eclipsed by Ticknor's three-volume study. For almost half a century, it stood as the only text of its kind in any language.

The emergence of Spanish literary history through Ticknor's work cannot be understood apart from the project to construct a national literature in the US undertaken in the middle decades of the nineteenth century. In the simplest of terms, Spain was to function as Other for the construction of an American imperial identity. In his first lectures as Smith Professor of French and Spanish and Belles Lettres at Harvard, Ticknor figured the national character of Spain as one of 'lofty enthusiasm' for chivalry and Catholicism. For his New England entrepreneurial and Protestant constituency, this was tantamount to pronouncing Spanish culture dead. The general decadence associated in Ticknor's intellectual milieu with both Spain and France would have a profound effect upon the initial moments of US Hispanism, for if the United States was an empire on the rise, Spain was an ominous emblem of an empire in ruins.

Madame de Staël had theorised nationality as a critical trope in her *De l'Allemagne* (1813). Her method there and in other works established the unfortunate precedent of making vast generalisations about national cultures on the basis of a minimal experience in the countries the critic sought to represent. But in reality Madame de Staël was less interested in constructing a typology of national identities than she was in figuring the alterity of those cultures against what in her opinion was the decadent and failed culture of France. In Ticknor's hands, a similar method cast the US as Other to Europe, and the idealist construct of national character became the basis for his own account of Spain. In a letter written shortly after the publication of his *History*, he stated: 'for a great many years I have been persuaded that literary history... should be made, like civil history, to give a knowledge of the character of the people to which it relates.'[3] Once the essential qualities of 'Spanishness' were catalogued they could be set over and against individual texts. The *comedia* was a privileged form in so far as it reproduced indigenous values: 'With all its faults, then, this old Spanish drama, founded on the great traits of the national character, maintained itself in the popular favor as long as that character existed in its original attributes....'[4] Those writers who abandoned or exaggerated the basic principles which constituted their nationality contributed to the decline of their culture. Thus Ticknor could condemn both the formal innovations of a Garcilaso and the repressive mechanisms of the Inquisition on similar grounds − the former abandoned the popular essence of Spanish literature whereas the latter had carried to an extreme the nation's innate religious faith.

4   Conflicts of discourse

The discourse of national character through which the first history of Spanish literature was written carried with it a variety of political implications, all of them conservative. The dominant ideology of the New England literary establishment was premised almost exclusively on the metaphor of the organic nation–state, an entity that flourished or decayed according to divine intervention and not because of social and material conditions. The issue of historical change was therefore displaced on to an all-powerful Providence that employed national character as a medium for its own projects. Thus Ticknor's verdict on the future of Spain was at best quietistic: 'The law of progress is on Spain for good or evil, as it is on the other nations of the earth, and her destiny, like theirs, is in the hand of God, and will be fulfilled' (quoted in Tyack, p. 141). In Ticknor's account we find very little of the voluntarism and rampant individualism which would inform those representatives of US Hispanism writing in the early decades of our own century.

But the submission to divine will did not preclude the literary critic from positing a cultural homogeneity designed to forestall social change. Ticknor's fundamental elitism was brilliantly outlined by Thomas Hart, Jr in a 1954 article.[5] What Ticknor admired most about Spain and those of its writers he selected for praise was the fact that the ideology of the ruling elite seemed to be happily accepted by all classes. It is quite a long historical but a rather short ideological leap from seventeenth-century Spain to nineteenth-century Boston, represented by the anecdote in which Ticknor lectured Thackeray that the mark of a gentleman is his appearance since 'good blood shows itself in good features'. But since in the American republic one could not claim status solely on the basis of blood, all social classes, in accordance with the essential character of the nation, must be governed by 'one costume of national manners'. In this way, both the status quo and more importantly propertied landowners were protected from the masses that threatened to rise up from below. The responsibility of the critic as the guardian of national culture was to be always alert to the potential threats posed by immorality, bad taste and (we can only assume) inferior blood.[6] Above all else, the professional scholar must keep himself 'saved from the enthrallment and degradation of party politics and party passions, and consecreated to letters' (quoted in Tyack, p. 21). The opposition between politics and criticism enunciated by Ticknor has remained firmly in place throughout the various permutations of Spanish studies.

The hegemony of national character within the discourse of literary criticism was relatively short-lived, but its elaboration into theories of race and culture would have grave consequences in our own century. That nationalism was the attendant ideology at the 'birth' of Hispanism is a symptom of a larger process through which the construction of nations necessarily coincides with the emergence of new disciplines and practices designed to regulate daily life. But in the case of the first history of Spanish literature, it was not so much the nation–state of Spain that was being produced as it was the national culture of the US. Through an economy of alterity and difference, Spain, the 'broken column' (Ticknor's image), played no small part in the invention of the young American empire.

A half-century after the appearance of Ticknor's *History*, the second comprehensive study of Spanish literature would appear, this time in England. In Spain, Amador de los Ríos had already published his *Historia crítica de la literatura española* (1865), but his investigations had reached only to the initial moments of the early modern period. The next attempt at an all-inclusive account of the literary production of Spain would again be made by an English-speaking Hispanist.

Not unlike Ticknor's earlier project, James Fitzmaurice-Kelly's *A History of Spanish Literature* (1898) proved to be anything but a stable text from the moment of its inception. The composition of Ticknor's *History* had been the result of a prolonged process of gathering materials across Europe carried out by an army of collectors and agents. By the 1840s, Ticknor was said to possess the largest private library of Spanish materials ever assembled. In a real way, therefore, his *History* was the product of intertextual scholarship and multiple authorship rather than the work of a single man. The collaboration of the young Spanish scholar, Pascual Gayangos, was an especially crucial element in the completion of Ticknor's project, and Ticknor himself continued to supplement each new edition. Through a similar process of revision and collaboration, Fitzmaurice-Kelly's *History* underwent continual changes in both form and content. The 1901 Spanish translation by Adolfo Bonilla, for example, offered the reader an additional 200 pages of Bonilla's own commentary; the 1913 edition was restructured and written in French by Fitzmaurice-Kelly himself. But despite the complex origin of these first two seminal texts of Anglophone Hispanism, the context through which each took shape was fundamentally different. To cite only the most obvious example: rather than the New England and Protestant ideology of Ticknor, Fitzmaurice-Kelly's *History* was informed by a Catholicism that compelled him to foreground many of the types of writing otherwise ignored by Ticknor (e.g. the mystics).

By the end of the nineteenth century, the ideology of national character had been supplemented by an emergent discourse of truth and human nature. The kind of literary history that could now be written was no longer as concerned with the imagining of nations as it was with the erasure of all boundaries thought to be artificial and contrary to the interest of representing bourgeois values as universal. This is not to suggest that the discourse of national character played no part in the production of Fitzmaurice-Kelly's project. On the contrary, the chapter devoted to the 'Golden Age' could not have been written without the figure of Spain as a sign of difference with relation to the other nations of the West: 'Her great writers were undoubtedly men of singular independence and originality; their work adds point to the saying that Spain is not quite in the European current of thought.'[7] And the idea of a 'Spanish mind', a construct that continues to prosper in our own time, is at the centre of all of Fitzmaurice-Kelly's judgements.[8] The truth of Spanish literature was contradictory at best in so far as the writing produced in Spain was 'derivative' (based on French and Italian models) yet had 'a characteristic savour of its own'. Nonetheless, the literary historian's ability to generalise and classify could ultimately reconcile all contradictions and reproduce the essential reality of both Spanishness and Spanish literature.

But in the work of Fitzmaurice-Kelly the trope of nationality was given a new function by linking it to the even more powerful humanist myth of a human nature that transcends local conditions and specific historical moments. The essential characteristics of this nature revealed themselves in studies of the 'great writers' who signify a body of values thought to be the common inheritance of Man. It was on the basis of such a cultural imaginary that Fitzmaurice-Kelly was able to cast Shakespeare, for example, against certain Spanish writers in order to situate them along a hierarchical chain of value. The case of Lope de Vega is representative of the ways in which being the poet of the national character was no longer sufficient grounds for praise as it had been for Ticknor's generation: 'Lope no doubt lacks Shakespeare's ample and embracing note. He does not portray universal human nature, but human nature as it manifested itself at a given time in given conditions. He is not the dramatist of humanity the world over. He is the typical dramatist of his own race ...' (*New History*, p. 305). In a similar vein, Quevedo is dismissed for being 'too immitigably Spanish, too representative of the seventeenth century to please generally' (*New History*, p. 362); Cervantes, on the other hand, is 'unquestionably the most glorious figure in the annals of Spanish literature, but his very universality makes him less representative of his race'.[9] Fitzmaurice-Kelly's language here sets him decisively apart from Ticknor's generation. For the emergent discourse of universality, the classic writer is no longer he who embodies a national essence, but rather he who 'overcomes' local circumstances and racial characteristics. The consequences of this revised paradigm for the formation of the Spanish canon were considerable; in its strongest form, the dualism universal/particular produced those oppositions (such as Cervantes/Quevedo) that continue to hold together all contemporary forms of Golden Age criticism. At the turn of the century, Cervantes was set against Quevedo on the basis of which of the two best represents Man's common heritage; in later moments, the same false dichotomy would be defended on the grounds of politics, style or the personal temperament.

II

> In this America of English language and origins I see a certain broadness of vision ... that is opposed to the exclusive narrowness of the island-dwelling English. [It is upon this that] I found my hope that the fruits of the Spanish genius ... will be better known and studied here than in Great Britain. Juan Valera, 1913

By the decades of the 1940s and 1950s, it was clear that the author of *Pepita Jiménez* had proven to be a poor prognosticator of the development of Spanish, especially Golden Age, studies. For it was precisely in Britain that a critical practice interested in early modern peninsular texts emerged and ultimately reconfigured the entire canon of Spanish literature. These developments were in no way the result of the critic's nationality as the quotation from Valera suggests. Valera's remark reminds us that the trope of national identity is a persistent one and cannot be easily displaced, not even by the powerful myth of human nature. But it was this latter construct that would reconstitute itself around the figures of the Individual and the Work in a critical enterprise that emanated from centres of cultural hegemony such as Cambridge. Just as the discourse of national character had first been spoken in the US through the disciplinary apparatus of Harvard, the developing ideology of liberal humanism would require similar institutional frames for its reproduction.

The period of the 1930s in and around Cambridge has been called by Francis Mulhern the 'moment of *Scrutiny*'.[10] Begun in 1932 by F. R. Leavis, L. C. Knights and others, the influential journal brought together a group of critics who took up a wide range of positions with regard to the relationship between the literary text, history and politics. What distinguished all of these critics from the generation of Ticknor and Fitzmaurice-Kelly, however, was the drive towards a technical language that transformed the literary text into what was to become an increasingly fetishised object. The nineteenth-century critic's function as the elite man of letters and guardian of culture had given way, under the pressure of bourgeois science and the specialisation of knowledge, to the professional critic who removed himself from the social world in order to become an expert reader. As a sign for this important shift in the genealogy of literary studies, *Scrutiny* remains an important cultural marker. The criticism produced by its contributors would reach far beyond English studies and extend even to the traditionally marginal discipline of Spanish Golden Age studies.

It was in the context of Cambridge and the rewriting of English literary history that Edward M. Wilson and Alexander A. Parker began their careers as interpreters of early modern Spanish culture.[11] But the scholarship written by this younger generation of critics would be produced by a different set of tropes than was that of their precursors. The emphasis on the autonomous work and on close textual analysis which informed the methodology of Leavis, James Smith and others associated with the *Scrutiny* circle would constitute the basis of the 'new' Golden Age criticism, and the fundamental tenets of a conservative humanism would underwrite the entire project. The influence of Smith was particularly strong upon the early professional development of both Wilson and Parker. In his 1978 memoir for Wilson, Parker claimed: 'He [Smith] exerted the greatest single influence on Wilson's formation as a literary critic', and in his own collected essays on Calderón, Parker pays special homage to Smith: 'To one man more than any other I owe my "training". He was never formally my teacher, nor was he even a Hispanist ....

He was James Smith, and at the end of my career as a literary historian and critic I wish to place on record this tribute to his memory.'[12]

For Smith, the literary text was a 'fragment [of life] that has been detached, considered and judged by a mind'.[13] But the goal of this criticism went beyond any simple act of isolating living fragments for interpretation. The early modern period in English literature had exercised a persistent fascination for the entire group of critics around *Scrutiny*, and what was at stake for them in the reconstruction of Elizabethan culture was much more than new readings of texts or even adding on to the historical record. According to Mulhern: 'The social and cultural conditions of Old England had, in *Scrutiny*'s view, fostered values of perdurable "human" significance. However, these values were not directly available. It was necessary to "re-create" them, by means of a literary criticism capable of recognising and assaying their significance, historical and contemporary' (Mulhern, pp. 135–6). The reconstruction of the Spanish Golden Age presented a similar opportunity for the recuperation of transcendent values. That the critical gaze of the young Cambridge Hispanists should ultimately fall upon seventeenth-century theatrical practice was logical, perhaps, given their commitment to a Christian world-view and the fact that in an earlier moment the German Romantics' fascination with Calderón had passed over to Cambridge through critics such as FitzGerald and Trench. Whatever the initial attraction to the *comedia* might have been, Parker recalls: 'Students and readers of Spanish literature in the 1930s had to realise that Calderonian plays could, through the ideas they developed, pass human life in review in a way not only historically important for understanding their age, but also universally significant (i.e. acceptable but not necessarily accepted) beyond the time and the place of their composition' (Parker, *The Mind and Art*, p. 13). One is tempted to ask what possible rationale there might have been in the early twentieth century for 'accepting' an aristocratic ideology founded upon a pre-scientific epistemology. More importantly, it is clear that by the late 1930s the ideology of Spanish studies had completed the shift from the imagined category of national character to the metaphysics of universal values. Spain was no longer Other to Anglo-American culture but rather a participant in the ongoing drama of an essential and undifferentiated humanity.[14]

In a process analogous to the one I have used to discuss Ticknor and the beginnings of Spanish literary history, I want to take the work of Parker not as an originary moment but rather as the inter-section of multiple discourses and practices that constituted literary culture in Britain in the pre-war period. It is not my intention to mount a full-scale description of what has come to be called 'the Parkerian method'. Since he first outlined his interpretive model in the influential 1957 article 'The Approach to the Spanish Drama of the Golden Age', Parker has remained faithful to his critical prin-ciples and has emphatically restated them in his latest book, setting them in opposition to more recent methods, especially the 'decon-struction theory of contemporary literary criticism' (Parker, *The Mind and Art*, p. 361). What interests me about what has come to be called Parker's 'thematico-structural approach' are the ways in which its emergence was determined by a specific ideology of the self-sufficient text that won hegemonic status in the 1930s.[15]

Much of the literary criticism produced around Cambridge in the 30s and 40s was constructed upon a number of shared presup-positions, one of the most important of which was a belief in the autonomous literary work and the 'universal values' contained within it. It was this ideological bias that led a number of working critics to scrutinise those texts which lent themselves to an allegorical reading. In the closing paragraph of a 1933 article on metaphysical poetry, for example, James Smith called attention to the *autos sacramentales* of Calderón as a series of texts worthy of critical examination because 'not the language merely, but the action is a metaphysical conceit: it is at once fleshy and spiritual'.[16] The idea of the literary text as an emblem for the mystical act of transubstantiation is a profoundly Catholic construct, and it strikes us today as not too surprising that Parker's first major publication was a study of the *auto* entitled *The Allegorical Drama of Calderón* (1943). I am by no means sug-gesting that this early work by a Hispanist can be traced directly to a casual remark made by an English scholar, despite the fact that the two critics shared an intimate relationship. Such influence-tracing would serve no useful purpose. Nevertheless, the emphasis on dramatic 'action' conceived as the textualisation of abstract ideas would become the structural centre of the reading method propagated by Parker throughout his career. In his laudatory review of Parker's book on the *auto*, Smith restates the idea that 'Calderón's poetry in the *autos* is dramatic poetry: such, that is, as accompanies and represents or "makes real" an action — an action of ideas, their growth, conflict and resolution, but action in the strictest sense of the word.'[17] The proposition that the dramatic text might be more productively read as poetry, traditionally viewed as the least historical genre, would soon become a dominant mode for reading all forms of early modern theatrical practice in Spain.

Given that the literary work was to be conceived as an organic whole, it became possible to break down the action of a dramatic piece, say, into its separate parts in order to show the chain of causality by which the moral message of the theme was conveyed. This procedure had been used by some of the contributors to *Scrutiny* such as Smith and Derek Traversi;[18] in Parker's hands it became a well-oiled mechanism for discerning the structural logic of the Spanish *comedia*. First delineated in 'The approach to the Spanish drama of the Golden Age' (1957) and elaborated later in 'Towards a definition of Calderonian tragedy' (1962), the principle of dramatic causality was designed to reveal the inherent rationality in the composition of the text. On this view, the potential for seeing irreconcilable contradictions both in the literary and the social text was effaced by a functionalism intent upon producing a totalised 'meaning'. In his most recent distillation of the method, Parker writes: 'In general it may be said that literary criticism in this book will aim at disclosing the total meaning of a play by analysing its structure — the way in which the structural elements, plots, characters, and poetic imagery are moulded to fit in with each other' (*The Mind and Art*, p. 24). These concerns continue to organise much *comedia* criticism even today, a fact that attests to the power and productivity of formalist discourse. But as I have already suggested, what is silenced by such a method are all of those cultural materials relegated to an 'outside-the-text' which is then cast as an inferior domain of experience in comparison to the aesthetic.

In a real way, the criticism of E. M. Wilson was more complex although less influential than that of some of his contemporaries, perhaps because of the apparent shifts that marked its development. Wilson's interest in an analytical model supplemented by comparative issues, popular culture and the history of ideas distinguished his method from that of Parker, for example, and Wilson was reportedly unhappy about being included in any so-called British School of Golden Age scholarship. Despite the peculiarly abstract nature of his defence of his methodology ('The words set down on paper are supremely important; to disregard the circumstances in which they were set down may lead to misunderstandings, mental confusions and a kind of spiritual anarchy'), his 1966 appeal for the contextualization of literary texts sets him apart from most of his colleagues and prefigured many of the concerns of present-day new historicists and cultural materialists.[19] But just as Wilson's earlier work on Calderón's imagery had been produced by the same tropes that organised the formalist project – poetic texture, images, structure – these same ideological figures continued to determine much of his later scholarship. It is not unusual, therefore, to find moments in the body of his writings when Wilson aligns himself with the strongest proponents of the autotelic work of art: 'Coleridge remarked that a work of art should contain in itself the reason why it was so and not otherwise (*Biographia literaria*, Chapter XIV). I try to show this in my discussion of *Peribáñez.*'[20]

From our vantage point in the 1990s, it is clear that both Wilson and Parker were above all else influential players in the establishment of formalist variants as the dominant practice within Anglo-American literary criticism. Not unlike the New Criticism of Richards, Eliot and other critics writing on English topics, the moment of the British Hispanists was inextricably linked to Christian values, the reification of the literary text, and the bracketing of history, and to a great extent it is a secular version of this same project that has determined the work of succeeding generations of Golden Age scholars both in Britain and the US. The hegemony of formalism has been continually although not seriously challenged by other forms of Golden Age criticism, and the ideology of universal Man which underwrote it has been reproduced in virtually all successive critical practices. It would be well beyond the scope of this chapter to trace even a fraction of the academic discourses that owe their existence to an investment in the imaginary realm of human nature and the construct of the self-sufficient Individual. Both of these figures have traditionally determined the ways in which the literary text is constituted as an object of study; thus the bourgeois self, in its enclosed isolation, continues to bequeath to us the all-inclusive and unified work of art.

The relatively minor deviation into so-called myth criticism that marked the 1950s did little to blunt the critical establishment's fascination with the formal properties of the literary artefact and a great deal to reinforce its belief in a transcendent realm of human nature. As Terry Eagleton has pointed out, the textual critic believed: 'the more rigorously criticism interrogated the literary object, the more richly it yielded up that sensuous concreteness and vital enactment of value which were of general human relevance'.[21] The move to myth within Hispanism under the influence of Eliade, Jung and Frye was accomplished with little fuss, and was even condoned by Parker himself in a recent statement that is striking in its ingenuousness:

> A sympathetic awareness of this [the function of myth] will be a great help in the understanding of Calderón. It is not that by applying these insights the literary critics is employing the findings of modern psychological and sociological science anachronistically where they cannot possibly apply, for symbols, archetypes and myths have been uncovering what have been aspects of the human psyche and sensibility throughout the centuries and across all frontiers. (*The Mind and Art*, p. 16)

On this view, the autonomous work represented as cut off from the surrounding sphere of human activity, as the more orthodox of the New Critics had wanted it, is suddenly the container of all human experience regardless of racial, class or historical difference. A mystified concept of culture such as this one was particularly compatible with a method that, rather than positing a radically closed work, had always sought to relate the structure of the text to the moral message which was taken to be its generative centre.

The move from a moral–formalist approach to the history of ideas was a relatively simple one in so far as the autonomy of the text was transferred to the autonomous sphere of literary discourse or culture. This realignment of the discursive formation of Golden Age studies seemed to reconcile once and for all the problem of how Spain might be both Other (nation-specific) and Self (universal) in relation to the Anglo-American tradition. More specifically, it made possible the work of one critic whose influence was always demonstrably less than that of Parker, Wilson, Wardropper and others, perhaps because his method was overly explicit in its unmasking of bourgeois criticism's terms. I am referring to Otis Green who, in his encyclopaedic *Spain and the Western Tradition* (1963–66), made the last great attempt to insert early modern Spanish writing into the canon of 'world literature'. Those of us interested in a materialist criticism cannot help but be attracted to the scope and range of archival documentation in Green's work, but in the end the idealism permeating his approach situates it in too close a proximity to the reigning formalisms against which it was conceived.

At the centre of Green's project we find the now familiar figure of the bourgeois individual, triumphant and self-sufficient. This should in no way strike us as odd. Universal Man in all of his various guises stands as one of the founding principles for all the critical paradigms we have discussed, from the earliest constructions of a literary history of Spain to the British Hispanists and beyond. But what sets Green apart from these other representatives of Anglophone Spanish studies is the explicit and unabashed fashion in which he promotes humanism's originary myth of the Individual, a myth that to a great extent has determined not only the literary and cultural history of the US but its political history as well.

A product of the era of manifest destiny, Green was born in the Midwest eight months after the outbreak of war with Spain and spent part of his childhood in one of the newly appropriated colonies – Cuba. The Manichaean world view of the McKinley–Roosevelt doctrine would resonate in a later academic discourse that Green claimed as his own: 'I see the genuine scholar as the preserver of truth ... in the long conflict of enlightenment with the powers of darkness ...'[22] If one were to appeal to the hoary trope of national character, one might argue that what is uniquely nationalistic about Green's work is his association of 'enlightenment' with US conservatism. More importantly, in the field of literary studies what marked his writing as distinctly American was his iconoclastic posture towards what he considered to be an earlier 'mistaken' criticism and his unshakeable belief in the unified Self. Green's iconoclasm, however, is curious in that it directs its complaints against established contemporary masters from a position of inferiority, especially with regard to scholarship produced in the Old World. In his preface to the first volume of *Spain and the Western Tradition*, he describes how his work on the context of courtly love was a revision of *idées reçues* and a reversal of *obiter dicta*. Such assertions, made in 1961, find their earliest expression in his 1937 article in which Green had proclaimed: 'The goal of research is not only to add to the store of knowledge, but to escape the atrophy which comes from relying on "authorities",' ('On the goal and method', p. 177). But later in the same piece, Green adopts a deferential tone and concedes that the American scholar can only serve the European patriarchs with humility and respect: 'Not everyone can be a Menéndez Pidal. But we can do what he does on a more modest scale', concluding: 'And if we ourselves cannot rise to the heights of genius, we can at least help furnish the genius with the facts he needs, and in the meantime pursue the studies that please us most.'

Green's eurocentrism and sense of his own belatedness with regared to Spanish criticism was mitigated to a certain extent by his belief that the fundamental goal of all criticism is the personal development of the individual critic. In his later writings, Green was able to unproblematically transfer this notion to the collective entity of the nation. Spain, as an agent of history, struggles to express its Self and so passes through the various stages of growth through which the bourgeois individual takes shape. Thus the title of the first section of volume three of *Spain and the Western Tradition*: 'Self-Realisation'; its goal to trace: 'the development of the national culture – primarily literary culture – from an unsatisfactory state in the fifteenth century to the point where the sense of inferiority to nations ancient or modern has been overcome [to› the problem of how Spain achieved full self-expression in literature' (p. v). The homologous relationship between the evolution of early modern Spain and the critic's own maturation process, in his Oedipal-like struggle with his precursors, is striking. Each volume of *Spain and the Western Tradition* in fact is presented as a moment in the trajectory of the nation. But now the nation is no longer understood as the natural essence of a people as it had been for Ticknor and Fitzmaurice-Kelly; for Green, nationality is reduced to an autonomous aesthetic second nature that germinated in the *Libro de Buen Amor* and bore its final fruit in Calderonian drama. By the end of the third volume (1965), the personification of Spain is complete. The decline of Spanish culture under the Habsburgs occurred because, according to Green, Spain 'failed to meet life's challenge'.

It would not be too much say that in the case of Otis Green the fundamental tropes of bourgeois humanism determined his life as much as his work. His involvement in the activities of hiking and mountain-climbing, the favourite Romantic pastimes which in an earlier time had been shared by Ticknor and Wordsworth, was to be expected since for Green 'meeting life's challenge' meant physically assaulting one's natural surroundings, even within the domain of literary studies. A book on the *cancioneros* (1949) was 'an exploratory tunnel into the "mountain" of fifteenth-century poetry'. Research on the seventeenth century was an attempt upon 'what seemed to be a less promising mountain'. A retrospective view from the age of Gracián is afforded 'from the top of the ridge [where] we shall see how we arrived at our vantage point and what sort of terrain we shall encounter on the other side'. Such language reveals Green's own personal involvements, but more importantly projects a peculiarly American *ethos* of rugged individualism and a deep-seated organicism that drives all of Green's writing back into the Romantic ideology of the unity of Art and Nature. Always on the look-out for 'fruitful fields of study' (Toynbee's phrase), Green describes his own scholarship and its products as the 'gathering of the sheaves', 'threshing' and 'spikes of grain'.

Not until the preface to the final volume of *Spain and the Western Tradition* (1966) do we notice a shift to the language of architecture and a more properly social space. The cornucopia of literary research has become the city or house whose foundations are the historical record waiting to be retrieved from contemporary documents. Suddenly, however, within the drift of Green's own rhetoric, the image of the city is used to signify the ideological foundations of early modern Spanish literature itself:

> Together with the body of religious, historical, and political literature, it [moral thought] forms the substratum of the art-literature which is at all times the vital interest of both the author and the readers of this series. That substratum, revealed as the pedestal that it really is, adds not only comprehensibility to Spanish literature, but a dignity and a beauty born of faith. That faith is not always on the surface; it may indeed be far beneath the surface. Yet one who has lived with that literature for most of his lifetime can scarcely fail to perceive that its authors sought – humbly, modestly, ecstatically, or fanatically – 'a city which has foundations, whose builder and maker is God.'

I have quoted this passage at length because it completes the binding together of the City of Scholarship and the City of God through which the moral authority of theological discourse is transferred to the sphere of literary criticism. Green might well have been unaware that by means of his analogy he had placed himself, as fabricator of the imposing edifice of *Spain and the Western Tradition*, firmly in the place of the Prime Mover or at least an Augustine-like Church Father. But such a conclusion was to be expected, given the brash confidence in 'Self' that informs Green's entire project. Contemplating his creation from above, the critic believes he has produced a dual vision of a past unaffected by the values and biases of his own historical and class position and of an 'art-literature' separate from every other form of writing. In the end, Green's historical method depends upon the same ideology of disinterestedness and truth that drove the formalist projects of his contemporaries.

During the height of New Critical hegemony in the late 1950s, Green would enter into a polemical exchange that revealed the contradictions inherent in his method. In 1957, five years after the publication of Green's *Courtly Love in Quevedo*, Amédée Mas had produced a lengthy study entitled *La Caricature de la femme, du mariage et de l'amour dans l'oeuvre de Quevedo* in which he argued that the influence of courtly love on Quevedo's poetry was virtually non-existent. Rather, Mas claimed, Quevedo's text formed part of a counter-discourse, popular and anti-aristocratic, that sought to undercut the idealisation of the lady. Green's review article (*Hispanic Review*, XXVIII, 1960) centred on the issue of whether or not Quevedo's supposed misogyny was real or merely a literary device. Only through a complete examination of the 'full armour of fact', in this case the evidence contained in the *Epistolario*, could one arrive at a definitive opinion. Green's argument that Quevedo's misogyny was a 'literary attitude' is built upon letters which the poet had directed to influential members of the court. Writing to the Duke of Osuna in 1615, for example, Quevedo had reported: 'Di la carta de v.ex[a] i besé la mano a la marquesa de Peñafiel mi señora, que es la más linda cosa del mundo después de mi señora doña Antonia' ('I delivered your excellency's letter and I kissed the hand of my lady, the Marchioness of Peñafiel, who is the most beautiful thing in the world after my lady Doña Antonia'). According to Green, such flattery proves that Quevedo was no woman-hater.

The issue of Quevedo's true feelings about women strikes me as only marginally interesting, although the record of the poet's life would seem to settle the question definitively in Mas's favour. What is more to the point is that, in the debate with Mas, Green's method fails to take into account the fact that Quevedo's rhetoric in the letters cited was already overdetermined by the dynamics of courtly power relations. By believing that the documents 'speak for themselves', the critic had failed to show that Quevedo, like all minor courtiers, was deeply embedded in aristocratic practice and stood to lose a great deal if he did not reproduce the kind of obsequious language we hear in the above excerpt. Sincerity, we can be sure, was not the most important sentiment motivating the epistolary mode in the early modern absolutist court. Green, however, steadfastly holds to the position that the written record allows the critic direct access to the past, and he sets up an uncanny opposition between text and interpretation: 'It was my intention that the light should come primarily from the texts. Of *thinking* there would inevitably be much, but I was convinced of the need for textual control of the imagination' (emphasis in original). Here, the critical faculty is restrained so that history might communicate to us directly.

This kind of empiricist approach, which claims extra-literary materials contain no rhetorical strategies of their own, allowed Green to assure his readers in 1964: 'My method is to avoid polemics, to refrain from writing a "notional" book, to let the Spanish texts speak for themselves.' If there is anything that has been consistently called into question during the last twenty years it is the belief that concrete facts can be considered outside the rhetorical system which seeks to organise them. This is by no means a new idea. As early as 1920, Croce himself had criticised the positivist enterprise for its lack of philosophical base (*Nuovi saggi di estetica*), and later had retreated from his own 'historicismo absoluto' in favour of a purely formal method. Green's work, therefore, remained within an earlier paradigm despite the fact that even its best-known practitioners had abandoned it, and so for Green it was still possible to speak of writing an objective history of medieval and early modern Spanish culture. His investment in the ideologies of historical truth and the Individual was so complete that his work may well stand as our most representative example of Hispanism as it has been practised in the US for the last 150 years.

III

the proper task of a history of thought [is] to define the conditions in which human beings 'problematise' what they are, what they do, and the world in which they live. M. Foucault, 1988

The process by which the recurring tropes of Spanish studies are isolated in the genealogy I have constructed bears a superficial resemblance to Green's description of the linear movement of the controlling ideas of Golden Age writing. But I want to insist that my account is not a narrative in the conventional sense (teleological and continuous), nor is it meant to suggest that the discursive elements that mark earlier moments of Hispanism have in some way been superseded or surpassed by our own. On the contrary, the dominant

ideology of Hispanism continues to reproduce its traditional *loci* —
the Individual, human nature, and national character — even in those
essays of the last twenty years that claim to represent a break with
the critical methods of the past. The powerful figures we have seen
at work since the movement of Ticknor's *History* cannot be simply
washed away. Still, by focusing on selected moments of the Anglophone tradition, we begin to see the ways in which all statements
about early modern Spain (including our own) are implicated in wider
social and cultural formations even as they constitute the object of
study called the Golden Age.

It is one thing to say that early modern Spanish literature
presents us with insights into the 'human condition'. It is quite
another to claim that this so-called human condition was essentially
the same for a seventeenth-century aristocrat as it is for a twentieth-
century academic, or as it may have been for a seventeenth-century
pícaro. I would not dispute the idea that there are certain inevitable
facts of material existence such as death that appear at the thematic
level in a significant number of literary texts, but I would insist
that these 'facts' are always constructed differently along cultural,
class and gender lines. For those of us interested in the relationship between writing and material reality, the invention of universal
values and essential notions of 'mind' or 'man' can only impede
our understanding of both the earlier historical moment and of
our own.[23]

Contemporary culture's investment in the idea of the Individual
may make it the most resistant of all inherited tropes to any future
rethinking. Traditional literary criticism's hostility to unorthodox
theories of subjectivity that call into question an autonomous and/or
unified consciousness is too often enacted without an awareness of
the ways in which such a construct blocks our ability to understand
how the subject was constructed in past cultures. For the early modern
period, particularly in Spain, the subject-position marked 'individual'
was still an emergent concept that was consistently opposed by
established discourses and practices. But because the 'Self' of
Anglophone literary studies is taken to be universal (yet almost
always signifies an Anglo-Saxon male and his bourgeois values, i.e.
the critic himself), centuries of ideological struggle over what the
subject could or could not be are effaced; from here, it is a relatively
simple manoeuvre to transform sixteenth-century nuns into Lacanian
case studies and seventeenth-century poets into schizophrenics.[24]

There may well be ideas worth reclaiming from liberal humanism (e.g. democracy), but to continue to defend a critical model founded on notions of human nature and the Individual is to preclude seeing the ways in which society and subjectivity were constituted for sixteenth- and seventeenth-century Spaniards and how we might problematise and ultimately transform our own. In the broadest sense, this is the goal of any political criticism. The refusal within English-speaking Spanish studies to see that early modern literature in Spain may have had a political function, that is, local rather than universal, cannot be separated from the ongoing desire to 'protect' contemporary critical practice from the anxieties of the social world. Such a strategy is merely another way of participating in a conservative agenda. When Ticknor, the elite arbiter of literary taste, railed against the 'wild sort of metaphysics' being proposed by Emerson and the younger generation of New England writers, he spoke through the art v. politics dichotomy that has structured liberal criticism in the US and Britain ever since. Hispanism's traditional resistance to emergent and potentially oppositional discourses in the academic setting is one other move within the same reactive strategy. Parker informs us that Wilson, for example, 'remained unimpressed by pure formalism, structuralism and semiotic and other extreme forms [*sic*] of contemporary criticism';[25] more recently, Parker warned against the 'extreme nihilism' of deconstruction' (see note 11). For most established Golden Age scholars, poststructuralism is nothing less than a frontal attack on the discipline itself.

The dismissal of certain kinds of theory as 'ideologies' (i.e. dogma, jargon, etc.) while remaining oblivious to the ideological biases of one's own method has been an unfortunate characteristic of the US literary establishment for some time. In 1937, for example, with Spain in the midst of civil war and capitalism poised on the brink of its bloodiest conflict, an official spokesman for the Modern Language Association of America lamented the developments in Europe:

> What is the American situation? We are not endangered by fanaticism yet, but young men, both authors and scholars, are taking up modes of interpreting literature which, though they make for simplification, must, if they are consistently followed through, give rise to similar 'ideologies'. Doctrinaire theory is in the air; volumes equating protestantism and capitalism, the bourgeoisie and the novel, poetry and the decay of civilisation have more than passing vogue; and other dogmas are being seriously discussed.[26]

We can only imagine the shock that the author of this passage would feel upon learning that not only had the first two daring propositions he lists become commonplace but that they had been surpassed by even more shocking suggestions such as the death of the author and a gender-based criticism. The liberal humanists' fear of politics blocks the elaboration of any method that might eventually expose traditional criticism's founding myths – the Work, the Individual, Human Nature – so that we are left with only the most idealist and mystifying forms of reading and the perpetual appeal for an illusory kind of pluralism made up of various methods that ultimately produce the same political consequences. Even some of those younger critics writing today, who seem relatively open to recent developments in theory, are no less committed to 'a genuinely pluralistic institution of literary criticism' and 'genuine humanistic inquiry'.[27]

The supposition that all methods are equal and must therefore have compatible results is a misguided one, and the desire for pluralistic humanism founders on the issue of who will decide what is 'genuine' and what is not. This is a problem endemic to traditional literary criticism in so far as the 'disinterested' individual critic has consistently been viewed as the sole origin of meaning. One of the most durable tropes that threatens to infiltrate my own account (proving that it is in no way outside these tropes) is that of the critic or the great 'initiator' of an 'original' discourse or 'school'. Hispanism has been no less susceptible than other local traditions to the mystification of certain 'great men'. We have already seen Green's subservient posture with relation to Menéndez Pidal and one might list numerous examples from previous and succeeding generations. But this and the other fundamental myths which we inherit from liberal humanism must be dismantled and historicised if we hope to understand the discursive formations and institutional power that make criticism possible. Only then can we contribute to the articulation of an emergent politics of culture.

Afterword

The title of this chapter is designed to invoke the memory of Stephen Gilman, in particular his 1946 article, 'An introduction to the ideology of the Baroque in Spain'. In the period immediately following the Second World War and before the 'golden age' of *comedia* criticism in the 1950s, Gilman ended his article with the following description of early modern Spanish culture: 'The dilemma was Baroque, but it was not born as the invention of a single generation; its period of gestation took decades of ideological warfare'.[28] Given what I have said about the need to eliminate the cult of the great man, I am not proposing that we install Gilman on the pedestal vacated by some other critic. On the contrary, I want to read Gilman's statement as symptomatic of what, in the earliest years of the Cold War, was an historical conjuncture in which there still existed the possibility of an Anglophone Hispanism interested in the relationship between literature, politics and society.

For a variety of reasons, the opportunity to develop such a criticism was lost. Institutional hostility in the US to the linking of concepts of ideology and literature as well as Gilman's commitment to liberal humanism and the individual artist together would block the elaboration of his fundamental insight. Nevertheless, as we enter the 1990s, there are several things about Gilman's statement that continue to strike us with a special force. That the phrase 'ideological warfare' issue forth from a non-Marxist pen is uncanny in itself, although not surprising given the moment in which it was written – on the heels of the great struggle between fascism and liberal democracy – as well as Gilman's profound belief in contextualising literary artefacts. In terms of the discipline of Spanish studies, what is particularly interesting is that Gilman's early account of Golden Age Spain as a site of ideological competition incorporates the insights of Américo Castro's first seminars at Princeton in the early 1940s, and prefigures by some fifteen years Castro's model of an 'edad conflictiva'. Castro's account was decisive for the deconstruction of the conservative model of 'Spanishness' defended by establishment historians and the Franco regime, but ultimately his caste-based reading, in its retention of various forms of bourgeois individualism, was to be more limited than the one that might have been theorised from Gilman's initial suggestion.

Within the discourse of English-speaking Hispanism, as we have seen, the decades of the 1950s and 1960s would witness the hegemony of formalist and mythopoetic approaches; in effect, the opportunity to construct a Spanish Golden Age literature on the basis of ideological warfare, social antagonisms and changing material conditions was dispersed in the thin air of increasingly idealist modes of reading. It is an undeniable fact that the majority of critics working in the field of Golden Age studies today continue to be attracted to those methods that are most easily reconciled with the idealisms of the past. But perhaps it is now, in the context of contemporary theory's attempted dismantling of essentialist concepts of literature, subjectivity, the author, and society itself, that we can renew the project of a political Anglo-American criticism of early modern Spain.

Notes

1 As Raymond Williams taught us: 'What we have to inquire into is not, in these cases, historical error, but historical perspective.' *The Country and the City*, New York, 1973, p. 10. My separation of English-speaking Hispanism from those critical practices produced elsewhere should be viewed as nothing more than a heuristic device. Anglophone Spanish studies are inextricably linked to the Spanish, French and other traditions; in their dominant forms, all of them reproduce the tropes of liberal humanism.

2 Göttingen has recently been discussed as the prototype for all modern universities and one of the sites where the myth of Aryan purity was first applied to classical studies. See Martin Bernal, *Black Athena: The Afroasiatic Roots of Classical Civilization, vol. 1: The Fabrication of Ancient Greece 1785–1985*, New Brunswick, 1987.

3 Letter to Sir Charles Lyell. Quoted in David B. Tyack, *George Ticknor and the Boston Brahmins*, Cambridge, Mass., 1967, p. 138.

4 *History of Spanish Literature*, Vol. II, new York, 1854, p. 453.

5 'George Ticknor's *History of Spanish Literature*: the New England background', *PMLA*, LXIX, 1954. See also John W. Rathbun, 'The philosophical setting of George Ticknor's *History of Spanish Literature*', *Hispania*, XLIII, 1960.

6 Confronted with the proposed annexation of Mexico by the US, Ticknor could not understand 'what we shall do with such a miserable conglomerate of undesirable peoples based on an effete civilization'. See Tyack, p. 197.

7 *A New History of Spanish Literature*, New York, 1926, p. 266. In his original *History* (1898), Fitzmaurice-Kelly had written: 'As with men of Spanish stock, so with their letters: the national idiosyncrasy is emphatic – almost violent. French literature is certainly more exquisite, more brilliant; English is loftier and more varied; but in the capital qualities of originality, force, truth, and humour, the Castilian finds no superior' (p. 1).

8 For example: 'Though Calderón does not incarnate the whole Spanish genius, he does present a temporary aspect of it with unparalleled splendour, with a barbaric intensity of romantic colour, with a most sumptuous scheme of decoration' (p. 385).

9 *Chapters on Spanish Literature*, London, 1908, p. 163.

10 Francis Mulhern, *The Moment of 'Scrutiny'*, London, 1979.

11 Wilson in fact would make several contributions on Spanish topics both to Eliot's *Criterion* and to *Scrutiny*, beginning with his translation of Góngora's 'De la brevedad engañosa de la vida' published in December

1933. See also 'Mr Maugham and Spanish literature, *Scrutiny*, IV, 1935–36: 209–13. According to Parker, both he and Wilson (and their mentor, James Smith) distanced themselves early on from the 'polemical and intransigent tone' of nonconformist Leavisism.

12 See *Bulletin of Hispanic Studies*, LV, 1978: 256 and *The Mind and Art of Calderón: Essays on the Comedias*, Cambridge, 1988, p. x. In their *Calderón y la crítica* (Madrid, 1976), Manuel Durán and R. González Echevarría, in an attempt to privilege the Spanish tradition, disregard the Cambridge context and rewrite the origins of Wilson's and Parker's early projects as a reaction to Menéndez y Pelayo mediated by D. Alonso.

13 'On William Empson's "Seven Types of Ambiguity" ', in James Smith, *Shakespearian and other essays*, Cambridge, 1974, p. 341.

14 Much of Wilson's comparative work was designed to draw similarities between English and Spanish literature in the early modern period. See, for example, 'A Hispanist looks at *Othello*' and 'Spanish and English religious poetry of the seventeenth century', both in *Spanish and English literature of the 16th and 17th centuries: Studies in discretion, illusion and mutability*, Cambridge, 1980.

15 For a critique of Parker's method, see R. D. F. Pring Mill, 'Los calderonistas de habla inglesa y *La vida es sueño*: Métodos del análisis temático-estructural', in Hans Flasche (ed.), *Litterae Hispanae et Lusitanae*, Munich, 1968, pp. 369–413.

16 'On metaphysical poetry', *Scrutiny*, II, 1933: 238. Smith would in fact convert to Catholicism in 1938 and remain a Catholic until the reforms of Vatican II. According to Wilson, Smith's conversion was precipitated by the death of a personal friend and his reading one of Parker's Calderonian essays. See Wilson's memoir in James Smith, *Shakespearian and other essays*, Cambridge, 1974.

17 'Calderón and the morality', *Scrutiny*, XIII, 1946: 318. Some years earlier, Smith had framed his analysis of George Chapman within the categories of 'action' and the 'moral world'. See 'Reevaluations (VII): George Chapman ii', *Scrutiny*, IV, 1935.

18 See James Smith, ' "Much Ado About Nothing" ', *Scrutiny*, XIII, 1946; Derek Traversi, ' "King Lear" ', *Scrutiny*, XIX, 1952–53. It is not an insignificant detail that during the Spanish Civil War, Traversi had contributed an attack on English leftists to the pro-Franco Catholic journal *Arena* (1937).

19 Given that various kinds of formalism still dominated Spanish studies in the late 60s, Wilson's appeal for a consideration of so-called extra-textual matters was a tentative one: 'Questions like: who was the author writing for? and: who in fact read him? may perhaps help us to understand and enjoy some literary works.' See the 1966 Taylorian lecture published as 'Some Aspects of Spanish Literary History', Oxford, 1967; Spanish version in *Entre las jarchas y Cernuda: Constantes y variables en la poesía española*, Barcelona, 1977. In his memoir for Wilson, Parker refers to this crucial historical material as 'cultural "marginalia" '. *Bulletin of Hispanic Studies*, LV, 1978: 257.

20 'Images and Structure in *Peribáñez*', in *Spanish and English Literature*, p. 260, n. 2.
21 *The Function of Criticism*, London, 1984, p. 83.
22 'On the goal and method of scholarship in the modern languages', *Modern Languages Journal*, XXII, 1937: 177.
23 The phenomenological concept of a 'mind' to which the literary critic can gain access is another of the dominant tropes in Golden Age studies. Thus Green's subtitle to *Spain and the Western Tradition*: 'The Castilian Mind in Literature from *El Cid* to Calderón', and Parker's most recent title: *The Mind and Art of Calderón*.
24 Although it is beyond the scope of the present essay, the much more serious issue has to do with how the ideology of bourgeois individualism excludes non-male and non-white human beings from the category of subjectivity itself. This exclusionary tactic persists in the criticism of those in the US who would surrender *Don Quixote*, for example, to the conservative agenda of 'cultural literacy' proposed by Allan Bloom and others.
25 Parker, 'Memoir', p. 258. In a polemical 1975 exchange with James Parr, Wilson mournfully inquired: 'Must literature become merely the hand-maid of sociology?' See 'A Defence of the "British Critics" of the "Comedia" ', *Hispania*, LXVIII, 1975: 481–2.
26 H. Carrington Lancaster in *Trends of Scholarship in the Modern Language Association of America*, New York, 1937, p. 17. Lancaster's remarks were made in direct response to the rising influence in the 30s of the vigorous Marxist criticism.
27 See, for example, C. Christopher Soufas, Jr, 'Speech act theory and Hispanic drama: a dialog with *Things Done with Words, Revista de Estudios Hispánicos*, XXII, 1988.
28 *Symposium*, I, 1946: 107.

This essay has benefited greatly from my conversations with Carlos Blanco Aguinaga, Lisa Lowe, Len Tennenhouse and Nancy Armstrong.

Teresa de Jesús and the relations of writing

'I beseech Him [the Lord] with my whole heart to give me grace to write this account of my life, according to my confessor's command, with complete clarity and truthfulness.'[1] This sentiment from the preface of the *Libro de la Vida* is often quoted as proof that Teresa de Jesús began to write only because she was ordered to do so by external authority. In all the spiritual writing she produced from 1561, when most researchers agree she began work on the *Vida*, until her death in 1582, Teresa emphasises her unworthiness for the task at hand. Protestations of her own inadequacy cover a broad spectrum: her lack of formal education, her inability to read or write Latin, poor physical health, a weak memory, the difficulty of creating time for writing amid her many responsibilities in the convent, and most of all, the double hindrance of being both female and sinful. Despite critical questioning of some of her specific complaints, these statements have been for the most part accepted as accurately describing her literary experience, and the bulk of Teresian commentary portrays her as an isolated, reluctant writer indifferent to the fate of her texts.

That these misconceptions persist is largely due to the narrowly textbound methodological approaches which have dominated discussion of her writings. The implications of poststructuralist theory have come late to studies of Golden Age writers and are only now beginning to be applied to Teresa's work, and to the experience of authorship which forms one of her major thematic concerns. However, much of this current analysis of Teresa's representation of writing continues to focus exclusively on the elements and operations of discourse at the expense of the material and cultural world of textual production.[2] Despite recognition of the importance of Teresa's Jewish ancestry and a growing interest in the political relationships between Teresa and her confessors, criticism remains largely limited, not only to issues of language and discourse, but to such issues within a single text (most often, the *Vida* or *Las moradas*). Our misunderstanding of her experience of authorship is thus compounded by a failure to allow for evolution or change during twenty years of writing and circulating her texts.

In contrast, I will consider Teresa's gradual emergence and development as a writer as a function of a series of relationships between the writer, her texts, and the contexts in which the act of writing takes place. Central to these relations is Teresa's specifically literary motivation, the desire to write and to be read, to enter into an intellectual and critical community − a form of desire which critics have been singularly unwilling to grant her.[3] In a much neglected article, 'La vocación literaria de Santa Teresa', Francisco Márquez Villanueva makes the only substantial challenge to the prevailing but limited construction of desire, arguing that Teresa had a true literary calling, a 'passion to write' amounting almost to an addiction.[4] His catalogue of evidence for her 'graphomania', ranging across many of her books and her letters, makes convincing reading. Once launched with the *Libro de la vida*, she turned feverishly from one book to the next, at times completing revisions for one book while drafting the following one. Besides writing books on mysticism and texts for the governing of the Reformed Carmelite Order, she also carried on a massive correspondence motivated by pleasure as well as by business.

Márquez Villanueva shows us a Teresa who possesses a 'rare talent for "inventing obediences" ',[5] who solicits or even creates institutionally acceptable opportunities to write, and who takes great pride in her completed work, to the extent of actively pursuing opportunities for its wider circulation. He notes that disclaimers within the text about her inability to write are weighted against a deliberate employment of literary models for the books' structures, an extensive thematic exploration of the act of writing, and a 'density of thought' apparent in her texts which, he argues, cannot possibly result from improvisational writing undertaken with utmost reluctance. Further, there is an enormous difference between what Teresa says about writing and about herself as a writer in the context of her mystic books and what she says in other modes of discourse: her correspondence in particular, but also satire, and conversations recorded or remembered by other nuns after her death. The evidence he marshals in support of his argument offers a tantalising opportunity to explore the interplay between the writer and institutional systems implicit in conventions of genre as this interplay allows, represses, or otherwise shapes Teresa's representation of her literary desires. But Márquez Villanueva bypasses this opportunity. Dismissing Teresa's comments about her reluctance to write and her lack of confidence in her ability to carry out the command as rhetorical strategies demanded by the conventions of spiritual writing and by her position as a woman, he poses her 'pleasure' — his key word — as uncomplicated by other forces, the road to what was in effect professional authorship as free of struggle.

While it would be difficult to overestimate the significance of Márquez Villanueva's article, the problems and gaps in his argument offer us the challenge of forming a more complex reconstruction of Teresa's experience as a writer. One possible direction we might pursue is that advocated by Michel Foucault in 'What is an author?'[6] Rejecting the Romantic legacy which equates authorship with individual creative genius, he offers us instead the 'author-function', a product of 'contemporary judicial and institutional systems', together with a series of social manoeuvres that we as critics perform. Foucault rightly alerts us to the ways in which genre, content, and style are shaped by means outside authorial agency and creativity. However, under his redefinition Teresa as agent, as author, disappears; there can be no interaction between author and text, author and literary community, but only between pre-existing subject positions in systems of discourse. To deny the power of agency is to limit our understanding of the act and circulation of writing in a manner analogous to the restrictive focus on agency which Foucault seeks to redress.

An approach I find more productive stems from the work of cultural and intellectual historians who define their field as 'the history of the book'. Attempting to map the general concerns of the field, Robert Darnton refers to 'the communications circuit' of textual production and transmission.[7] The label suggests the interactive focus of this approach; Darnton and his colleagues place the book at the actual and symbolic centre of a variety of interactions, both within the writer and between writers, patrons, printers, copyists, readers, government agencies and cultural traditions (both oral and written) of signification and interpretation. Historians of the book urge us to investigate books both as material objects and as carriers of ideas; this dual focus allows us to consider what both traditional, text-oriented criticism and Foucault's 'author-function' neglect: the material manuscript as a product of the relations between a writer and her text. It allows us to consider both Teresa's manuscripts as they acquire a history of relationships, passing through the hands – and under the pens – of readers, as their circulation is encouraged or restrained, and Teresa's changing views of her books over time.

At its best, this perspective posits each of the various elements of her texts, including the conditions under which it was written, its language, generic conventions, themes, materiality, and the history of its transmission, as a potential site for tension between the acceptable contemporary representations of female authorship and her own literary ambitions. Taking the concept of relations as a guide, I will argue that it is this tension in all its manifestations which constitutes Teresa's experience of authorship; that her desires, satisfactions, and frustrations took shape within an intellectual and literary community which fostered her move to writing and which at the same time prohibited her from representing the full extent of her desires.

I The conditions of writing

Acceptance of Teresa's own description of her turn to writing has promoted a picture of her literary life as divided into two distinct and separate parts. On one side of the command (or, in the opinion of Rossi and of Márquez Villanueva, the decision) to write, Teresa is a reader, and on the other, she has suddenly and mysteriously become transformed into a writer whose vivid, colloquial prose style enchants biographers and critics. She is often described as a born writer whose talents lay untouched until released, fully developed, by this command, rather like Athena stepping armour-clad and battle-ready from Zeus's head. Most critics view her connection with any wider literary community as tenuous, and tend to define any such connection in terms of her early reading, during which, they claim, she absorbed stylistic and structural conventions which she then incorporated into her own work. Virtually all of the inquiry into Teresa's life before the command centres on a search for sources which may have influenced her later writing.[8]

But there were also a number of other events and forces which contributed to what instead was her gradual emergence as a writer: her decision to enter a convent, the relationship of mysticism to writing, the *Index Librorum Prohibitorum*, Teresa's reform activities, her choice of confessors and their relationship to the written word.

Teresa's literary desires developed not in isolation but in relation to one of the few historical and cultural contexts in sixteenth-century Spain where the activities of reading and writing played such a prominent role. Her exposure to the pleasures of reading began early. Teresa grew up in a literate household where her father read religious works as well as classics, while her mother was a fan of *novelas de caballería*.[9] In the *Libro de la vida* Teresa recounts how, during adolescence, she became so avid a fan of these chivalric romances that without a new book, she says, 'I was never happy' (ch. 2). She could continue to allot this level of importance to books in her adult life only because the twin fears of damnation and of marriage drove her to the relatively leisured life of the Unreformed convent, where her enthusiasm for reading could be transferred to spiritual texts. Although her motives for reading underwent a radical change when she turned to religious works, the medium through which she attained her ends remained the same; thus in the early stages of her mystic development Teresa was unable to enter into an appropriate state of prayer without either receiving communion or perusing a book (ch. 4).[10] Throughout her life, reading remained important, and the Constitutional Rules she created for the Discalced or Reformed Carmelite Order urged the prioress of each convent to 'see to it that there are good books ... for sustenance like this is in its way as necessary for the soul as is food for the body' ('On what days the Lord is to be received', in the Constitutions).

In embracing the tenets of mysticism, Teresa reinforced her connection with books. The phenomenon of mysticism, which reached its peak in Spain during Teresa's lifetime, continually linked experience with textuality. The ineffable, incontrollable nature of its manifestations meant that new practitioners relied on books about mysticism as guides, while those who had reached its further stages attempted to shape and understand their experiences through writing, laying out definitions, charting mysticism's more abstract reaches so far as that was possible. The flourishing genre of mystic writing may have presented a potential space for the expression of women's spirituality through its belief in the equality of the souls of men and women, but ironically, it was the Inquisition's attempt to repress mystic texts that led to a key event in Teresa's turn to writing. Targeting translations of Scripture and spiritual writings in the vernacular, the 1559 Index of Forbidden Books most affected those without formal training in Latin and those who practised mystical forms of spirituality. Women comprised the majority on both counts. The publication of the Index under Inquisitor General Fernando Valdés was followed by rigorous examination of the collections in shops, monasteries, universities and private libraries. Teresa's personal library was not exempt. In 1560 her library was examined, and all offending volumes confiscated.

Chronicling the event in the *Vida*, Teresa is conscious of the fine line between expressing her real sense of loss and appearing to criticise the Inquisition's actions. She comments:

> When a great many books written in Spanish were taken from us and we were forbidden to read them, I was very sorry, for the reading of some of them gave me pleasure and I could no longer continue this as I had them only in Latin. Then the Lord said to me: 'Be not distressed, for I will give thee a living book'.... And the Lord showed me so much love and taught me by so many methods, that I have had very little need of books – indeed, hardly any. His Majesty himself has been to me the Book in which I have seen what is true. (Ch. 26)

Ironically, the Inquisition's attempt to control Teresa liberates her. At this pivotal moment she responds to the confiscation of her library by redefining the nature of the book so that she no longer needs those which have been taken from her. God becomes a metaphysical text, and the physical process of reading, which leads to intellectual knowing, is replaced by mystic experiences in which God conveys to Teresa a higher level of spiritual understanding. In this 'living book' Teresa has access to the same truths and funds of wisdom which her scholarly confessors find through exegesis of biblical and other Latin texts. However, she now sees physical texts as an imperfect, inferior source of understanding, since they engage the intellect and the emotions, but do not connect the reader directly with God's will. Texts function as a barrier rather than as an entrance to a higher truth. In addition, although the connection is not made explicit, Teresa responds to the confiscation by hearing a call to write herself. She claims that she has no need of earthly texts once she achieves this relationship with her living book, and her mention of reading other texts does indeed taper off after this event is narrated. But structurally, the incident of the confiscation is surrounded by references to the *writing* of *her* text. The confiscation of her library coincides almost exactly with Teresa's shift from reader to writer.

One of the most crucial events which made writing not only possible, but necessary, was Teresa's decision to found a Reformed branch of the Carmelite order. She came to this decision in 1560 – the year of the loss of her library, and the year in which she wrote the earliest *Relación*, or short account of the state of her soul, that has come down to us. During the period when she was drafting the *Vida*, from about 1561 to 1565, Teresa was also corresponding with a number of men about her projected foundational plans. Her belief that the Discalced convents should not be funded through 'possession of revenue' led to protracted arguments on paper: 'I kept on disputing about it with learned men. I wrote to that effect to the Dominican friar who was helping us, and he answered me in a letter two sheets long, full of refutations and theology' (ch. 35). The paper flow increased greatly over the next few years, the same years in which Teresa completed her draft of the *Vida* and then revised it. Matters relating to the establishment of the Discalced Carmelites immersed Teresa in written documents of all sorts: letters, financial agreements, licences from Church officials, real estate documents. In 1562 Pope Pius IV authorised creation of the Discalced Constitutions, which were completed and approved in 1565. Teresa, then, did not write the *Vida* in textual or personal isolation. Its composition was both preceded and surrounded by other writing which contributed in various ways to her evolution as a writer.

Teresa's affiliation with the world of writing was again reinforced by her connections with confessors who came from the more scholarly monastic orders, one of whom requested the 1560 *Relación*. Despite her emphasis on the importance of a confessor who possessed spiritual understanding rather than academic knowledge alone, when choosing her own confessors Teresa consistently showed a preference for men of very scholarly orders – Dominicans and Jesuits, who enjoyed a particularly intimate connection with the written word. In the 1550s, after a difficult stint with Calced Carmelites unsympathetic to her mystic experiences, she began confessing to Jesuits, whose scholasticism combined with an acceptance of mystic experience to create an ideal emotional environment in which her mystical bent would not be repressed, where her intellectual enthusiasm would be welcomed rather than discouraged.

Teresa's first short *Relaciones* arose as writing tasks that confessors routinely required of nuns in their charge.[11] She progressed gradually from these smaller pieces of writing to the more extended first draft of the *Libro de la Vida*. Critics speculate that many of the earlier *Relaciones* were incorporated into the version of the *Vida* that exists today. The text's evolution was closely overseen by three prominent Dominican theologians, each of whom served as Teresa's confessor during part of the book's composition: Pedro Ibáñez, Domingo Báñez, and García de Toledo. Many of her confessors also held professorial posts at the prestigious theological university in Salamanca or at other colleges; an impressively large number were writers themselves. A number of Jesuits and Dominicans with whom Teresa had contact produced spiritual writings in both Spanish and Latin.[12] Through her intimacy with this select group of confessors, she was situating herself in a community of men who were nominally her superiors but who would over the years gradually become, in effect, her theological and literary colleagues.

II Writing the first book

If it is reductive to view Teresa's literary experience on one side of the 'command' as solely that of a reader, it is equally a misreading to view her motives, attitudes, and experience of authorship over more than twenty years of writing as fully developed in the *Vida* and unchanging thereafter. Far from being representative of her entire body of work, the *Vida* is instead a testing ground for issues of authority and authorship. The two major contrasting representations of the experience of writing in the *Vida* − I will summarise them rather simplistically, for lack of space in which to elaborate, as denial and assertion of authority − each operate in the context of the other. Rather than pointing to either one or the other as the true nature of Teresa's literary experience, as is often the case with critical analyses, I believe that it is their simultaneous existence, their interworkings, that helps form her early experience of authorship.[13]

The text took shape under the jurisdiction of her confessors, and Teresa accepted their jurisdiction (in theory if not always in practice, as we shall see). There are many explicit references to her confessors as her readers, and in a sense, as her co-authors, whose demands will shape both the fine points of her theological statements and the general shape of the text; she has been commanded to describe her method of mystic prayer and to avoid dwelling on her unworthiness and sinful nature, and her discussion of mysticism will be amended by the prominent theologians who serve as her confessors. The instances of her self-depreciation, and of her realisation that in many instances she has no authority to write, have been thoroughly documented.[14]

As Márquez Villanueva rightly observes, these passages do serve as rhetorical conventions common to mystic writing. But to label them as such to dismiss their importance is to do Teresa a disservice. Teresa's employment of these conventions is significant in more than one way. Through them she signifies not only her recognition of the literary tradition but also her desire to place herself within that tradition. At the same time, these passages constitute formal recognition of the contemporary strictures placed upon women's access to authority and to public speech or writing. That she was responding to very real strictures which inevitably affected how she experienced authorship becomes clear in Jerónimo Gracián's *Dilucidario*. In the opening pages he contends with possible arguments against Teresa, and the primary objections he expects are those of her gender and her lack of education. He spends an inordinate amount of time justifying her writing by listing historical instances of other women who have been inspired or otherwise received approval to write. Other possible problems, which he lists and then defends her against, are her unlearned status, her mystic raptures, her lack of rhetoric, and the fact that the subject she addresses cannot be proven in any way, but stems from personal experience. The arsenal of logic, historical examples and persuasion that Gracián brings to his task shows the strength, potential or actual, of contemporary attitudes. Teresa's constant references to her weaknesses represent the inevitable impact of this way of thinking upon her experience, *and* a rhetorical manoeuvre to bypass or ameliorate it. I would describe her constant invocation of her scholarly male readers and judges as evidence of one element in a multi-faceted relationship with her text, an element that is culturally established and imposed, yet no less real for being so.

This imposed relationship is counterbalanced by Teresa's establishment of a more assertive relationship between herself and the text. I mentioned in opening that the preface to the *Vida* has often been quoted in support of the claim that Teresa wrote solely in obedience to her confessor's command. Yet even here it is apparent that Teresa has a plan of her own for her text's development:

> As I have been commanded and given full liberty to write about my way of prayer and the favours which the Lord has granted me, I wish I had also been allowed to describe clearly and in full detail my grave sins and wicked life. To do this would be a great comfort to me; but it has been willed otherwise — in fact, I have been subjected to severe restrictions in the matter. So, for the love of God, I beg anyone who

reads this account of my life to bear in mind how wicked it has been —
so much so that, among all the saints who have been converted to
God, I can find none whose life affords me any comfort. (Preface)

In the preface Teresa suggests that picking up the pen is a response
to external authority. But her own desires have not been completely
dominated by those of her confessor. In fact, her own will manifests
itself in a variety of ways. Note that the command to write, which
she claims is fuelling her work, is presented within a subordinate
clause, while the main clause of the first sentence of this preface asserts
Teresa's own wishes for the construction of the book; in the original
Spanish her first two words are 'Quisiera yo' ('I would wish').
Ostensibly directed to her confessor, the statement actually takes in
a potentially wider audience ('anyone who reads this account of my
life'). Her address to this audience is an instruction; although she is
constrained by her confessor's perception of what the text should
contain, she wants her *Vida* to be read in the light of her sinful nature
and unworthiness, which to her mind would reflect even greater glory
to God.

Most of the time the presence of her confessor in the text as an
immediate audience is necessary as part of Teresa's careful negotiation
of the territory of mysticism itself. In accepting, even stressing the
importance of the priest's role in guiding her spiritual development,
she submits herself to priestly authority, and thus brings her practice
of mysticism away from the edge of the heretical cliff, claiming a space
for mystic practice within Church doctrine. Augustine's *Confessions*,
one of the models for the *Vida*, is structured as a dialogue between
God and the soul. Teresa's situation as a woman and a mystic, however, requires that she include both God and her confessor as par-
ticipants in her writing. But Teresa also constructs an alternative mode
of writing, one which for short segments of the text allows her to
exclude her confessor entirely and to put some of her own plans for
the text into effect. She figures this other experience of writing as a
private, interior one, largely through the claim that the book's mystic
content spills over into and affects the method of its composition.
In his discussion of mystic speech Michel de Certeau describes the
'place' of the *Vida* as 'a journey to the center'.[15] Teresa's later book
Las moradas fits this description in its very structure: the journey of
the soul through the rooms of the interior castle, moving from the
outside world toward the innermost places where the soul attains
union with God. The interior focus of the *Vida*'s treatment of

mysticism becomes intense, particularly during those times when Teresa writes that she is 'not yet recovered from this holy heavenly madness' (ch. 16).

She refers periodically to the state of mystic communion from which she writes, a state often precipitated by the quintessentially private experience of communion.[16] At such times she refuses to be governed by the restrictions her confessor has set upon her, because his instructions to her spring from *letras,* or intellectual, scholarly knowledge, which is to be distinguished from the deeper understanding which results from mystic communion with God. This understanding is not irrational so much as it is beyond the bounds of the merely rational. If mysticism can be likened to a journey of the soul towards God, the scholarly confessor whose knowledge of union with the divine essence comes only from books is an armchair traveller. Teresa's gradually attained status as an advanced or 'expert' mystic gives her authority to override her confessor's perception of what she ought to write, and to write instead in the way she thinks can best express her understanding: 'For there is no reason strong enough to keep me within the bounds of reason when the Lord takes me out of myself' (ch. 16). By defining reason (and by implication, the intellectualism of the scholar) as a limitation, rather than an aid, in the soul's intimacy with God, Teresa gives validity to her writing despite her lack of erudition.

However, it is significant that to do so, she must claim that she is taken out of herself, that she is not in control of her writing. The apparently paradoxical link between assertion of literary authority and this denial of control over the self who writes can be seen in a representative passage where she excuses herself for having made a long digression: 'Your Reverence must forgive me for wandering from my subject: as I am speaking with a purpose in mind you must not be surprised. I am writing what comes to my soul' (ch. 14). While Teresa's religious rapture fell, however narrowly, within acceptable boundaries, the confluence of intellectual and textual pleasures apparent in this quote was not welcome in a world which reserved these forms of experience for men. Her assertions of literary authority, and expressions of the desire to write and to be read, are more often than not present in carefully disguised or displace forms in the language of the text.

If we conceive of this desire, ambition, and fulfilment as enacted exclusively on the level of discourse, as much of current theory would have it, we overlook other possibilities for the expression of desire; in particular, we neglect the text as a material object.[17] The autograph manuscript of the *Vida* rests in the royal library of the Escorial, where it was brought, along with the original copies of three other of her books, by Philip II after Teresa's death. The paper, watermarked at Valladolid and Salamanca, is of high quality.[18] There are few erasures or revisions in the text. Every so often the margins, or the spaces between lines, bear notes in the hand of one of her confessors, Domingo Báñez. Despite the lack of punctuation or paragraphing, Teresa's handwriting is large, regular, surprisingly clear and legible. One particularly enthusiastic report goes so far as to say that the harmony of the lines, spaces, and pen-strokes suggests that the writing on the page represented something almost alive for Teresa.[19] Although as partisan biographers Efrén de la Madre de Dios and Otger Steggink wax romantic on the manuscript's appearance, these details do express the meticulous care and attention Teresa took with the materials and the presentation of her writing, a care which hardly points to indifference on her part, much less an expectation or a desire that her work will be read in secret and then destroyed. The very length of her manuscript is itself an important piece of evidence that Teresa found pleasure in the act of composition. Although pressed for time to carry out her convent duties, her Reform activities, and her necessary correspondence, she eventually produced a manuscript of over 400 folio pages, a length her confessors could hardly have anticipated when they encouraged her to set down her 'way of prayer'. It is difficult to imagine a manuscript of this length, to say nothing of the books that followed, originating in a reluctant writer who claimed that she would much prefer to be going about her other religious duties.

Between the time that Teresa was requested to expand her original draft and the completion of the revision in 1565, two key events took place which affected the transformation of the original confession into a book, events in which Teresa played an active, rather than a passive role. First, in 1564 she approached an official of the Inquisition, Francisco Soto y Salazar, requesting a definitive judgement on the nature of her mystic experiences, which had stirred controversy among the various theologians she consulted. Soto y Salazar suggested that she write an account of her visions and send it to Juan de Avila, a respected scholar and authority on mysticism. Teresa not only accepted, but wholeheartedly embraced the idea.

Despite her immediate confessor's nominal control over the content and purpose of her writing, a letter normally appended to the *Vida* as a postscript reveals that her ambitions for the text's circulation ranged beyond the limits he wished to impose upon it. She states that she considers herself to be writing for Juan de Avila, and presents this as her own wish, detached from the original conversation with Soto y Salazar.

The second event, if it can be called that, occurred during the process of revision. We know from a short note in Domingo Báñez's hand at the end of the manuscript that the first draft of the *Vida* was unpunctuated, unparagraphed, and evidently much shorter than the revised version. The traditional claim is that Teresa expanded the book against her will, her confessor having ordered her to add a new section narrating the founding of her first Discalced Carmelite convent, and finally, to relate the visions she had experienced since the completion of the earlier draft in 1562. But Teresa made an additional, apparently independent change during revision which took her further than her confessor's 'orders'; she divided the rather amorphous mass of the manuscript into chapters. The change in structure in the manuscript is an important landmark in the evolution of her writing from the genre of shorter confessions/professions into the format of a book dealing not only with autobiographical matters, but also with theology and mysticism. As a book, the manuscript no longer reflects the original occasion of writing, the command to write out a general confession. It reflects a new series of relationships between writer, text, confessors and potential audience. Making the chapter breaks, declaring her text as a book, signals her desire to enter into a much wider, specifically literary community, to classify her work as something more than a private confession.

In one of the last sentences of the book, Teresa describes how she sees her own text. In order that more glory may be given to God, she says, 'I have ventured to put together this story of my unruly life, though I have wasted no more time or trouble on it than has been necessary for the writing of it, but have merely set down what has happened to me with all the simplicity and truth at my command' (ch. 40). But of course she has done nothing of the sort. Far from writing simply, she has constructed a complex text which bears obvious marks of having been thought out carefully before she even started to write. Márquez Villanueva even dates Teresa's first outlines and projections for the *Vida* to her reading of Augustine's

Confessions in 1555, seven years before she completed the first draft, ten years before she penned the final lines of the revised version.[20] Furthermore, she has explored in great detail her own relationship to her text through an extended anlysis of the effects that literature had on her spiritual development, and through attempts, however limited, to control the manner in which her text unfolds. Her project has not been restricted to relating her 'way of prayer' or to describing her mystic experiences, as it was originally conceived of by Soto y Salazar and by her various confessors. It has been much more; in the materials and in the content of the *Vida* Teresa has discovered her literary vocation, and from the time of its composition until her death some twenty years later, she led the life, as Márquez Villanueva remarks, 'of an authentic professional writer'.[21]

III The book in the world

Besides being portrayed as a reluctant writer, Teresa has also been widely regarded as a humble one, humble to the point of indifference to the eventual fate of her manuscripts. I do not wish to claim that Teresa is insincere in her humility, but only that this humility can coexist with other, more complicated emotions about her texts. Her humility, after all, emerges in the context of surrendering up that which she has written, relinquishing control of her words to her confessors, who as representatives of the Church then mediate its circulation and, to a degree, its interpretation. This surrender was not a matter of choice, but of necessity.

Over and over Teresa acknowledges the authority of her confessors to correct or even to destroy her writing. But while she relinquishes control of her manuscripts with one hand, she is busy reclaiming it with the other. Her attempts to gain control over the transmission of the *Vida* include sending the book secretly to Juan de Avila in flagrant disobedience to her confessor's command. She allows what she claims in Avila's 'wish' to read the manuscript (see letter of 27 May 1568), which coincides with her own desires, to override her confessor's authority. Márquez Villanueva conjectures that Teresa entertained the idea of publishing her book in 1568, despite multiple attempts on the part of her confessors, who on this occasion were of one mind with Juan de Avila, to limit the book's audience. Márquez Villanueva interprets this as evidence that her opinion of her own work had soared to great heights; he continues: 'She did not hide from her friends the fact that her writings would be of great worth after her death; she even boasts that they might be compared to Scripture.'[22] The plan for publication does even more; it demonstrates Teresa's awareness of the mutability of a manuscript compared with the relative security and permanence of a printed text. She wanted her writing preserved as she had written it.

There is further evidence that although she surrendered her drafts to her confessors with repeated protestations of her inadequacy as a writer (protestations which, although they surface repeatedly, come to have a more perfunctory tone in her later books), she actually minded very much that her work was tempered with and changed. For obvious reasons she could not directly criticise her confessors, but she could vent her feelings to other nuns. In his biography, Ribera quotes Ana de Jesús giving evidence for Teresa's beatification and canonisation: 'When she received the translations, she said: "God forgive my confessors who have returned what they commanded me to write, transforming it and changing certain words, some of which are not mine." And then she erased their changes and in her own hand [replaced the original] between lines.'[23] In a similar manner, in the *Vida* itself she gives credit to God for passages which are particularly lucid explanations of difficult points in mystical theology: 'The Lord ... set these comparisons before me, and taught me how to express all this and to describe what the soul in this state must do' (ch. 16). But later, in private moments with individual nuns to whom she felt close, she confesses to a satisfaction with her own work, and God's contribution is noticeably absent. Isabel de Santo Domingo relates: 'The Saint often told her, as she read to her from the book she had written, that she never thought it would turn out so well. She was amazed that, without thinking, it had turned out to be so coherent, especially since her subject was such a lofty one.'[24]

Such moments of self-satisfaction are obviously incompatible with the spiritual ideal of humility, and Teresa cannot express them publicly. She apparently does not confide even in Gracián, to whom she felt particularly close. She turns instead to other nuns. Most of the comments Teresa makes about women in the forum of the *Vida* repeat cultural stereotypes of female inferiority. But these other stories hint that she expected other women's sympathy for private expressions of her own authority and the pleasure she found in writing. This expectation is surprising in the flight of the steps she took to bar other nuns from pursuing the same major writing tasks (namely, mystic texts) she herself undertook, preserving her own status as an exception, a woman able to enter into a territory otherwise restricted to men. To enter that world, however, she had to remain conscious of her own marginal status within it, and she was not able to express the full extent of her literary vocation within the bounds of her mystic writing or her correspondence with her confessors.

If evidence of Teresa's pleasure in writing is largely indirect in her books themselves or is confined to discussions with other nuns, her letters provide a place where she can safely display, even parade, enthusiasm, knowledge and aesthetic concerns. She lectures her brother Lorenzo on the best way to read and write letters, chastises other correspondents on the quality of their penmanship and the infrequency and brevity of their replies in comparison with her own textual onslaughts. She is particular about the kind of ink she uses, and even more particular about her pens, having them sent to her specially because the ones available locally are poorly made and make her writing look uneven: 'Before I forget (as I did before), I must ask you to tell Francisco to send me some well cut pens, for none can be got here, much to my disgust and trouble' (27 and 28 February 1577). Her aesthetic sense extends to every aspect of textuality, from the border of birds and flowers which adorns a letter of condolence to the seal she uses.[25] She writes to her brother Lorenzo with marked impatience: 'Kindly forward my seal as well; I cannot endure this death's head one; I want the seal with the name which I wish was stamped on my heart as it was on that of St. Ignatius' (2 January 1577). This attention to sensory detail and the freehandedness which allows her to discard a sheet of paper if the ink had soaked through contrast markedly with the philosophy behind Teresa's prescriptions for her Discalced nuns, which stress economy and function over ornament of any kind. Their habits are to be of coarse black cloth, made with the smallest amount of material possible; for reasons of economy as well as of moral principle, not even pleats are allowed. They are allowed no mattresses, no bed hangings, and are enjoined to eschew any hint of decoration or colour, 'even in so small a thing as a girdle' ('Of fasts', in the Constitutions). Teresa evidently allowed herself luxuries in writing that she denied herself and other nuns in almost every other area of monastic life.

Although Teresa's status as a woman and spiritual protégée barred her from expressing an unedited version of her literary desires and ambitions to her confessors, neither was the literary relationship between Teresa and her confessors a fixed hierarchical one. Actually, her letters and manuscripts reveal that if indeed the relationship began in this manner, it nevertheless developed into an interactive one. By the 1570s she was keeping herself informed of the writing projects her confessors undertook, and she felt free enough to comment upon them. In a letter she teases Gracián, 'I can assure you that I am amused at hearing that you are writing a treatise on confession – as if you had nothing else to do!' (9 January 1577). Her joke implies a shared authorial experience of the struggle to find time to write amid the duties of religious life. Francisco de Ribera's biography includes an account given by Gracián describing the process of revision for her later book *Las moradas*. Editing sessions were attended by himself, the Dominican theologian Diego de Yanguas, and Teresa. The manuscript itself shows erasures and marginal notations in both Teresa's and Gracián's hands. E. Allison Peers conjectures from these two sources of evidence that the three of them discussed potential changes together as equals, and that Gracián would enter corrections in the manuscript once an agreement had been reached.[26] Later still, Teresa writes to another confessor, Don Sancho de Avila, about a biography of his mother he has just completed: 'You have done well to write the history of so saintly a life: I could bear witness to its sanctity. I kiss your hands for promising to let me read it' (9 October 1581). The passage suggests that Teresa and some of her confessors exchanged manuscripts, acting as each other's early audiences. The two examples cited come from the small fraction of her correspondence that still exists; we can only guess as to when this practice began, and to what extent it developed.

Other texts reveal Teresa's participation in a community of writers much different than the isolated and hierarchical relationship between confessor and penitent suggested by her mystic texts. We have the *Vejamen* or letter of rebuke from January of 1577 as a prime example. On this particular occasion Teresa, confused by a vision in which God had told her to 'Seek thyself in Me', had solicited a variety of opinions. Her brother Lorenzo, Juan de la Cruz, Francisco de Salcedo and Julian of Avila all contributed written interpretations which Teresa's letter playfully judges from the position of devil's advocate (typically, she begins by proclaiming that she writes only from obedience to an external command). On at least one occasion she may have written in collaboration with one of her confessors. Authorship of a parody of monastic rules and regulations entitled

El Cerro has recently been attributed to Teresa 'in virtual collaboration with her right arm, P. Jerónimo Gracián'.[27] Of another vital
spiritual and literary relationship we have only indirect record; Juan
de la Cruz, generally acknowledged as the finest mystic writer in
Spanish history, destroyed every trace of his correspondence with
Teresa out of a mixture of personal scruple and political caution.

Teresa's evolving literary relationship with theologians and
scholars is paralleled by a shift, over time, in the way she conceives
of her own work. Her growth to authorial confidence and to an
attitude that can perhaps best be described as professional is clearly
marked by two metaphorical representations, written ten years apart,
of the *Libro de la Vida*. Shortly after revising the *Vida* in 1565, she
sends the manuscript to Doña Luisa with instructions to pass it on
to Juan de Avila with speed and caution, because, as she says: 'Since
I have entrusted my "soul" to you, will you return it safely as soon
as possible' (23 June 1568). This brief passage carries enormous
power. Despite her claims that her confessors can — even must —
correct, change, or even destroy the manuscript if they consider
any part of it inappropriate or in error, the metaphor of the soul
emphasises that Teresa, with the novice writer's inability to distance
the self from the text, equated her writing with her own identity,
indeed, with the deepest and most valuable part of herself. Here, the
entire manuscript is a material manifestation of her own spirit. Like
her passion for the objects of the material world of writing, however
— the inks, the pens, the seals — this intense early response to the
physical manuscript can only be expressed to a safe audience, once
again outside the convent walls, outside the hierarchy of authority
which possesses power over her text.

Almost ten years later, in December 1577, Teresa writes to
Gaspar de Salazar in a completely different tone:

> Tell Carillo that the business about which she wrote to a certain person
> in Toledo has never been settled. Undoubtedly he has the jewel in his
> possession, in fact, he praises it highly and will not return it until he is
> tired of it. He says he has a reason for examining it. But if Señor Carillo
> came here, Peralta says he would see another gem which, she believes
> [,] is much more valuable, as there is nothing outside to take from its
> beauty. It is more delicately enamelled and wrought, as the goldsmith
> says he knows his work better than when he made the other. The gold
> is purer though the gems are not as conspicuous. It was made after
> the Jeweller's design, which people say is evident. (7 December 1577)

The air of stepping back, of scrutinising her work from arm's length and being pleased with the results, is unmistakeable. Moving away from a spiritual, intensely emotional description of her writing, Teresa chooses instead a very material metaphor, one with a long tradition in Renaissance poetics: the precious gem. She still attributes her success at least in part to God, who in his role as master craftsman provides her with the structuring principle of *Las moradas*, the book she compares to the *Vida* in this passage. But her effectiveness as a writer has evolved considerably since the *Vida*, and she knows it. She has come to consider herself as a craftsman, an artisan, who despite her gender has become part of a male-dominated and male-defined literary tradition whose metaphor she appropriates for herself. Even more striking is the fact that Teresa addresses this comment not to another nun or to her brother Lorenzo, recipients of previous statements of her authorial confidence or satisfaction, but to a male reader who holds a position of some power in the ecclesiastical hierarchy, one who had served as her confessor. Although she still attributes much of her accomplishment to God's help, she no longer feels it necessary to conceal all of her satisfaction in the act and product of writing. Composition of *Las moradas* has taken Teresa only six months, and despite pleading an initial reluctance to undertake the task, at the end she confesses openly that 'it has cost me very little' (Postscript).

With the metaphors of the soul and the jewel I have touched upon the first and last of Teresa's mystic writings (the *Fundaciones*, her last book, is more historical in nature). I have tried to suggest both the extent of her development during the intervening years and the general complexity of the relations which shaped the expression, or sometimes the repression of that development. The intricacies and historical particularities of this development have yet to be explored, and would of course include many more issues, discussed with more exact chronology, than I have been able to outline here. In my choice of examples and quotations I have stressed Teresa's specifically literary motivation, her desire to achieve recognition and status not only with the nuns who, after her confessors, formed her immediate audience, but also with the male scholars, theologians, and writers who constituted the literary community where she sought acceptance. To see clearly Teresa's ambitions, her frustrations, and her satisfactions as she gains confidence and control of the act and circulation of her writing, we must move away from exploring a single text's language and content, toward examining the relations between Teresa's various texts and the contexts in which they are written. Only by recognising the extent to which her achievement, crowned in 1970 by papal granting of the title Doctor of the Church, remains displaced or limited by the conditions under which she wrote can we take the full measure of her desires and her accomplishments.

Notes

1 Translations of Teresa's major writings are from E. Allison Peers, *The Complete Works of St Teresa of Jesus*, 3 vols, London, 1982. Her letters have been translated by the Benedictines of Stanbrook (*The Letters of Saint Teresa*, London, 1926). I would like to thank George Mariscal for help with translations from Francisco de Ribera and Francisco Márquez Villanueva.

2 This generalisation holds true for criticism based on a wide range of otherwise very different poststructuralist approaches: psychoanalytic readings (Gari LaGuardia, 'Santa Teresa and the problem of desire', *Hispania*, 63, 1980: 523–31); discussions of mysticism and the limits of language (see the section on 'Lenguaje y estilo' in Manuel Criado de Val's collection of essays, *Santa Teresa y la literatura mística hispánica*, Madrid, 1984); the fragmented subject in autobiography (see Antonio Carreño, 'Las paradojas del "yo" autobiográfico', in Criado de Val, *Santa Teresa*, pp. 255–64; see also Louis Renza, 'The veto of the imagination: a theory of autobiography', in James Olney (ed.), *Autobiography: Essays Theoretical and Critical*, Princeton, 1980, pp. 268–95); Foucaultian analysis (Lillian Manzor-Coats, 'La relación poder-saber-placer en Santa Teresa', in Criado de Val, *Santa Teresa*, pp. 75–80); and exploration of feminist issues, particularly that of a female narrative space or relation to language (Paul Julian Smith, 'Writing women in golden age Spain: Saint Teresa and María de Zayas', *Modern Language Notes*, CII, 1987: 220–40).

3 I want to acknowledge Rosa Rossi's excellent discussion of Teresa's political activities and the impetus they gave to her writing (*Teresa de Avila: biografía de una escritora*, Barcelona, 1984). However, Rossi's exclusive focus on religious politics preludes consideration of literary ambitions and satisfactions, and the book, despite its title, remains a portrait of a foundress and activist who wrote rather than of a writer.

4 Francisco Márquez Villanueva, 'La vocación literaria de Santa Teresa', *Nueva revista de filología hispánica*, XXXII, 1983: 355–79.

5 Márquez Villanueva, 'La vocación literaria', p. 362.

6 Michel Foucault, 'What is an author?', *Language, Counter-memory, Practice: Essays and Interviews*, Ithaca, NY, 1977, pp. 141–60.

7 Robert Darnton, 'What is the history of books?' in Kenneth E. Carpenter (ed.), *Books and Society in History*, New York and London, 1983, pp. 3–26.

8 Dámaso Chicharro's introduction to his edition of the *Libro de la Vida* (Madrid, 1981, pp. 19–95) details traditional work focusing on Teresa's possible reading and its influence on her later writing. Juventino Caminero ('Actitud intelectual de Santa Teresa en su ambiente social', in Criado de Val, *Santa Teresa*, pp. 535–70) has written one of the rare studies of the relationship between textual authority and spiritual understanding in Teresa's mystic texts, but he does not consider reading in general as an important thematic strand of the *Vida* with both direct and indirect links to her treatment of writing.

9 The division along sexual lines that she imposes upon these two types of reading forms a significant contrast to Maxime Chevalier's argument that the readership of *novelas de caballería* is a function of social status and class rather than of gender (Maxime Chevalier, *Lectura y lectores en la España de los siglos XVI y XVII*, Madrid, 1976).

10 Teresa consistently implies a connection between the effects of receiving communion and reading or writing. So far critics have passed over the potential significance of this connection, but it is an issue which deserves further exploration.

11 Electa Arenal and Stacey Schlau, *Untold Sisters: Hispanic Nuns in their Own Works*, Albuquerque, 1989, especially p. 14.

12 I have not seen a discussion or even a list of writings by Teresa's confessors as a group (although there are certainly studies of individual works, or of individual confessors as authors), much less of the impact her contact with writers had on her own literary development. But the list is extensive, including Baltasar Alvarez, Domingo Báñez, Diego de Yanguas, Felipe de Meneses, Pedro de Alcántara, Bartolomé de Medina and Jerónimo Gracián, who wrote two books, *Dilucidario espiritual* and *La peregrinación de Anastasio*, dealing in part with Teresa's writing (P. Silverio de Santa Teresa (ed.), *Obras del P. Jerónimo Gracián*, Burgos, 1933).

13 Dámaso Chicharro is representative of more traditional critics (whose work is also summarised in his introduction) who tend to downplay examples of Teresa's assertion of authority and authorship; Márquez Villanueva and Rossi, on the other hand, dismiss as rhetorical devices any elements which conflict with that assertion.

14 Dámaso Chicharro's introduction to the *Vida* is again a useful compendium of previous criticism in this area.

15 Michel de Certeau, *Heterologies: Discourse on the Other*, Minneapolis, 1986, p. 95.

16 Access to communion comes through the priest, as permission to write comes theoretically through her confessors, or through Soto y Salazar. But the relationship between God and the communicant is private in a manner analogous to the way in which, I think, Teresa can at times represent the act of writing once permission has been given.

17 See Carlo Ginzburg's plea for renewed critical attention to material details in 'Morelli, Freud, and Sherlock Holmes: clues and scientific method', *History Workshop*, IX, 1980, especially p. 16.

18 Detailed information about the paper on which the *Vida* was written comes from several sources. See Guillermo Antolin, *Los Autógrafos de Santa Teresa de Jesús que se conservan en el Real Monasterio del Escorial*, Madrid, 1914, pp. 19–20; Vita Sackville-West, *The Eagle and the Dove*, London, 1953, p. 88; Efrén de la Madre de Dios and Otger Steggink, *Santa Teresa y su tiempo*, Salamanca, 1982, I, p. 88.

19 Efrén and Steggink, *Santa Teresa y su tiempo*, p. 88.

20 Márquez Villanueva, 'La vocación literaria', p. 365.

21 Márquez Villanueva, 'La vocación literaria', p. 358.

22 Márquez Villanueva, 'La vocación literaria', p. 369. Teresa's boast was evidently delivered, with great satisfaction, not to a nun, but to one of her confessors, Diego de Yepes. Yepes went on to write her second biography (Francisco de Ribera's, published in 1590, was the first) which was published in 1606. I would guess that she was able to speak so directly of her satisfactions to a man because in doing so here she was only repeating what others had said to her, and also because their conversation seems to have occurred later in her life, when her confidence and her reputation as a writer were more firmly established. See the discussion of metaphors at the end of this chapter.

23 Francisco de Ribera, *Vida de Santa Teresa de Jesús*, Barcelona, 1908, p. 645.

24 Efrén de la Madre de Dios, quoted in Márquez Villanueva, 'La vocación literaria', p. 369.

25 The original letter is displayed in the Teresian museum of the convent of San José in Avila.

26 E. Allison Peers, introduction to *The Interior Castle* in *The Complete Works of St. Teresa of Jesus*, II, pp. 193–4.

27 Márquez Villanueva, 'La vocación literaria', p. 359.

Confidence and the *corullero*: *Guzmán de Alfarache*

Many works of Spain's sixteenth- and seventeenth-century boom period, as well as its designation the 'Golden Age', have recently come under scrutiny by critical readers seeking a more accurate understanding of the contexts from which both the texts and their evaluations arose.[1] The 1980s have witnessed numerous examples of self-conscious criticism of 'Golden Age' works, following upon the historically oriented re-evaluation proposed by Anthony Close in *The Romantic Approach to Don Quixote*.[2] In all genres, literary studies have come to acknowledge the importance of assessing the influence of modern thought as well as of contemporary sociopolitical reality upon our characterisation of aristic representation and its function in late imperial Spain. Particularly revealing, for example, has been the realisation that modern reverence for 'Golden Age' texts as superior, timeless cultural artefacts may in fact date from the search by modern nationalist thinkers for models of self-legitimisation.[3] In addition to questioning critical motives for the overly portentous manner in which the lively creativity of this literary period has been characterised have come a series of fresh looks at what, in different authors and their works, was innovative and questioned the period of their production.

While it has sparked its own series of debates and re-readings, Mateo Alemán's *Guzmán de Alfarache* has remained almost wholly exempt from such considerations.[4] Sieber's deconstruction of linguistic subversion and its social implications in the *Lazarillo*, Cros's and Bataillon's contextualisation of political barbs and examination of levels of social parody in the *Buscón* and *Pícara Justina*, respectively, and Zahareas's and Spadaccini's study of the juncture of history and art in *Estebanillo González* are examples of a moment that has left this primary innovator of picaresque narrative, for many readers, quite literally in the dust, on the shelf of perennially boring books.[5] This essay is not intended to convince its readers that the *Guzmán* is a work for modern tastes or that it should excite the same enthusiasm as do its successors, which were overtly acknowledged to be *libros de entretenimiento* (text books). I will argue, nevertheless, that Mateo Alemán's fictive autobiography, the driving force behind a highly influential vogue in narrative 'self-writing', must be considered in re-reading the Golden Age, on two accounts: (1) the disjunction between modern critical assessments of this novel and the response evidenced among its original readers, from Spanish imitators to James Mabbe, is a prime example of the contextual issues I have just cited; and (2) the *Guzmán* has a crucial role, as the work identified by its original readers to be the prototype for *libros de pícaros* (books of picaros), in the sudden burgeoning of narratives that followed to question the limits of àrt and history.

Readings during the last fifty years have for the most part described *Guzmán de Alfarache* as the heavy-handed account of a tortured soul, seen variously as a sincere Catholic convert or recalcitrant *converso*.[6] Yet moralising readings of Alemán's convict's tale segregate the ponderous religious code from the represented social context of deviance in which the narrator has found it expedient to deploy this discourse of his superiors. In so doing, such readings thereby neatly effect the monumental closure of a work that, according to its author (Prologues, 'Declaración para el entendimiento deste libro' ('Declaration for the understanding of this book')), Barros (Eulogy) and later theorists such as Gracián not only lacks a clear, univocal voicing, but in fact achieves its didactic warning precisely through discursive ambiguity, or *agudezas compuestas* (complex wit).[7] This chapter is intended to demonstrate that Alemán's narrator grounds himself in a represented social 'reality' that radically questions his use of moralising discourse: the service of his adversaries, jailers and ministers of justice, with his person and with the text of his person, as a deviant in whom they can have confidence − an informant. This created context does not simply, as critics favouring the *converso* position argue, criticise religious orthodoxy. By parodying the very discourse that seeks to regulate his behaviour, the narrator subverts the hierarchical relationship underlying his communication with destinaries who judge him. For in speaking their language both within the story he tells − the *historia* he claims to have lived while writing − and in the re-telling of that reality to inform posterity, the fictive author Guzmán not only denigrates himself, he also controls with impunity the fate of his powerful subjects, as the privileged criminal upon whose double-edged word their well-being depends.

Guzmán's composition of his life thus represents, while it is coetaneous with, this paradoxical relationship to authority. Foreshadowed by his decision earlier to study preaching as a source of income and safe cover (II, 3, 4, pp. 363−4), the convict's sanctimonious narrative of the present from which he writes discloses a series of recent service relationships that have culminated in one literally parodying the expression it evokes: as an informant aspiring to the patronage of ever higher placed authorities, Guzmán is ultimately branded a 'brown-noser', in a final episode whose indelicacy has sheltered it from discussion by modern critics.[8] And it is upon this note that Alemán's monumental fiction closes. I have chosen this episode, which consists of Guzmán's work as *corullero* (stowage slave), as the focal point of this chapter because it is my opinion that this defining context of the novel's articulation demands reinterpretation by modern readers of the novel, or perhaps more accurately, a return to the reaction of Alemán's initial readers, summed up in the wit of James Mabbe's 1622 English translation. The *corullero* episode however cannot be read in isolation; to position it intratextually, within the developing code of religious terminology and social obeisance that confers the convict's concealed authority, it is necessary first to examine the section on Guzmán's intentions at Alcalá and then the series of final service relationships that culminate in his demotion to the *corulla* (stowage).

First, let us reconsider the function that the narrator himself assigns to his use of religious language, preceding the 'conversion' that modern critics so commonly ascribe as the cause. At the University of Alcalá in II, 3, 4, pp. 378−80, Guzmán admits to having plotted the use of religious discourse for secular purposes − to guarantee an income and, somewhat cryptically, to protect himself from future dangers occasioned by past *casos* (incidents):

> Determinábame a ser bueno; cansábame a dos pasos. Era piedra movediza, que nunca la cubre moho, y por no sosegarme yo a mí, lo vino a hacer el tiempo. Vime desamparado de todo humano remedio ni esperanza de poderlo haber por otra parte o camino que de aquella sola casa. Púseme a considerar: «¿Qué tengo ya de hacer para comer?» Morder en un ladrillo hacíaseme duro; poner un madero en el asador, quemaríase.

Vi que la casa en pie no me podía dar género de remedio. No hallé otro mejor que acogerme a sagrado y díjeme: «Yo tengo letras humanas. Quiero valerme dellas, oyendo en Alcalá de Henares, pues la tengo a la puerta, unas pocas de artes y teología. Con esto me graduaré. Que podría ser tener talento para un púlpito, y, siendo de misa y buen predicador, tendré cierta la comida y, a todo faltar, meteréme fraile, donde la hallaré cierta.

Con esto no sólo reparé mi vida, empero la libraré de cualquier peligro en que alguna vez me podría ver por casos pasados. El término de pagar lo que debo viene caminando y la hacienda va huyendo. *Si con esto no lo reparo, podríame ver después apretado y en peligro. Bien veo que no me nace del corazón, ya conozco mi mala inclinación*; mas quien otro medio no tiene y otra cosa no puede, cometer debe a lo que hallaré.» (II, 3, 4, pp. 363×4, emphasis added)

I had often resolved to be good, but I was quickly weary of well-doing; I was that rolling stone, that never gathers mosse. And because I could not tame my selfe, time had now tamed me. I saw my selfe abandoned of all humane remedie, and had no hope of any other helpe, then that onely of my house. I began then to consider, and to say with my selfe; What have I now in the house, to staunch my hunger withall? Shall I bite upon a brick-bat? that is but tough feeding, and somewhat too hard a crust to gnaw upon. Shall I roste one of my rafters? That will be burnt away upon the spit: I found that a naked house, without something to maintaine it, could not afford me any kinde of remedie. I could thinke upon no better thing, then to betake my selfe to sacred Orders, and to become a Churchman: Saying to my selfe; I have humane learning; I will make benefit of that, by hearing those Lectures read in Alcala de Henares. I have some little smackering also in the Liberall Arts, and Divinitie, and when I have studyed these a-while, I will take my Degree, then shall I be qualified for the Pulpit, and being able to say Masse, and to preach a Sermon, I shall be sure to have wherewithall to eat; and if all should fayle, I would turne Fryar at the last, whereby I should not onely live upon certainties, but should also lead a very safe and secure life .... *By this course, I shall not only repayre my life, but I shall free it likewise from any danger whatsoever, which I might have incurred by my former misdemeanours.* The time, for the payment of my debts, drawes on a-pace, and my wealth goes away fast; *if by this meanes I did not provide for the storme, that was now a coming, I might afterwards see my selfe oppressed, and in great perill to be utterly lost.*

> *I knew that this came not from my heart, for I was not ignorant of mine owne evill inclination*; but he that hath no other meanes, and is put to his shifts, must doe as he may. (Mabbe, IV, pp. 184–5)

These ponderings at Alcalá, which Guzmán wishes us to 'overhear', clearly anticipate his use of preacherly discourse in the novel's final pages, warning that his ends at that point may be secular as well. Immediately following is another carefully planted slip that incorporates Alemán's introductory allusions (I, p. 89) to the fictive author's final state as a galley slave: 'No tengo más que barloventear; esto es, echar la llave a todo, antes que preso me la echen' (II, 3, 4, p. 364) ('Now that I am imbarked, I must play the cunning Mariner, and seeing I cannot sayle with a fore-winde, I must fetch boords, and come about with a side-winde' [Mabbe, IV, p. 185]); Mabbe does not translate the segment following the semi-colon, which in my own terms, is: 'that is, try the key in every door, before, as prisoner, they throw the key to mine away'. In a curious shift of register from the previous discussion of letters, the nautical term *barloventear* (come about) foreshadows from four chapters ahead Guzmán's final straits aboard ship. The studious *pícaro* knows prior to his capture that it behoves him to 'take a new tack', which will enable him to close the previous chapter in his life or, in effect, to put it behind him, before they 'throw away the key', leaving him to end his days a prisoner.[9] The context of this reference, of course, is not elaborated by the fictive author, and with good reason. Guzmán structures his life story shrewdly, assuring that crimes coinciding temporally with his role as author do not receive undue – or ironically, even due – consideration. The admission of his current deceptions may be hoped to bring him praise as an earnest regenerate who submits himself to public censure, but Guzmán, quite rightly, does not want the nature of his recent crimes to detain our attention. Thus he passes from allusions to ships and looks on to other matters without further ado.

Guzmán's self-narrative passes from Alcalá to a dizzying series of increasingly grave crimes that he committed against persons of social substance, before once again picking up the thread of references to the profit potential in religious discourse, in the description of his alleged penitence and conversion, after he has been caught and sent to serve sentence near the novel's end. As in the first mention of this recourse, the *pícaro*'s deployment of the gesture is again evidently an interested act. This is made clear a second time by the context in which it is placed. After being made a convict, Guzmán undertakes the establishment of a series of service relationships intended to better his circumstances and, ultimately, to free him from his sentence. Ascending in order of social rank and benefits, from the commissary who first transports him to the galley to the authority who may commute his sentence, each relationship offers provisional gain. In the course of this process, Guzmán attempts the transition from a materially-based personal service, in which he himself is the commodity, to the less taxing, empowered service offered in the artfully narrated text of his person. Reference to his relationship with God occurs mid-point in this sequence, after the commissary and boatswain, and before the captain's relative and the implied destinary of his final ploy, *Su Majestad*, the master of royal galley slaves who may himself write the final chapter to the convict's life. In each relationship, Guzmán establishes his worth to his master by telling the truth – informing – both on himself and other convicts; ironically, the devious manner in which the truth benefits these superiors compromises the authority they represent, for Guzmán's divulging of the truth is in itself an exercise in the *engaño* (deceit) that they police.

If we are to appreciate critically the importance for his entire narrative of the mature *pícaro*'s claims to reliable, even sanctimonious intentions in the writing of his personal history, we must take a closer look at the string of service relationships in which information – the 'truth' – exacts a pay-off at the novel's end, or present tense of its articulation. In the first relationship, that of Guzmán and the commissary, Guzmán incites the chain gang destined for the galley to steal a number of suckling-pigs by encircling them on the road to Las Cabezas. He uses his own booty to ingratiate himself with the commissary who is marching them to the coast, offering to prepare it for his dinner. Correctly identifying the commissary's sensual weakness, Guzmán thus obtains freedom from chains to cook the feast and, incidentally, to rob other wayfarers of two small but heavy packages containing valuable rosaries. He passes these to another slave, Soto, with what would seem to be either prudence (to avoid detection with them himself until back on the road) or a surprising lack of it (Soto has already broadcast his unreliability, informing on Guzmán in prison, and may well keep the goods). The resolution of this episode is highly instructive, for we then learn that, as might have been expected, Soto later denied knowledge of the packages and Guzmán succeeded in motivating the commissary's participation in the reappropriation of the jewels, both to the *pícaro*'s own *provecho* (advantage) as well as his own. While confessing quite readily to his theft of the packages, Guzmán forestalls his own punishment and authors that of Soto by bribing the commissary with offers of recovered plunder. Not only is he exempted from punishment by his confession; Guzmán assures for himself at least temporary preferential treatment. Guzmán tells the truth about his own actions and those of Soto, but the carefully planned effects of his words reveal the dangerous nature of his duplicity. While Guzmán could have arranged to win the commissary's friendship by transferring the rosaries directly to him, he instead creates the role of accomplice for Soto who, although greedy, is innocent of the theft in question. The torture of Soto's genitals that produces the goods serves to repay the slave in terms that are particularly ugly for his previous 'singing' in jail, at the same time that it establishes Guzmán's dominance over both men. The context of this particular series of transgressions (II, 3, 8, pp. 446–51) clearly defines the value of Guzmán's confessions, confirming suspicions that readers have been led to harbour earlier: the *pícaro*'s confessions are carefully composed to ensure favour and the freedom that enables him to create the terms of his existence as well as that of others.

Once aboard ship, this sequence is duplicated with another slave and a more powerful master (II, 3, 8, pp. 451–63), as Guzmán's astuteness enables him to distinguish himself quickly and to curry various rewards that result in the redefinition of his status as a slave. The pursuit of greater goals this time leads Guzmán to play dirtier pool, and this sequence is narrated with a series of metaphors and ellipses that evoke the *Lazarillo* all too clearly. Quickly identifying the authority whose favour may make or break his daily existence, Guzmán sets about enslaving the will of his overseer, the boatswain, whom he blasphemously refers to as his chosen 'ángel de guarda' (guardian angel). Identifying the same sensual weaknesses in this master that he mobilised in the commissary, Guzmán assiduously ministers to first the physical needs of the boatswain and then to his taste for a good story. While our narrator devotes more narrative to highlighting the latter (retelling two of his anecdotes in II, 3, 8, pp. 455–7), repetition of a more elliptical nature highlights the former theme in terms that, as Brancaforte argues, can only be seen as unfavourable.[10] An initial rundown of his tasks:

> Desta manera me fui poco a poco metiendo cuña en su servicio, ganando siempre tierra, procurando pasar a los demás adelante, tanto en sevirlo a la mesa, como *armarle la cama*, tenerle aderezada y limpia la ropa, que a pocos días ya ponía los ojos en mí. (II, pp. 454–55, my emphasis)

> Thus, little by little, I went scruing my selfe into his service, getting more ground still upon him, and striving to out-strip the rest: As well in my attendance at his boord, as in having him to bed; I trickt up his Cabin, brusht his Cloathes, kept them neat and handsome, lookt to his linnen, and was in every other respect so diligent about him, that within a few dayes I was the onely man in his eye. (Mabbe, IV, p. 318).

finds clarification in two following references. Guzmán works for his master, at night:

> Matáble *de noche* la caspa, traíale las piernas, hacíale aire, quitábale las moxcas con tanta puntualidas, que no había príncipe más bien servido (II, p. 455)

> 'A nights I did ridde the Dandruffe out of his head, rubb'd his feet, fann'd his face, destroyed the Gnats, and waited on him with that observance and punctualitie, that the greatest Prince in the world would not be better served. (Mabbe, IV, 319)

and although he is soon taken to live in the boatswain's quarters in round-the-clock service of his person and freed from a galley slave's normal toils, Guzmán makes a voluntary show of rowing and sleeping occasionally with the convicts to avoid gossip: 'por no querer apartarme de allí *ni dar ocasión a murmuración*, dejando de la mano lo que una vez quise de mi gusto poner en ella' (II, p. 458) ('because I would not leave my Oare, *nor give occasion to others to murmur*, by withdrawing my hand from that, which for mine own pleasure I had voluntarily undertaken' [Mabbe, IV, p. 324]). Although it is possible for twentieth-century readers perhaps to assign neutral values to 'armarle la cama', 'de noche', and 'murmuración', the text of Lázaro's Tratado Seven as well as similar use of ellipsis in Tratado Four were bound to have been present in the minds of the original public of the *Guzmán*.

Guzmán's currying of favour takes a nastier turn in this episode in other ways as well. Once again concealing prohibited items of value – coins sewn in his shirt – Guzmán predetermines a sequence of events that will further his ends. The money, known to his fellow convicts, challenges one to rob him at night, and by confessing his own transgression − their ownership − as well as presenting the lure of material gain, Guzmán incites his master to search, beat and whip eight rows of slaves, nearly killing many and rubbing salt in their wounds in order to produce the money with which the slave will ply him (II, 3, 8, pp. 459−61). Once again, Guzmán confesses one wrong in order to successfully commit another. Clearly impenitent, the convict exhibits his old flair at *engañar con la verdad* (deceive with the truth), wishing, ironically, to draw the distinction between his honesty and the other slaves' duplicity that will ensure for him the bed, food, and company of the powerful aboard ship. Readers should note with some suspicion that in the episodes within Chapter Eight his communication apes that routinely reserved for *discretos lectores* (prudent readers): deception with the truth, which guarantees that they will not perceive themselves to be victimised and thus will not retaliate.[11]

Before discussing the brief interior monologue of repentance that we find within the narrative of Guzmán's service for the boatswain, it is important to look at the third relationship in this series of communications with his superiors aboard ship. By Chapter Nine, his closing lines, Guzmán's efforts have paid off, for the captain, noticing his diligent care of the boatswain, has requested that the convict serve a close relative who is accompanying him. Guzmán's relocation to the gentleman's quarters marks the pinnacle of his influence or, we might say, the 'cumbre de toda buena fortuna' (pinnacle of his good fortune) of his existence aboard the galley, for he displaces the man's own servants to enjoy the prestige and comforts of − he tells us pointedly − his own sleeping quarters in the *despensilla* (pantry) of his new master's cabin and direct access as a trusted servant to his clothing and jewellery (II, 3, 9, p. 466). While attempting to persuade us as to his true loyalty − 'de quien *él y yo* teníamos menos confianza y más recelaba, era de sus criados' (p. 466) ('But that which he and I, had least affiance in, and were most jealous of, was, of his owne servants' [Mabbe, IV, p. 335]) − Guzmán's other allusions refer to his ulterior motives. His service of this new master, who obviously has influence with the captain, is ultimately aimed at obtaining Guzmán's complete freedom:

> De todo se me daba un clavo, mi cuidado era sólo atender al servicio de mi amo, por serle agradable, pareciéndome que podría ser − por él o por otro, con mi buen servicio − alcanzar algún tiempo libertad. (II, p. 467)

> I made no reckoning of it, ... all my whole care being now taken up, in the diligent atending of my new Master, and in doing him all faithfull service, that I might procure his love and good liking towards me; hoping it might one day so fall out, that either by him, or by some other, in recompence of my good service, I might chance to purchase my liberty. (Mabbe, IV, p. 336)

In the meantime, with a brazen defiance of the risks involved, the convict does not hesitate to rob the same benefactor who may obtain for him this freedom. Alerting us with brief allusions to his relative physical freedom ('me pusieron una sola manilla', 'they placed on me only one manacle') and with the term 'ágil' (nimble), whose reference to his increased mobility reminds us of his theft while virtually free with the commissary ('Desta manera quedé más ágil para poderle mejor servir' [II, p. 466]) ('By which means, I was inabled to doe him the quicker and nimbler service'), Guzmán clarifies the nature of his [Mabbe, IV, p. 335]) loyalty. In passing references that, not surprisingly, find no moralising self-criticism, he writes:

> Ellos [sus criados] dormían con el capellán en el escandelar y el caballero en una banca del escandelarete de popa y yo en la despen-silla della, donde tenía guardadas *algunas cosas* de regalo y bastimento. Yo me hallaba muy bien; bien que trabajaba mucho. Mas érame de mucho gusto tener a la mano *algunas cosas con que poder hacer amistades a forzados amigos.* (II, 3, 9, p. 466, emhasis added)

> They cabbin'd with the Chaplaine, neere to the maine Mast; and the Gentleman, he had his cabbin within the Poope; and I, in a little Dispense, or Pantrie, where I kept some *regalos*, and dainties, besides other necessary provision.
>
> I liked very well of my service, though I tooke a great deale of paines, but it was a pleasure unto me, and gave me much content, that I had now *the power, by those things that past thorow my hands, to performe many kindnesses toward such Slaves as were my friends and acquaintance* (Mabbe, IV, p. 335)

Hiding things to be stolen, as he had done while a *pícaro de cocina* (Kitchen boy), in the place where they are normally stored, the *despensilla* that doubles as his sleeping quarters, Guzmán freely dips into the gentleman's supplies to run a small black market among the slaves. A parody of suppressed references to transgression in the *Lazarillo*, 'algunas cosas' here alerts us to Guzmán's continued deviance. Either no longer obliged to perform for this master base physical ministrations or carefully not discussing possible connections between this material economy and sex, Guzmán helps himself to his new master's physical wealth, laundering it in an equally unsavoury and potentially more dangerous underground economy. We are made to notice that the gentleman whom he now serves receives the ostensible treatment of a *discreto* (prudent reader), which for much of the novel has been equated with the social elite. Far more important than Guzmán's care of the man's personal effects is his entertainment of the courtier with witty anecdotes and tales, and Guzmán's astuteness as a politic adviser: 'dejaba mi amo de conversar con sus criados y muy de su espacio parlaba comigo cosas graves de importancia' (II, p. 467) ('My Master had now left off conversing with his other servants, and would at large discourse with mee of grave and weighty matters'; [Mabbe, IV, p. 337]). Yet the fictive author's references to the liberty he plots and the appropriation of his master's supplies clearly indicate that this supposed *discreto* has no more defences against Guzmán's wiles than do the *vulgo* (common public). Guzmán simply 'plays' him with a more sophisticated set of *burlas* (jokes).

When the resentment produced by Guzmán's power among the convicts causes Soto to frame him with the theft of a small silver plate (II, p. 470) and then, we must assume, of the gold-encrusted hatband (II, p. 472), the power wielded by the three parties of this third relationship − master (captain−cousin), Guzmán, and slaves − comes into open strife that threatens to redefine Guzmán's fate in ways beyond his control. For once words are of no use to him − he cannot try to bargain by confessing the truth or resort to bribery because he has not authored the *burla pesada* (injurious joke) and has nothing to show for it. Furthermore, any cries of religious repentance − he admits − would be seen as hypocrisy:

> Palabra no repliqué ni la tuve, porque, aunque la dijera del Evangelio, pronunciada por mi boca no le habían de dar más crédito que a Mahoma. (II, p. 473)

> I reply'de not so much as one word, nor had I the power to speake; And if I should have sought to justifie my selfe, had it beene Gospel, that I should have delivered unto them, comming out of my mouth, no more credit would have beene given unto it, then to Mahomet (Mabbe, IV, p. 345).

Guzmán's lack of control in this deception leads, when his near-death fails to produce the stolen goods, to a punishment that is highly appropriate for a base currier of favour such as himself – his reassignment to the bowels of the ship as *corullero*.

Thus, finally, at the end of this series, coinciding with the end of his account and present from which he writes, the antithetical relationship between Guzmán's material status and the superior company he seeks is highlighted by the price of the accumulated betrayals wrought by his truthfulness. After having acted both as an informant upon other slaves and satisfier of his masters' pleasures aboard the galley, the fictive author, even while consecrating his life to literary posterity by composing the experiences we read, has been condemned by the ship's captain to suffer public ignomy as the ship's *corullero*, among other duties, a dispenser of bung wipes. As Guzmán tells us ruefully, in referring to this last tribulation,

> que aquésta es la ínfima miseria y mayor bajeza de todas. Pues habiendo de servir con ellos para tan sucio ministerio, los había de besar antes que dárselos en las manos. (II, 3, 9, p. 477)

> this was the utmost of all miseries, and went most against my stomake, as being of all others the meanest and the basest Office; for being to serve them with these, for so beastly (that I may not give it a worse word, for feare of turning thy stomake) a piece of businesse, I must first be forced to kisse it, before I give it into their hands, so that by an Attourney, I must kisse, you know what. (Mabbe, IV, p. 349)

Not to be outdone, the *pícaro* manages to triumph through this punishment, however, masterminding as an informant the fatal betrayal of his rivals in order to regain the comfort of life on the upper decks. Readers learn that the fictive author informed superiors of a plot of mutiny to which he, allegedly innocent, was privy. As a result, Guzmán's counterparts among the galley slaves suffered hideous fates. The leaders, including his nemesis Soto, were drawn and quartered between four galleons, many co-conspirators were executed by hanging, and the *moriscos* lost their ears and tongues. Guzmán tells readers that he, for his own – supposedly meritorious – role, anticipates at the closing of Part Two royal pardon, which should enable him to live and write Part Three of his life, pending 'la cédula' (certificate) of the King, master of royal slaves. Readers should be perplexed if not suspicious when they recall the last line of Alemán's opening 'Declaración' (I, p. 89). Since Guzmán's life story is delivered, according to the real author, in verbose parody of a typical convict's 'sermoncito', 'para en la escalera', the context suggests that he is still under suspicion as a co-conspirator and in danger of being hung in punishment. The *Guzmán* thus closes upon unresolved tension between Guzmán's claims to innocence, as the confidant of his superiors, and Alemán's simultaneous characterisation of him as an incorrigible criminal and joker figure, whose own brazenness has led him from life as a slave to the threat of the death-sentence.

Many critics have confused Guzmán's assistance of authorities in this final civil case with motives of the narrator's religious penitence in the preceding chapter. But, as Brancaforte argues eloquently, pointing out the fictive author's continued transgressions aboard ship during both final chapters of the novel, the interior monologue of Chapter Eight taken to substantiate his recent conversion does not justify their readings;[12] if anything, it should cause heightened suspicion of the *pícaro*'s innocence in the explosive test of authority posed by the plot of mutiny. Brancaforte's analysis is very much on target. The immediate narrative context in which the religious monologue is embedded provides no logical motivation for serious or 'sincere' meaning of the discourse employed. First, it occurs during a period of Chapter Eight when Guzmán enjoys considerable favour with the boatswain, is given shore leave, allowed to make money on the side, and to sport a new 'vestidillo' (suit) for summer (II, 3, 8, p. 461). Second, the opening lines of his reflections draw attention to the irony of Guzmán's language, for although he protests that he would die before doing 'cosa baja ni fea' ('anything base or ugly'), it is his 'torpe sensualidad' ('filthy sensualitie' [Mabbe IV, p. 328]) that has brought him to the height of misery from which he might 'con facilidad, alzando el brazo, alcanzar el cielo' (II, p. 461) ('easily, by raising an arm, reach Heaven'). Since he has succeeded in winning the good will ('ganarle la gracia') of the demanding boatswain, his lesser or lower-case 'señor' (master), Guzmán reflects that he should have no difficulty in acquiring for himself the greater benefits that his upper-case master, 'Dios', (God) dispenses for a less painful price. As Brancaforte (*Degradación*, p. 67) points out, 'Guzmán pone en la balanza lo que se gana con el cómitre y lo que se gana con Dios. Es una forma tosca de apuesta pascaliana. El peso se inclina hacia Dios, *ergo* hay que elegir al más poderoso.'

Fraught with economic metaphors ('precio', 'cuenta', 'paga', 'cornadillo', 'acaudalar', 'comprar' and 'valor'), the entire monologue is articulated in what Longhurst (97) has accurately identified as 'the language of a business deal', as Guzmán, in effect, transfers temporal values to the consideration of eternity. Just as he has succeeded in 'comprarle la gracia' ('buy favour') (II, p. 461) aboard ship, he audaciously decides to negotiate the Afterlife − 'comprar la bienaventuranza' ('by "eternal bliss"') − hoping for a bargain. Guzmán clearly is not sufficiently unhappy with his life under the boatswain to renounce it; the language of his narrative tells us that he simply aims to capitalise on his wrongs, as currency for redemption:

> Ya con las desventuras iba comenzando a ver la luz.... De donde vine a considerar y díjeme una noche a mí mismo: «¿Ves aquí, Guzmán, la cumbre del monte de las miserias, adonde te ha subido tu torpe sensualidad? Ya estás arriba y para dar un salto en lo profundo de los infiernos o para con facilidad, alzando el brazo, alcanzar el cielo. Ya ves la solicitud que tienes en servir a tu señor, por temor de los azotes, que dados hoy, no se sienten a dos días. Andas desvelado, ansioso, cuidadoso y solícito en buscar invenciones con que acariciarlo para ganarle la gracia. Que, cuando conseguida la tengas, es de un hombre y cómitre. Pues bien sabes tú, que no lo ignoras, pues tan bien lo estudiaste, cuánto menos te pide Dios y cuánto más tiene que darte y cuánto mejor amigo es. Acaba de recordar de aquese sueño. Vuelve y mira que, aunque sea verdad haberte traído aquí tus culpas, pon eses penas en lugar que te sean de fruto. Buscaste caudal para hacer empleo: búscalo agora y hazlo de manera que puedas comprar la bienaventuranza.» (II, 3, 8, pp. 461−2)

> Now (thinking upon my former mis-fortunes) I beganne to have a glimpse of that light .... And as I was thinking and considering on these things, I said one night with my selfe; Guzman, thou seest heere the top of that Mountaine of miseries, where-unto thy filthy sensualitie hath brought thee: now art thou come to the highest part of it, and must either make a speedy leape downe to the bottomlesse pit of hell, or which thou mayest more easily do, by lifting up thy arms, take hold on Heaven. Thou seest now the care that thou hast to serve thy Master, for feare ... and to purchase his favour, which when thou hast obtained, is but of a man, and a masters-Mate ....
>   Now thou well knowest, and canst not be ignorant of it, for thou hast beene a profest Student, and hast studied that point; how much lesse God requires at thy hands, and how much more he hath to

conferre upon thee, and how farre a greater friend hee is, then any man can be unto thee.

Rouze up thy selfe therefore, and awake ... consider, that though it be true, that thy sinnes have brought thee hither, yet so apply this thy punishment unto thee, and lay it so neere to thy heart, that thou mayst make good use of it, and that it may turne to thy good. Thou hast sought after a stocke to imploy it for thy profit; seeke now to obtaine eternall happinesse, and lay out all that thou hast, that thou maist buy it. (Mabbe, IV, pp. 327–8)

In ironising the discussion of redemption with a parody of economic discourse, Guzmán's musings on his planned penitence hardly reassure the reader of his sincerity. Just as he has won the favour and subverted the authority of the boatswain and others before him by carefully picking the behaviour most desired by his audience, so he considers the appropriate angle for efficacious dealings with God:

Sírvele con un suspiro, con una lágrima, con un dolor de corazón, pesándote de haberle ofendido. Que, dándoselo a él, juntará tu caudal con el suyo y, haciéndolo de infinito *precio*, gozarás de vida eterna' (II, p. 462, emphasis added)

Serve him with a sigh, with a teare, or with a true heart-sorrow, grieving for thy sinnes .... And so by giving him that which thou hast, hee will joyne thy stocke with his owne, and making it of an infinite *price*, not by thine, but his merits, thou shalt enjoy life everlasting. (Mabbe, IV, p. 329)

While Guzmán wishes readers to believe that the ensuing trials and tribulations that he suffers prove the firmness of the penitence that he has just ironised, they clearly point to the opposite, representing poetic justice slated by Alemán for the unrepentant convict who has chosen to boast of his wrongs.[15]

The dilemma that frames the narrative of *Guzmán de Alfarache* could hardly be described as humorous. But it should cause us to reconsider the tenor of the implied dialogue that Guzmán undertakes with *discretos lectores* and, presumably, the King, in hopes of guaranteeing favourable outcome for himself. Although Guzmán invokes discourses of high seriousness, applying religious and judicial argumentation to his own case, he cuts a risible, if not ridiculous, figure in so doing. More importantly, through the same hybrid articulation of his relationship to society, he succeeds in laughing at readers who consider his beguiling communication. While he cannot confess, for his usual profit, to the crime that sent him to the *corulla*, because he does not possess the objects stolen, the able narrator can and does resort to confessions of another type: Guzmán first confesses the plot of mutiny that his rival, Soto, has masterminded, and then, to emphasise the intent to co-operate with his masters to the fullest, if returned to the deck and their company, he proffers the account of his life as a sinner, both as evidence of contritition and to entertain them.

While the lenient response of censors to Alemán's novel attests to the didactic value that Guzmán's religious argumentation has, in and of itself, modern criticism has assigned the narrator a serious character altogether inconsistent with the context in which he uses such argumentation to support his own case. Although its indelicacy has excluded the *corullero* episode at the novel's end from 'serious' critical discussion, it is the most revealing indication we have that Alemán intended his fictive author to be perceived not in earnest or serious terms, but as a currier of favour from courtiers and God alike, one whose behaviour identifies him both a metaphoric and a literal 'brownnoser', of whom readers should well be wary. James Mabbe clearly echoes the perceptions of Alemán's original reading public in his 1622 translated version of the *Guzmán*, giving us the characterisation of Guzmán that modern readers have stubbornly ignored.[13] Remarking (Vol. I, p. 4) in the Dedication of the English version to 'Don Ivan Estrangwayes', 'gentilhombre de la Camara de Su Serenissima Magesdad de la gran Bretaña' that his Guzmán is assured a warm reception since 'los Picaros tienen entrada en las Casas de Señores', Mabbe characterises him (p. 5) as a 'graçioso'. In 'To the discreet reader' he repeats (p. 17) Alemán's rejoinder that readers will suspect Guzmán's story to be intended not for 'publicke good' but 'Interest' and 'ostentation of wit'. The wit announced in the opening volume closes the last, as Mabbe translates Guzmán's description of the episode in question here. In Volume IV he writes:

> The care was laid upon me ... of old ends of Ragges, or of Flax and Tow, to make wads and wisps for that that go to the Long-house (you know what I meane) and this was the utmost of all miseries, and that went most against my stomake, as being of all others the meanest and the basest Office; for being to serve them with these, for so beastly (that I may not give it a worse word, for feare of turning thy stomake) a piece of busínesse, I must first be forced to kisse it, before I give it into their hands, so that by an Attorney, I must kisse, you know what. (IV, p. 349)

Telling the truth or 'informing' in the *Guzmán* is an admitted act of obeisance – a didactic affirmation of the rules broken by Alemán's convict and his counterparts – but it simultaneously constitutes the act of defiance that negates Guzmán's jailers' power to castigate him. For in setting the record straight about his life as a dangerous deviant, by way of the extensive apology that comprises his autobiography, Guzmán pre-empts the authority of his superiors both to suppress such questionable exemplarity and to impose their own assessments of the history he represents. In particular, the convict's diligent confessions usurp his superiors' right to guarantee their own visage of infallibility, for he alone articulates the terms of reality. Guzmán's life story does not simply tell the truth about *engaño* – it deceives with the truth, providing in the process a striking study of the power of art and the limits of discourse to structure reality.

The *Guzmán* is not a light or comic novel, but its articulation, through the convict Guzmán, is a masterful study in the humour with which language may subvert the very terms of the communication it serves. Alemán's novel is a *libro de entretenimiento* with a serious message, that has suffered ossification under modern criticism. It not only contains *burlas*; its narration by the fictive author Guzmán in itself constitutes an edifying *burla*.[14]

Notes

Where I have cited it, English translations of quotes from Alemán's text are taken from James Fitzmaurice-Kelly's 1924 edition of James Mabbe's *The Rogue or the life of Guzman de Alfarache* (edition cited in note 13). Otherwise, the quotes are mine.

1 Examples of this recent proliferation are too numerous to cite exhaustively. There are studies of a primarily textual nature, which consider the relation of specific works to the so-called literary canons of the Golden Age, while other studies focus on extratextual aspects of artistic production. The following indicate the breadth of focus and variation of method in recent American Golden Age criticism alone: John R. Beverley's Marxist study, *Aspects of Góngora's 'Soledades'*, Amsterdam, 1980; Ruth El Saffar's feminist *Beyond Fiction: Recovery of the Feminine in the Novels of Cervantes*, Berkeley, 1984; Walter Cohen's comparatist Marxist analysis, *Drama of a Nation: Public Theater in Renaissance England and Spain*, Ithaca, 1985; Diana de Armas's gender study, 'Cervantes's *Labors of Persiles*: "Working (in) the in-between" ', in Patricia Parker and David Quint (eds.), *Literary Theory/Renaissance Texts*, Baltimore, 1986, pp. 150–81; John J. Allen's historical sleuth work, *The Reconstruction*

of a Spanish Golden Age Playhouse: El Corral del Príncipe 1583–1744, Gainesville, 1983; Marcia L. Welles's examination of intertextual parody in *Arachne's Tapestry: The Transformation of Myth in Seventeenth-Century Spain*, San Antonio, Tex., 1986; Wlad Godzich and Nicholas Spadaccini (eds.), *Literature Among the Discourses: The Spanish Golden Age*, Minneapolis, 1986, collected essays on popular culture and literature; and the following studies, whose orientation is self-evident: Anne J. Cruz, 'Spanish petrarchism and the poetics of appropriation: Boscán and Garcilaso de la Vega', in Maryanne Cline Horowitz, Anne J. Cruz and Wendy A. Furman (eds.), *Renaissance Rereadings: Intertext and Context*, Urbana, 1988, pp. 80–95; María Cristina Quintero, 'Translation and imitation in the development of tragedy during the Spanish Renaissance', in *Renaissance Rereadings*, pp. 96–112; Anthony N. Zahareas, 'The historical function of picaresque autobiographies: Toward a history of social offenders', in Nicholas Spadaccini and Jenaro Talens (eds.), *Autobiography in Early Modern Spain*, Minneapolis, 1988, pp. 129–62; Margaret Rich Greer, 'Art and power in the spectacle plays of Calderón de la Barca', *Publications of the Modern Language Association of America*, CIV, III, 1989: 329–39. Since this piece will concern itself primarily with American readings of the *Guzmán de Alfarache*, I have not cited the numerous British counterparts to the above. Paul Julian Smith's deconstructive study, *Writing in the Margin: Spanish Literature of the Golden Age*, Oxford, 1988, is an excellent recent example.

2 Anthony Close, *The Romantic Approach to Don Quixote: A Critical History of the Romantic Tradition in 'Quixote' Criticism*, Cambridge, 1977. Although Close's conclusions have been queried, most scholars now agree with his argument for the major reevaluation of ideological presuppositions operative in modern criticism. Shorter pieces in the same vein include Roberto González Echevarría, 'The life and adventures of Cipión: Cervantes and the picaresque', *Diacritics*, X, III, 1980: 15–26; Javier Herrero, 'Dulcinea and her critics', *Cervantes*, II, 1982: 23–42; Peter Dunn, 'Cervantes de/reconstructs the picaresque', *Cervantes*, II, 1982: 109–31; John Beverley, 'Can hispanism be a radical practice?', *Ideologies and Literature*, IV, XVI, 1983: 9–22; George Mariscal, 'History, the Subject, and the Spanish Golden Age', forthcoming in *The Seventeenth Century*; and Peter Evans, 'Golden-Age dramatic criticism now', *The Seventeenth Century*, II, I, 1987: 49–53.

3 Wlad Godzich and Nicholas Spadaccini, 'Popular culture and Spanish literary history', *Literature Among Discourses: The Spanish Golden Age*, pp. 41–61, argue (p. 45) that 'Spanish literary history has inherited, though not always understood, the privileging of its own early modern times. It has especially failed to appreciate the fact that this privileging, whose consequences for the remainder of Spanish cultural development would condemn it to a representation of decline and backwardness and a deprivation of inner dynamics, was an alibi for someone else's project: the literary history of the Germans.' The use of Spain's literary production in the sixteenth and seventeenth centuries by German Romantics, who formulated its literary history and laid the groundwork for criticism to

follow, in order to exemplify and thus legitimise the representation of
nationalist ideology in modern Germany, as Godzich and Spadaccini
assert, has had many negative effects on our perception of their model.
Not only is Spanish literature after the 'Golden Age' seen in terms of
decline; artistic representation and its function during that period, because
of its atemporal privileging, has until recently not been considered by
modern criticism to be a vigorous process, one open to question, as well
as one that challenged the literary and social givens of its period.

4 The two dominant modern movements in *Guzmán* criticism consist of a
trend that has been referred to as the 'catholic–apologetic school' and one,
largely American, favouring the interpretation of the protagonist as an
unrepentant *converso*. While both are historically-grounded, to the extent
that they focus on the articulation of post-Tridentine doctrine in the
novel, neither tendency examines the representation of historical context
in which this religious discourse is formulated; they instead question the
individual spirituality of the character Guzmán. The first trend is
represented by Enrique Moreno Báez, *Lección y sentido del 'Guzmán de
Alfarache'*, Madrid, 1948, who develops ideas expressed earlier by Miguel
Herrero in 'Nueva interpretación de la novela picaresca', *Revista de
Filología Española*, XXIV, 1937: 343–62; and by Angel Valbuena Prat
in the Prologue to his edition of the *Guzmán* in *La novela picaresca
española*, Madrid, 1943, p. 159; also Carlos Blanco Aguinaga, 'Cervantes
y la picaresca. Notas sobre dos tipos de realismo', *Nueva Revista de
Filología Hispánica*, XI, 1957: 313–42; A. A. Parker, *Literature and the
Delinquent*, Edinburgh, 1967; Donald McGrady, *Mateo Alemán*, New
York, 1968; Francisco Rico (ed.), *La novela picaresca española*, Barcelona,
1967, pp. xviii–cli; *idem*, 'Estructuras y reflejos de estructuras en el
Guzmán de Alfarache', *Modern Language Notes*, LXXXII, II, 1967:
171–84; *idem, La novela picaresca y el punto de vista*, Barcelona, 1969.
Peter Dunn ('Cervantes de/reconstructs the picaresque', pp. 109–31)
reminds us, however, that readings by Spanish intellectuals of the *Guzmán*
as an authoritarian text during this period may have contemporary
ideological notives, and should be considered in the context of the Franco
era (pp. 116–17, n. 10).

The second movement is represented by Américo Castro, 'Perspectiva
de la novela picaresca', in *Hacia Cervantes*, 1957, revised edn., Madrid,
1967, pp. 118–42; and *idem, De la edad conflictiva*, Madrid, 1961,
pp. 188–9; J. A. van Praag, 'Sobre el sentido del *Guzmán de Alfarache*',
in *Estudios dedicados a Menéndez Pidal*, V, Madrid, 1954, pp. 283–306;
Marcel Bataillón, 'Les nouveaux chrétiens dans l'essor du roman
picaresque', *Neophilologus*, IV, 1964: 283–98; Edward Nagy, 'El anhelo
de Guzmán de Alfarache de "conocer su sangre"', una posibilidad inter-
pretativa', *Kentucky Romance Quarterly*, XVI, 1970: 75–95; Alberto del
Monte, *Itinerario de la novela picaresca española*, trans. Enrique Sordo,
Barcelona, 1971, p. 80; Joseph H. Silverman, 'Some aspects of literature
and life in the Golden Age of Spain', *Estudios de literatura española
ofrecidos a Marcos A. Morínigo*, Madric, 1971, pp. 133–70; Eugenio
Asensio, 'En torno a Américo Castro. Polémico con Albert A. Sicroff,

Hispanic Review, XL, 1972: 365−85, esp. pp. 380−3; A. A. Sicroff, 'Américo Castro and his critics: Eugenio Asensio', *Hispanic Review*, XL, 1972: 1−30, esp. pp. 9−15; Victorio Agüera, 'Salvación del cristiano nuevo en el *Guzmán de Alfarache*', *Hispania*, LVII, 1974: 23−30; Joan Arias, *Guzmán de Alfarache: The Unrepentant Narrator*, London, 1977; Richard Bjornson, '*Guzmán de Alfarache*: Apologia for a "converso" ', *Romanische Forschungen*, LXXXV, 1973: 314−29; *idem*, 'The dissemination of the picaresque: *Guzmán de Alfarache* and the *converso* problem', in *The Picaresque Hero in European Fiction*, Madison, 1977; M. N. Norval, 'Original sin and the "conversion" in the *Guzmán de Alfarache*', *Bulletin of Hispanic Studies*, LI, 1974: 346−64; Carroll Johnson, *Inside Guzmán de Alfarache*, Berkeley, 1978; Benito Brancaforte (ed.), *Guzmán de Alfarache*, 3rd edn., Madrid, 1984, pp. 17−51; *idem, Guzmán de Alfarache: ¿Conversión o proceso de degradación?*, Madison, 1980; Giuseppe Bellini, 'Guzmán de Alfarache: Juez-penitente', in Giuseppe Bellini (ed.), *Aspetti e problemi delle letterature iberiche: Studi offerti a Franco Meregalli*, Rome, 1981, pp. 61−78; Carlos A. Rodrìguez, 'Guzmán de Alfarache, narrador: La poética del gracioso', *Kentucky Romance Quarterly*, XXXI, 1984: 403−12; *El narrador pícaro: Guzmán de Alfarache*, Madison, 1985; Judith Whitenack, *The Impenitent Confession of Guzmán de Alfarache*, Madison, 1985.

5 Harry Sieber, *Language and Society in 'La vida de Lazarillo de Tormes'*, Baltimore, 1978; Edmond Cros, *L'Aristocrate et le carnaval des gueux: Etude sur le 'Buscón' de Quevedo*, Montpellier, 1975; Marcel Bataillon, *Pícaros y picaresca*, Madrid, 1969; Nicholas Spadaccini, 'Clues and sources: Imperial Spain and the secularization of the picaresque novel', *Ideologies and Literature*, I, 1976−77: 59−62; 'History and fiction: The Thirty Years' War in *Estebanillo González*', *Kentucky Romance Quarterly*, XXIV, 1977: 373−87; Nicholas Spadaccini and Anthony N. Zahareas, 'Introduction', *Estebanillo González*, Madrid, 1977.

6 See note 4.

7 A detailed analysis of the Prologues, 'Declaración para el entendimiento deste libro', and Barros's Eulogy is provided in my forthcoming book, *Autobiography as 'Burla' in the Guzmán de Alfarache*. Baltasar Gracián cites Alemán's book as an outstanding example of the use of *agudeza* to creae extended argumentation, 'agudeza compuesta' or 'agudeza mayor', in Arturo del Hoyo (ed.), *Agudeza y arte de ingenio, Obras completas*, 3rd edn, Madrid, 1971, pp. 364, 372−3, 435, 477−9, 482, 508; also in *El criticón, Obras*, pp. 875, 1143.

8 All citations of the *Guzmán* are taken from Brancaforte's 1984 edition.

9 *Diccionario de autoridades*, s.v. *barloventear*, gives: 'Puntear ù dár bordos el navío quando no tiene viento favorable para navegar, à fin de ponerse sobre el viento' and 'Metafóricamente es andar de una parte à otra sin firmeza ni estabilidád'; s.v. *echar la llave*, 'Vale lo mismo que Cerrar'. Guzmán evidently articulates a play on *cerrar* and the literal meaning of the individual words that compose the expression, *echar* and *llave*.

10 *Degradación*, pp. 60–5, 118.

11 Chapter One of my book on the *Guzmán* analyses in detail the communication established in the narrative with this problematic group, and considers the social function assigned to *discretos*.

12 *Degradación*, Chapter Three.

13 Citations are taken from James Mabbe, *The Rogue or the life of Guzman de Alfarache*, ed. James Fitzmaurice-Kelly, 4 vols., I and IV, London, 1924.

14 Monique Joly, *La Bourle et son interprétation. Recherches sur le passage de la facétie au roman (Espagne, XVIe–XVIIe siècles)*, Atelier National, Reproduction des thèses, Université de Lille, Toulouse, 1982, argues in a long overdue study that *burlas* are a structuring principle of Guzmán's narrated story; in his book and article (note 4), Rodríguez locates jokes in the present of Guzmán's narration itself, but sees their use as limited to one of four discursive functions attributed to Guzmán. I suggest, instead, that the articulation of the entire narration is an extended *burla* or study in *agudeza compuesta*.

15 C. A. Longhurst, 'The problem of conversion and repentance in *Guzmán de Alfarache*' in *A Face Not Turned to the Wall: Essays on Hispanic Themes for Gareth Alban Davies*, ed. C. A. Longhurst, Leeds, 1987, pp. 85–110 asserts (101) that the narrator's expression of a desire for spiritual emendation, in this context, must be seen not as evidence of convictions, but rather as a last-ditch attempt. His thorough review (91–101) of sixteenth-century conceptions of conversion presents convincing evidence that the narrator's experience would not have been perceived by Alemán's readers as having constituted any of the three basic types.

Constructive testimony: patronage and recognition in *Don Quixote*

I Deconstruction's premises

My aim in this chapter is to consider how far 'deconstruction' is applicable to *Don Quixote*; the conclusion that I shall reach is negative. My scepticism about this critical approach is based on philosophical conviction, which I have expressed elsewhere.[1] I recognise that French and American avant-garde theory has salutarily forced literary criticism to become more alert to its unexamined premises, and to take account of linguistics, philosophy, psychology, anthropology, Marxism, and semiotics. Less fortunately, it has fostered the impression that it provides an ironically aloof overview of the whole tradition of Western literature and thought, and that its methods constitute a ready-made kit which may be applied to any part of that tradition with equal efficacy. After a preliminary exposition of deconstruction's premises, I propose to test them in relation to the theme of 'recognition' in *Don Quixote*.

The avant-garde theorists alluded to above include Jacques Derrida, Roland Barthes, Julia Kristeva, Paul de Man and J. Hillis Miller. They share certain key assumptions.[2] They object to 'Western' thought's 'onto-theological' tradition, its metaphysics of 'presence', its 'logocentrism', its belief in the conscious self as ground of meaning, its endemic dichotomies of signifier and signified, culture and nature, history and origin, writing and speech.[3] They maintain that, with respect to all these dichotomies, the 'Western' tradition has treated the first term as convertible into the second, rather like a currency bill which promises the bearer that it may be encashed for a determinate weight of gold at the Bank of England. Thus, the sign may be exchanged for the signified; history may be traced back to an origin; 'In the beginning was the Word (*Logos*).'[4] Derrida's gospel is that the currency is fraudulent: the promised conversion is barred by the nature of language.

Derrida begins *Of Grammatology* (original French version, 1967) by calling attention to the Western tradition's tendency to give pre-eminence to speech over writing.[5] In this he sees self-deluding repression: a lurking sense of lack camouflaged by a metaphysics built on the promise of restitution. The promotion of speech is motivated by the sense that this is a form of expression intimately trnsparent to the speaker's consciousness, assuring the convertibility of sign into signified. Yet, argues Derrida, when one examines linguistic signs in the flight of Ferdinand de Saussure's theory of language, one perceives that they exist in an inter-linked, differential chain which quite discredits that illusion. Saussure declares: 'In the linguistic system there are only differences, *without positive terms.*'[6] The value of signs, just like that of currency bills, is not primarily determined by a positive relation to some 'object of exchange' (e.g. a concept or referent), but by a negative and contrasting relation to signs of the same 'denomination'.

According to Derrida's leading American follower, the 'differential' property of language opens up 'vertiginous possibilities of referential aberration', particularly in literary texts, which continually skew, subvert and overspill their margins of sense.[7] This effect is compounded by the 'citability' or repeatability of linguistic signs, which causes them to escape the determinations of specific context, and also, to carry with them the hidden traces of all their previous usage. Since language conditions the form of man's knowledge and experience, what is true of 'text' is true of man's whole universe: 'there is no beyond-the-text'. This is the axiom of Derrida's thesis of supplementarity, which, in the second part of *Of Grammatology*, he develops in relation to the writings of Jean-Jacques Rousseau. Taking Rousseau as exemplary of the Western tradition, Derrida argues that his overt insistence on the merely supplementary status of education, masturbation, mother-substitutes and writing is belied by a practice which repeatedly finds the 'real thing' deficient and in need of supplementation.

An essential aim of Derrida's deconstructive enterprise is to problematise the concept of self; he rebels against a tradition of French/German philosophy which takes a metaphysical encounter with Self as the ground of knowledge. Another aim is the cast doubt on the possibility of catching the self in a net of interpretation.[8] If the 'I' which originates the text is a mirage of language, there can be no pontifical arbiter of its true intentions. This subversion of authority over the text is extended, notably by Barthes and Kristeva,[9] though not by Derrida's American followers, to Authority in general, bourgeois/capitalist society and the Christian–humanist tradition. The humanist assumptions of traditional literary criticism are prime targets of this subversion: they include the idea of literature as mimetic representation, as expression of an individual mind or of some historic world-view, as part of a specific tradition. The concept of the work *of* an author yields to that of 'text': the place of pure linguistic freeplay without origin or reference to truth, and of a polyphony of cultural discourses entering into relations of dialogue, contestation, and parody.

J. Hillis Miller's essay on Dickens's *Bleak House* – introduction to the Penguin edition of the novel (Harmondsworth, 1971) – is a good early example of the deconstructive method, and may usefully illustrate how it could be applied to *Don Quixote*.[10] It typifies deconstruction's practice of picking away at the fine stitching of a text – e.g. its metaphors, its rhetoric, its key-words and their associations – in order to disclose a paradoxical contradiction between what it implies and what it asserts. The paradox concerns some form of intuition of the short-circuit of The Sign; and the intuition is less the author's than the Text's. As Hillis Miller describes *Bleak House*, the novel sets out to offer a representative panorama of the English society of Dickens's time. It features two narrators who are engaged in the task of discovering the causes of England's decline, and it continually prompts the reader to emulate them, and all the characters, in deciphering the written signs – wills, parchments, letters – that elicit their investigative curiosity. 'The interpretation of signs or of texts', Hillis Miller roundly asserts, 'may be said to be the fundamental theme of this novel' (p. 17). The motive for all this archival activity is the investigators' desire to learn their origins and identity, hence their rightful place in the social system. Surprisingly, much of the activity fails; and the implication is that the culprit is the nature of the sign-system itself, which alienates man from knowledge of self and others. Yet the Derridean disquiet implicit in *Bleak House* conflicts with a residual theocentrism. At the heart of the novel Hillis Miller finds 'a tension between belief in ... a stable centre outside the shadows of the human game, and ... the shade of a suspicion that there may be no such centre, that all systems of interpretation may be fictitious' (p. 32). In all the ways that he describes it – the social realism; the characters' obsession with origins; the dramatisation of the activity of interpretation; the metaphysical tension just mentioned – *Bleak House* corresponds to *Don Quixote* as modern criticism has interpreted it.

II   Recognition and patronage in Cervantes's romantic mode

The fundamental question that has beset Cervantine criticism since Américo Castro's *El pensamiento de Cervantes* (1925) has been how to reconcile 'the two Cervantes'. Roughly speaking, one side of Cervantes is represented by the romantic works (*La Galatea, Persiles y Sigismunda*, some of the *novelas*, the interpolations in *Don Quixote*). These, by virtue of their sentimental tone, idealised settings and characters, and black-and-white morality and life-philosophy, appear very different from the fictional creations of the 'other', better-known Cervantes, such as *Don Quixote* and the more famous *novelas* (e.g. *Rinconete y Cortadillo, El coloquio de los perros*). These works, which are comic in tone, are acutely perceptive about the prosaic quality of ordinary human existence; they seem to exude indulgent approval for colourful idiosyncracy, even lawlessness; a notoriously genial and noncommittal irony apparently puts every opinion in inverted commas, as merely a viewpoint to be set against other viewpoints.[11] The ideology explicitly formulated by the 'two Cervantes' shows no disaccord; broadly speaking, it is aligned with Counter-Reformation Catholicism and the values of the Spanish Golden Age. The disaccord, if any there is, lies rather in the contrast between what is quizzically implied in one area and rhetorically emphasised in the other.

I shall argue in this chapter for the essential continuity between the two sides, and, leaving moral/religious ideology somewhat to one side, shall concentrate on matters which affect the apologetics, hermeneutics and epistemology of the fictional work, and involve the various ways in which it seeks to validate itself: that is, to lay claim to aesthetic and moral persuasiveness and 'truth'. On the surface, Cervantes's fiction, in both its modes, should lend itself to deconstructive analysis in this direction, since both tend to portray surrogates for the reader and the author at the centre of the fictional world, hence to dramatise the process of their own reading, writing and valuation. The ultimate concern of these readers-by-proxy is recognition, understood in various ways: *anagnorisis* (dramatic recognition of one personage by another); discovery of origins; restitution of status;

clarification of mysteries and of moral truth. One of these readers, by virtue of his authority, typically has the status of a patron. *His* function is to validate recognition. By considering *Don Quixote* in this light, we come face to face with a difficulty that any deconstructive approach to a Spanish Golden Age text must confront: here is a literary work which overtly insists on the recoverability of Sense and Origins, and does so, not just on a conceptual level, but in diverse aspects of its style and form. How, then, can it be plausibly claimed that this insistence is radically flawed?[12] The contrast between the 'two Cervantes' suggests a way of making the claim good.

I choose one of the principal interpolations of *Don Quixote* Part I as an example of how 'recognition' works in the romantic mode; it is the episode featuring Cardenio, Dorotea, Fernando and Luscinda (*DQ* Part I, Chapters 23–29, 36).[13] It typifies the principal features of Cervantine 'romance': the sentimental, exemplary, and genteel tone; the ingeniously Byzantine structure; the free use of prodigious peripeties and adventures which imperil or save love, life and honour. Despite its treacly improbability for the modern reader, it is designed to yield truth of an artistic kind – i.e. lifelikeness. This is a fundamental concern of Cervantes in both his fictional modes.

The episode artfully dovetails two narratives of unhappy love, Cardenio's and Dorotea's. Cardenio is the forlorn, crazed, savage personage encountered by Don Quixote in the *sierra* (I, 23–24). He tells his story in two instalments; the first is addressed to Don Quixote (I, 24), and the second to the priest and barber (I, 27). The story's gist is as follows. Fernando, son of an Andalusian Duke and Cardenio's best friend, cruelly abused the confidence of that friendship by secretly arranging to marry Cardenio's sweetheart, Luscinda. Previously, Fernando had been infatuated by the daughter of one of his father's vassals, and had confided to Cardenio his intention to seduce her under pretext of a promise of marriage. Cardenio did his best to dissuade his friend from this dishonourable purpose. When, warned by Luscinda, he heard of her imminent wedding to Fernando, he just had time to attend it, hidden behind an arras, but not to prevent its occurrence. Assuming that he had been betrayed by his fiancée, he went off in despair to the *sierra*.

No sooner has Cardenio finished his story, than the priest hears a voice raised in lamentation (end of Chapter 27). Peeping round a rock, he sees a young peasant who proves to be a maiden in manly disguise. Prevailed upon to account for herself, the girl relates that she is a rich farmer's daughter, whose previously blameless existence has been shattered by the amorous attentions of a certain Duke's son, Don Fernando. When entreaties failed, he resorted to more high-handed means. In circumstances which left her little option, she submitted to his will, but not before extracting from him a solemn vow of marriage. Subsequently, he abandoned her, and, so she heard, married a beautiful lady called Luscinda. Furious at this perfidy, she resolved to pursue him to keep him to his vow. Soon she got to hear of the secret marriage, including certain particulars suggesting that its outcome was less clear-cut than Cardenio imagined. Such is Dorotea's story. Much of its drama lies in a circumstance extrinsic to it: the fact that its listeners already know the background of her plight, and that one of them has a vital interest in it, because he shares it. As she drops the significant names in her story, enabling us to identify her relation to the other protagonists, we savour the dramatic irony, particularly the anticipated moment of Cardenio's recognition of her.

Barthes, in *S/Z* — a detailed structuralist commentary on Balzac's novella *Sarrasine* — analyses the narrative in terms of five 'codes', i.e. implicit rules for understanding the purpose of any narrative sequence.[14] If one applied his analysis to Cardenio's and Dorotea's stories, one could easily show that they converge relentlessly on the ultimate recognition. Thus, *no sooner* has Cardenio finished his story than Dorotea's lament is heard, as though in promise of picking up its broken thread. Barthes's 'hermeneutic' code, concerned with posing and clarifying mysteries, is the one which chiefly concerns us. It works overtime, giving the whole episode and its sundry dovetailed components some resemblance to a whodunit. Its functioning is bound up with the reactions of the audience, notably the priest, to the two narratives and their sequel. The audience's role, apparently merely a matter of packaging, gives Cervantine romance a distinctive character and constitutes its chief originality.

In this genre, Cervantes tends to abandon 'omniscient', impersonal, chronologically linear narrative, and to favour instead a form of presentation calculated to achieve the maximum impact and illusion of immediacy. The viewpoint is that of the hand-held camera, which shows events as casually seen and overheard by unsuspecting witnesses. These persons are launched into the drama at or near its crisis, and are given explanations retrospectively, as it continues to unfold. Though merely passive spectators, their role is essential:

to transmit the above-mentioned impact to us, the readers. They are, implicitly, proxies for us; the priest's relation to Cardenio and Dorotea duplicates ours to *him* and both of *them*. Cervantes effects successive chance encounters between his witnesses and the protagonists, each of whom gives his or her subjective version of events at a stage when the memory of injuries received is still raw and the predicament is still unresolved. These flashback narratives – fragments of a jigsaw puzzle – are inset in a paradigmatic sequence which forms the basic structure of a significant part or the whole of Cervantes's romantic *novelas* and interpolated episodes. His fondness for this sequence shows where his priorities lie: not so much in exciting contingencies such as escapes, seductions and the like, as in the tantalising process by which the mystery surrounding the narrator–protagonists is removed, and such questions as 'Who is he?' and 'What's his secret?' are completely answered for the witnesses' benefit. The culminating chance encounter is the one which brings these narrators face to face with the original troublemaker (in this case, Fernando). Then the predicaments are resolved and the jigsaw is triumphantly completed. In effect, the paradigmatic sequence turns story into theatre, and the author–narrator into a noncommittal, self-effacing presenter of the show.

I propose to highlight the sequence's tendentious, teleological operation in its hermeneutic aspect by subjecting it to the kind of narratological analysis that Vladimir Propp employs in *Morphology of the Folktale* (original Russian version, 1928).[15] In this seminal study of one hundred Russian fairy-tales, Propp discovers that they reveal a morphological structure akin to that of a natural species; all their individual differences of plot, setting and character may be seen as variations upon a sequence of thirty-one constant functions, which pass from 1: 'One of the members of the family absents himself from home', to 31: 'The hero is married and ascends the throne'. With Propp, I make these assumptions: in determinate cases there may be some variation of the sequence's basic pattern; part of the sequence may be repeated several times in the same story; individual characters are not limited to one type of functional or 'actantial' role. Yet, unlike Propp, who treats the functions as an unconscious, universal substrate of the wonder-tale, I see them as reflecting Cervantes's conscious and distinctive practice. Moreover, I perceive them at work, not in the whole story, but in the organising framework and chief turning-points.

I base my analysis on the climax of the interpolated episode (*Don Quixote* I, 36): the fateful arrival at the inn of a party of distinguished travellers, whose faces are masked to protect them from sun and dust. Note that the sequence of functions set out below has unfolded at each previous stage of the episode: first discovery of Cardenio (I, 23–24); second discovery (I, 27); discovery of Dorotea (I, 28). The impact of this repetition is cumulative and plethoric.

1 A mysterious stranger (or strangers) becomes an object of curiosity for a witness (or witnesses)

Four men and a lady on horseback, accompanied by two grooms, arrive at the inn (beginning of Chapter 36). The innkeeper, Cardenio, and the priest note their arrival with interest. The narrator contrives an air of naturalness (Barthes's *effet de réel*) by a realistic detail: the innkeeper, anticipating wealthy clients, is the one who sights and describes the party. While feigning ignorance and impartiality, the narrator lightly draws attention to the signs that whet curiosity, deepen the mystery, and offer clues: e.g. the lady's deep sigh and infirm condition. These circumstances are, logically, of greater concern to the priest than the innkeeper; the priest, as an embodiment of *discreción*, assumes the role of witness-in-chief in function 2.

2 A witness takes steps to clarify the mystery

The priest asks one of the grooms for information about the party. It is noteworthy that Cardenio, who, for no obvious reason, goes inside, and Dorotea, who modestly veils her face, adopt the opposite attitude to the priest's. Their curiously uncurious attitude is explained by the build-up to *anagnorisis*, which is a dramatic, tantalising *process* of revelation by signs. Revelation, for Cardenio, will be triggered by the sound of Luscinda's voice. Thus, *her* place on the porch, and *his* in the interior, reveal the narrator's artful disingenuousness; each casually insignificant detail has its precise function in the sequence. Function II is undeveloped at this stage of the episode; yet at previous stages (e.g. Don Quixote's search for and meeting with Cardenio [I, 23–24]), it is more protracted. To it correspond the characteristic *comedimientos* (courtesies) and *ofrecimientos* (offers of help, good-will) with which witnesses presume to intrude on the private grief of these mysterious stranges, by eliciting their stories.

3 The witness receives an evasive or incomplete reply

The groom can tell the priest little about the party, except that its members are of high social standing, and that they have travelled in marvellous silence, broken only by the sobs and sighs of the lady, who is probably being taken to a convent. Note the disarmingly natural recourse once again to an insignificant, plebeian informant: the groom. He stands for any casual onlooker − including us − and, more particularly, for an onlooker lacking the requisite sagacity or inside information − an unprivileged situation from which we will soon be rescued. At the first stage of the episode, this function was elaborately developed, comprising the goat-herd's narrative (I, 23) and the first instalment of Cardenio's (I, 24). Its purposes are obvious: to tantalise by means of merely partial clarification, to sustain the *effet de réel*, and to enhance the ultimate enlightenment by contrast with incomplete states of it.

4 The impediment to clarification is removed, and the witness discovers the stranger's secret and identity

Hardly has the groom finished speaking than Dorotea makes an *ofrecimiento* to the mysterious lady; and this triggers a chain-reaction leading to *anagnorisis*. Masks or veils slip or are removed from faces; Cardenio rushes outside; and everyone beholds everyone else. The drama of all this is due to two principal factors: the recognition's likeness to a theatrical 'discovery', and, even more, its shocking or scandalous nature. Characteristically, these *anagnorises* reveal the mysterious stranger as being the troublemaker, the arch-rival, the opposite of what he or she seems, the beloved. The significance of this one is summed up by the sentence specifying the precise address, in each case, of that quadrilateral exchange of looks: 'Callaban todos y mirábanse todos: Dorotea a don Fernando, don Fernando a Cardenio, Cardenio a Luscinda y Luscinda a Cardenio' ('They all kept silent, looking at each other: Dorotea at Don Fernando, Don Fernando at Cardenio, Cardenio at Luscinda, and Luscinda at Cardenio') (I, p. 449).

At this climactic moment, the priest ceases to be witness-in-chief. We might say that this role devolves on each of the protagonists, with one of them standing out in importance: Dorotea. *Her* skilful pleading is required to remove the impediment to a happy outcome: Fernando's prickly possessiveness regarding Luscinda. The role of witness, combined now with that of patron, will devolve on the priest again near the beginning of Chapter 37: 'Todo lo ponía en su punto el cura, como discreto, y a cada uno daba el parabién del bien alcanzado' ('The priest found the right words for everything, and congratulated each of the lovers on the happy autcome that had been attained') (I, p. 457).

4a The stranger relates his predicament

In earlier phases of the episode, this step is co-extensive with function 4, and corresponds to Cardenio's and Dorotea's narratives. In this phase, it represents Fernando's explanation of what happened after the secret wedding, and follows function 6 so as not to disperse the tension of the imminent resolution. Function 4a is an inset narrative which permits the author to unfold a substantial part of the plot. It is where a story told in traditional, chronologically linear order would begin; Dorotea's narrative in I, 28 starts: 'En esta Andalucía hay un lugar de quien toma título un duque' ('Here in Andalusia there is a town from which a certain duke takes his title') (I, p. 347). Yet it differs from the traditional model in that it gives a partial and subjective, not an omniscient, view of events, and serves either as explanation of a discovery or as prelude to another one. Its location in the paradigmatic sequence highlights its subordinate function.

4b The witness reveals his/her own identity

Not relevant at this stage, though at a previous stage (second discovery of Cardenio) it provides an opportunity for a return to 4 and 4a and a reversal of roles: Cardenio becomes the stranger with the interesting secret, and Dorotea the witness.

4c The witness offers sympathy and help in the quest for the troublemaker

Omitted at this stage.

5 They meet either another stranger, victim of a related predicament (return to step 1), or the troublemaker

Irrelevant here.

6 The injured party or an intermediary entreats the troublemaker to make good the injury or renounce his claims

We may pass over the details of Dorotea's argument, merely noting that it is essentially concerned with the restoration of status, social and moral, to each of the protagonists, including Fernando; that it is endorsed by all the bystanders – that is, by society; that it formulates some leading ideas in Cervantes's ethical code, e.g. about the relation of the individual destiny to Providence.

7 The troublemaker confesses his error, and the injury is repaired amidst joyful reconciliations

7a The patron bears witness to the exemplary, prodigious and veridical nature of the case

The two steps are often co-extensive. In his nauseatingly sentimental reconciliation scenes, Cervantes saturates recognition with communal tears. Step 7a, though seemingly no more than an epilogue, is, from the hermeneutic standpoint, the most significant of the whole sequence, since it imposes society's stamp of validity on recognition. For this to be effective, the patron should have the requisite status – e.g. nobleman, ecclesiastic, magistrate – and the whole case should seem certifiably true. Hence, this step often assumes a notarial tone. The most interesting example of this occurs in *La española inglesa*. In this *novela*, the paradigmatic sequence only figures prominently at the dénouement; yet the whole of the preceding story is, by implication, based on an explanatory inset narrative in the sequence (Function 4a), hence made dependent on it.[16] This narrative is the heroine's account of her and the hero's travails. She offers it to an audience which includes the magistrate and two prominent ecclesiastics of Seville, who later request her to set it down for the benefit of the Archbishop. The hero proves his credentials by producing the certificate of the act of contrition that he made in Rome. The location of Isabela's family lodgings is identified – 'opposite the monastery of Santa Paula' – and so is the *hidalgo*, Hernando de Cifuentes of Burgos, from whom the freehold was later acquired. Cervantes implicates himself in the relay of testimony. Of Isabela's narrative he says: 'el cual le reduzco yo a que dijo todo aquello que ...' ('which I summarise by saying that she related all that which ...') (p. 94). This casual statement carries undertones of which Cervantes's contemporary readers could not have been aware. In the early years of the seventeenth century, about the time when he wrote *La española inglesa*, Cervantes himself contributed to a literary miscellany for the entertainment of Archbishop Niño de Guevara of Seville. So, the first-person narrator who makes the above-mentioned summary is, implicitly, the historical Cervantes, who does Isabela the honour of putting her on the same plane of reality as himself and making her co-contributor to the very miscellany to which he contributed.

Thus, the disquieting implications that Hillis Miller finds in *Bleak House* are decidedly not present in Cervantine romance. Here, signs are straightforwardly assumed to be convertible; tokens and warrants serve their purpose; characters seek and discover their social origins. That quest is affirmed to be extensible beyond the shadows of the human game to the divine sphere. Are matters any different in Cervantes's comic mode?

III Recognition and patronage in Cervantes's comic mode

As we might expect, the paradigmatic sequence works less obviously and systematically in Cervantes's comic mode than his romantic mode, and to different effect. Yet its underlying premises remain firmly in place, as we may verify by examining a particular aspect of *Don Quixote*: its pretence to be a kind of history.

Effectively, the basis for the pretence is laid in *Don Quixote* I, 9, where Cervantes reports his discovery of an Arabic manuscript by a *morisco* of Toledo, Cide Hamete Benengeli, containing the veridical record of the heroic deeds of a contemporary knight of La Mancha. After getting it translated from Arabic into Castilian, Cervantes has made it available to the public, acting simply as editor of what Benengeli wrote. Such is the author's overt, tongue-in-cheek pose as narrator of the story. Obviously it is a preposterous spoof, and he cheerfully advertises the fact. Its most striking improbability concerns the ethnic origins and character of the historian. The *moriscos*, in 1605 (date of Part I), were a despised community, notorious amongst the old Christians for their apostasy, disaffected spirit and untrustworthiness — quite the wrong qualifications for reliably hymning the deeds of a Spanish hero. By 1615 (date of Part II), all the *morisco* community had been expelled from Spain. Moreover, the character and doings of Don Quixote, bound up with his crazy delusions of being a knight-errant, are evidently not the stuff of history, but of a comic fiction, which, as we know, has been invented by Cervantes. Much of Cervantes's play with the figure of Benengeli insistently reminds us of this: e.g. comments on Benengeli's scrupulousness, or quibbling equivocations about a precise term or number or species or etymology, when the facts in question are patently footling or ridiculous. A delightful example of this occurs in Part II, Chapter 12, in a passage which sends up humanistic lore and history's moralistic digressions. 'Editor' Cervantes reports that there is a tradition from father to son that the author of this true history devoted particular chapters to extolling the friendship of Rocinante and Sancho's ass, but suppressed them in order to respect the decorum due to his heroic theme. Yet sometimes he strays from this purpose, and writes that the two beasts would congregate in order to scratch each other, and once satisfied, would remain with Rocinante's neck across the ass's for three days together. Cervantes comments: '*Digo que dicen que dejó el autor escrito que* los había comparado en la amistad a la que tuvieron Niso y Euríalo, y Pílades y Orestes' ('I say they say that the author recorded that he had compared them in friendship to Nisus and Eurylus, and to Pylades and Orestes') (II, p. 123; my italics). The italicised words nicely suggest how preposterously diffuse and amorphous is the chain of intermediaries linking what Benengeli wrote to what we read, and by implication, what he wrote to 'the facts'. It all appears very remote from the quasi-historical pretensions of *La española inglesa*.

Yet the flippant insistence on Benengeli's punctiliousness is not just a joke; it alludes to the novel's lifelikeness, hence its difference from chivalric romances. Moreover, if we turn our attention from the pretence which frames the story, to the picture within the frame, we find that it keeps featuring, in various quiet and incidental ways, the chain of information and communication that bears the news of Quixote's and Sancho's adventures to the world around them. To be sure, these allusions to sources are often humorous, yet not as preposterous as the example mentioned above. Since Don Quixote's world is depicted as historical and contemporary, the chain stretches, by implication, from Don Quixote to Cervantes. *Don Quixote* thus creates the impression of being a vast contemporary gazette, focused on the two central figures, and compiled from the multiple testimonies of all the personages featured in it, and from archives, notarial documents, rival chronicles, folk-tradition, police records. The narrative continually says or implies whose version is being followed at any given stage.

I offer a number of examples of how this impression is created. *Example 1.* In Part I, Chapter 4, Don Quixote meets a party of travellers who, 'como después se supo' ('as later transpired'), were

Toledan merchants on their way to Murcia to buy silk. Clearly, the quoted words are not those of an omniscient narrator. They hint at the gradual assembly of the facts of the matter from different sources at different times. Which source apart from Don Quixote himself? The end of the chapter alludes to it: 'Los mercaderes siguieron su camino, llevando que contar en todo él del pobre apaleado' ('The merchants continued their journey, having much to tell in the remainder of it about that poor drubbed wretch') (I, p. 102). *Example 2.* When verses are cited in the novel, we are usually told who remembered or recorded them. Of those that Don Quixote engraved on trees or in the sand during his penance in the *sierra* (I, 26), only three were subsequently discovered, hence recorded, by his deliverers — the three featured in the text. These persons guessed the reason for the ridiculous termination 'del Toboso' at the end of each verse, and the knight subsequently confirmed it. Here, the process of subsequent divulgation that is merely hinted at in Example 1 is explicitly alluded to. *Example 3.* The guide who conducts Don Quixote to the Cave of Montesinos is chief witness of the events related in Part II, Chapters 22 to 24. Like the official chronicler designated to record Sancho's every word and deed in the governorship, he is a sort of counterpart to Benengeli within the novel — a believable counterpart, and not, as the Moor is, a preposterous figment. His correspondence to Benengeli is augmented by his authorship of two books which are thematically matched to the hero's story of what happened in the Cave, in that both are burlesque accounts of the origins of things. A self-styled humanist, he is preparing a send-up of Ovid's *Metamorphoses* and a flippant supplement to Polydore Virgil; he declares in II, 24 that Don Quixote's narrative is cloth cut exactly to his measure. Thus, in Cervantes's comic mode, as in his romantic mode, events tend to be presented in terms of their impact on just the right kind of observer, potentially or actually envisaged as author, witness, or source.

Example 4. In both the comic and the romantic modes, reunions and recognitions have the purpose of showing how complementary versions of events fit together and of making the relay of testimony plausibly manifest. Often in *Don Quixote* these connections are artfully contrived and cover a wide span of chapters, hence a corresponding span of space and time. In Part II, Chapter 64, Sansón Carrasco, *alias* the Knight of the White Moon, challenges Don Quixote to a joust on the sands of Barcelona, defeats him, and imposes on him the penalty of returning to his village and retiring from knight-errantry for one year. Soon afterwards (II, 65), Sansón reveals his identity and his motive to Don Quixote's host in Barcelona; yet he does not answer a question that rises naturally in the reader's mind: 'How did Sansón, starting from that place somewhere in La Mancha, manage to track Don Quixote to the *ciudad condal*?' Let us momentarily leave that question, going back to Part II, Chapter 50, which tells how a page comes to Don Quixote's village bearing news of Sancho's governorship of an island, a letter from him to his wife Teresa, and, also for Teresa, a rich coral necklace from the Duchess accompanied by an amusingly familiar letter from her requesting a gift of two dozen acorns. The chapter contrasts the artless euphoria of Teresa and her daughter, who take the news and tokens at face value, with the predictable bafflement of the priest, Sansón Carrasco, and the barber, who doubt the news but cannot doubt the tokens. The page teasingly keeps this trio in suspense by confining his report, at least in Teresa's earshot, mainly to the bare facts, without divulging the inside story, which the priest extracts from him at supper. The page does, however, clearly hint that the island of Barataria is not really an island, but a town of one thousand inhabitants. We may note that the events and reactions featured in this chapter correspond to functions 1 to 4 of the paradigmatic sequence (note particularly the comments on function 3), and that the page's equivocation or reticence about 'the facts' is jocularly motivated, as is apparent to the intelligent members of his audience. At the priest's table, we may assume, the mystery is unravelled, and tokens, news, and 'facts' are proven to be in alignment.

Let us now jump ahead to Chapter 70. Here we have detailed clarification of several mysteries, including the question how the Duke's servants manage to intercept Don Quixote and Sancho on their way back from Barcelona, in order to force them to participate in the charade of Altisidora's 'resuscitation'. The explanation answers our original question about how Sansón Carrasco managed to locate Don Quixote in Barcelona. Sansón, informed by the page of Don Quixote's whereabouts, resolved to pursue him and bring him back in the manner described. When he arrived at the Duke's castle, he was briefed about all that had happened there, and told of Don Quixote's recent departure for the jousts at Zaragoza. He went to Zaragoza, but, not finding his quarry there, proceeded to Barcelona. After defeating Don Quixote, he returned via the Duke's castle, as he had promised, and gave the Duke a thorough account of what had happened. Thus was the Duke able to intercept Don Quixote on *his* return. Such is Benengeli's explanation (II, pp. 563–4); note the punctiliously factual tone. We are given the impression that the world of *Don Quixote* is full of avidly curious witnesses of the two heroes' doings, all united by this curiosity, and tirelessly engaged in tracking them, spying on them, reporting on them, and keeping each other informed about them by letters, chronicles, emissary's reports, public romour, and so on. Some of this is comic *mis*information or embroidery; but, in general, the veil draped by jest over truth is provisional and transparent to *discreción*. The communications network stretches from Barcelona to Seville, and includes persons directly or plausibly linked to the historical world, not least because they are readers of the book that we read. Thus, Cervantes's jests about the fallibility of the network's central node, Benengeli, contrast with his habitual practice of telling us how events were witnessed, evaluated, and later divulged, which imply something very different.

It is a commonplace of modern Cervantine criticism that *Don Quixote* is a novel which systematically presents multiple viewpoints on the same event, or versions of it. The foregoing examples corroborate that observation, but suggest a different conclusion from the one that is usually drawn. They point to the motives examplified by 'the paradigmatic sequence': to achieve effects of realism, suspense, immediacy and enhancement; to supply necessary clarifications; to create an illusion of quasi-historical truth. That is, motives intrinsic to the business of bringing a story alive, and not to the relativistic outlook that Américo Castro and others have diagnosed. The epistemological stance of this novel, like that of a whodunit, is realist. Facts are facts; individual versions of them converge on them, clarifying mysteries and equivocations – except, of course, the footling ones. A further interesting conclusion may be drawn. One of Cervantes's chief contributions to the development of the modern novel has been held to be his sophisticated subversion of the premise, rife in Medieval and Renaissance prose romances, that fiction must portentously masquerade as history in order to overcome the prejudice that it is merely mendacious fable. According to this view, Cervantes gave fiction its Aristotelian birthright, claiming for it autonomous purposes separate from history's, even while pushing it down a parallel, socially realistic road.[17] No doubt this was the effect of what he did, but I doubt whether it was the clear intention. Though, in his major novel, he pokes persistent fun at the solemnity and explicitness of the masquerade, he is nonetheless deeply influenced by it.

Thinking of Dr Johnson's refutation of Bishop Berkeley's idealism — 'I refute it *thus*' (kicking a stone) — we might call *Don Quixote*'s underlying epistemology Johnsonian. What stones are to Dr Johnson, the *hombre de carne y hueso* (man of flesh-and-blood) is to Cervantes. His novel is one that revolves around two personalities; and it presupposes that their extravagant, lifelike individuality is what makes it prodigiously funny, fascinating, and 'true'. This premise is basic to Part II.

Part II differs from Part I in this principal respect: it incorporates the historical fact of the first part's publication and immense popularity in contemporary Spain, and, in large measure, bases the fiction upon it. Part II thus has a celebratory purpose, and a new and complex third dimension. Many of the characters have read Benengeli's 'chronicle', and their knowledge of it determines their reaction to the two heroes, just as awareness of having a literary 'image' affects the heroes' attitude to themselves, each other, and the world around. One can think of various reasons why Cervantes chose to give his novel this curiously reflexive character; one reason is particularly pertinent here.

By means of the new twist to the story, Cervantes is able to give full effect to the validatory purpose of the paradigmatic sequence; several adventures and episodes of Part II may be seen as successive replays of the sequence, culminating in Function 7a. The publication of Avellaneda's *El Quijote* (1614), the sequel to Cervantes's Part I which appeared one year before the publication of Part II, and which attracts disparaging allusions from Part II, Chapter 59 onwards, gave an added spur to validation. Notaries are now brought on stage: a mayor and a scribe to authenticate the identity of the real Don Quixote in Part II, Chapter 72; another scribe to attest his death and thus forestall further sequels in II, 74. Cervantes even appropriates Don Quixote's protector-in-chief in Avellaneda's novel, Don Alvaro Tarfe, and converts him into the chief witness at the authentication proceedings just mentioned. These testimonials add bite, if not weight and authority, to all the accreditation that has gone before: the reception of Don Quixote and Sancho by a Duke and Duchess in Aragon (II, 30ff.), the interest in him shown by the Spanish Viceroy in Barcelona (II, 64) and by the famous Catalan outlaw Roque Guinart

(II, 60–61). Though the activity is led by prominent patrons like these, it represents the tribute of a whole community. In this respect, it corresponds to the acts of homage mentioned in Function 7a. Yet it differs from them in a gratifying way: the tone is not cloyingly sentimental, but merry, gay and convivial, uniting man to man in the salutary fellowship of laughter. The splendid description of the scene that greets the two heroes' eyes at daybreak outside the city of Barcelona, on Midsummer's Day, typifies the mood: hallooing horsemen riding out to greet them, white dawn at the balconies of the Orient, flowery meadows, warships with streaming banners conducting manoeuvres on the placid sea, cannons shooting from the city walls. Despite its burlesque motive, the pageant is worthy of a royal entry; and it is all in Don Quixote's honour:

> Bien sea venido a nuestra ciudad el espejo, el farol, la estrella y el norte de toda la caballería andante, donde más largamente se contiene. Bien sea venido, digo, el valeroso don Quijote de la Mancha: no el falso, no el ficticio, no el apócrifo que en falsas historias estos días nos han mostrado, sino el verdadero, el legal y el fiel que nos describió Cide Hamete Benengeli, flor de los historiadores

> Welcome to our city to the mirror, beacon, star, and pole of all knight-errantry, as elsewhere it is more fully set down. Welcome, I say, to the valiant Don Quixote de la Mancha, not the false, fictitious, and apocryphal one offered to us in mendacious histories, but the true, legal and loyal one described by Cide Hamete Benengeli, flower of historians. (Part II, Chapter 61; II, p. 507).

Barcelona, the Spanish Navy, and Nature herself unite to impose the stamp of validation on recognition.

Of course, *what* is hereby validated is different, in one notable respect, from what is validated in Cervantine romance: the extravagant comicality of the two heroes, rather than their heroic virtue. The typical purpose of these scenes of recognition is to show the two heroes 'being themselves': that is, exhibiting their familiar bees-in-the-bonnet to *aficionados* of Benengeli's chronicle, who can thus delightedly verify that the flesh-and-blood originals correspond exactly to the portrait that Benengeli has drawn. In Part II, Chapter 58, Don Quixote and Sancho meet two beautiful girls dressed as shepherdesses who, with other members of the local gentry, have come to a wood to enact a *bergerie*. After the knight has introduced himself, one of the girls, expressing her delight to her companion, refers to him in these terms: 'el más valiente, y el mas enamorado, y el más comedido que tiene el mundo, si no es que nos miente, y nos engaña una historia que de sus hazañas anda impresa, y yo he leído' ('the most valiant, the most loving, and the most courteous knight in the world, if one may believe a history of his deeds that has been published and I have read'). She adds: 'Yo apostaré que este buen hombre que viene consigo es un tal Sancho Panza, su escudero, a cuyas gracias no hay ningunas que se le igualen' ('I'll bet that this good fellow with him is a certain Sancho Panza, his squire, whose jests are incomparable') (II, p. 478). The flattering epithets bestowed on Don Quixote are ironically euphemistic; they correspond exactly to Cervantes's official pretence about his hero: 'el más casto enamorado y el más valiente caballero que de muchos años a esta parte se vio en aquellos contornos' ('the most chaste lover and the most valiant knight who has been seen in these parts for many a year') (prologue to Part I; I, p. 58). Cervantes pays his readers – those depicted in the novel, and by implication, those outside it – the compliment of assuming that they understand his irony perfectly. In the sequel to the meeting of Don Quixote and the shepherdess, the knight makes a *characteristically* elegant and verbose post-prandial speech, which includes a *characteristically* gallant and rash undertaking to the shepherdesses: to maintain for two days on the highway to Zaragoza that they are the most beautiful and courteous maidens in the world, save only for the peerless Dulcinea. Predictably, the undertaking ends in abortive ignominy when the hero is trampled by a herd of bulls. Thus, the essential point of this adventure is to show Quixote and Sancho providing precise confirmation of the recognition originally accorded to them – recognition which precisely doubles ours.

The manner of confirmation carries interesting implications about the relation of literature to life. After a series of conversations early in Part II between Sansón Carrasco and the two heroes, Sansón reflects that though he had read the first part of the history, he had never believed that Sancho was as funny as he was portrayed in it, but now he confirmed the truth of the portrait, and declared him to be one of the prize nitwits of the age (Part II, Chapter 7; II, p. 91). The comment is somewhat analogous to one made by Cardenio about Don Quixote's madness in Part I, Chapter 30: 'tan rara y nunca vista, que yo no sé si queriendo inventarla y fabricarla mentirosamente, hubiera tan agudo ingenio que pudiera dar en ella' ('so rare and unprecedented, that I do not know if one could find an intelligence subtle enough to invent it fictitiously') (I, p. 381). Adverting to the extraordinariness of the two personalities, the two passages imply their flesh-and-blood vividness by audaciously referring to them, from within the fictional world, as though they literally had ontological status outside it. That is, both passages take for granted what the jests about Benengeli imply to be false. Beneath their disarming self-congratulation, one discerns rampant Johnsonianism. Flesh-and-blood characters have a tangible identity, transparent to inimate acquaintance or self-knowledge. Sancho declares to Don Alvaro Tarfe:

> El verdadero Sancho Panza soy yo, que tengo más gracias que llovidas; y si no, haga vuestra merced la experiencia, y ándese tras de mí, por lo menos un año, y verá que se me caen a cada paso.' (Part II, Chapter 72; II, p. 577).

> I'm the true Sancho Panza, and I've got more jests than you can count; if you don't believe me, make the test, sir, and follow me around, for a year at least, and you'll see that they drop from me at every step.

Nobody in *Don Quixote* challenges Sancho's right to make this claim. The whole apparatus of validation supports it. Now, because living characters have this clear-cut identity, the historical representation of them has an equally clear-cut, true-or-false status, and so has the fictitious portrayal of them by figurative extension. To find out if a character has been accurately depicted in a history, it is enough simply to juxtapose one with the other to see if they match. Considered as a fiction, Benengeli's version has undisputed copyright over the heroes thanks to the same reasoning. *His* Quixote and Sancho, contrasted with the spurious phantoms who have usurped their names, have a substantive presence and individuality, part-and-parcel of their aesthetic superiority. Upon this basis, Cervantes ringingly asserts the origin of Quixote in *his* mind, hence his undisputed authority in determining and identifying his qualities: 'Para mí solo naciá don Quijote, y yo para él; él supo obrar, y yo escribir' ('For me alone was Don Quixote born, and I for him; he found the deeds, and I the words') (Part II, Chapter 74; II, p. 592). The 'speaker' here is Benengeli's quill, speaking for Cervantes. To Derridean supplementarity, Cervantes would oppose total convertibility; to Derridean doubt about the recuperability of origins, radiant certitude. We can now see that the apparent opposition between the 'two Cervantes', at least in the aspect of *Don Quixote* that we have studied, is a many-faceted effect of Cervantine humour that camouflages an essential unity.

Offshoot of various 'unmasking' ideologies which have dominated modern thought (Marxism, Nietzsche, Freud), deconstruction has assumed the right to unmask an epistemological unease endemic to a whole tradition of culture. Yet the unease seems to me a relatively modern phenomenon – a symptom of 'the disinherited mind' and of its mistrust of totalising explanations, whether scientific or metaphysical. The obvious affinities between deconstruction and some major movements of modern literary art are scarcely coincidental. So, not surprisingly, the deconstructive approach is at ease with literature which either experiences that spiritual 'disinheritance' directly or may be claimed to anticipate it (Rousseau, Dickens's *Bleak House*). With older books, written in epochs still heavily gripped by 'theocentrism', it finds itself less naturally at home. The evidence of *Don Quixote* should make us sceptical of the value of re-casting two and a half millennia of cultural plurality in an image of a post-1960s hermeneutics, politics and anthropology, or treating them as mere staging-posts on the way to the discovery of these verities.

Notes

1 See my article, 'Centering the de-centerers: thoughts on Foucault's analysis of Velázquez's 'Las Meninas', *Philosophy and Literature*, XI, 1987: 21–36.

2 This account of deconstruction's ideology is, for reasons of space, deliberately simplified. For a general panorama of the movement, individual positions within it and theories bordering on it (e.g. Foucault, Lacan, Deleuze and Guattari), see Vincent B. Leitch, *Deconstructive Criticism: An Advanced Introduction*, London, 1983. See also the essays in John Sturrock (ed.), *Structuralism and Since: From Lévi-Strauss to Derrida*, Oxford, 1979, and in Josué V. Harari (ed.), *Textual Strategies: Perspectives in Post-Structuralist Criticism*, New York, 1979.

3 Herewith a glossary of the jargon, typical of avant-garde theory: *onto-theological*: concerned with questions of being, essence, and ultimate causality; *presence*: state of being present to consciousness, fully knowable; *logocentrism*: tendency to seek a *logos*, or rational first principle.

4 For the importance of these dichotomies in deconstructive thought, see J. Culler, *DeConstruction: Theory and Criticism after Structuralism*, London, 1983, p. 85 ff.

5 *Of Grammatology*, trans. Gayatri Spivak, Baltimore, 1976. Spivak's preface is a helpful introduction to Derrida's thought.

6 See Ferdinand de Saussure, *Course in General Linguistics*, ed. Charles Bally and others, trans. Wade Baskin, New York, 1966, p. 120.

7 Paul de Man, *Allegories of Reading*, New Haven, 1979, p. 10.

8 Since, in this chapter, I shall be asking of *Don Quixote* the kind of
questions posed by Yale Deconstruction, prominently represented by
Paul de Man and J. Hillis Miller, it is pertinent to mention at this point
that these two Derridean aims are of paramount importance to these
two critics. See, for example, the essays collected in de Man's *Allegories
of Reading*, and the two programmatic articles by Hillis Miller entitled
'Stevens' rock and criticism as cure', *Georgia Review*, XXX, 1976:
5–31, 330–48.

9 I single out Barthes and Kristeva, amongst other reasons, because of their
representativeness: in France, they were leaders of the so-called *Tel Quel*
group, whose collective manifesto is *Théorie d'ensemble*, Paris, 1968.
See, e.g., the essays by Barthes collected in *Roland Barthes: Image Music
Text*, ed. and trans. Stephen Heath, New York, 1977, including 'The Death
of the Author' (142–48) and 'From Work to Text' (155–64); also Julia
Kristeva's *Semiotike: Recherches pour une semanalyse*, Paris, 1969, and
the selection of her essays in English translation entitled *Desire in
Language*, ed. Leon S. Roudiez, Oxford, 1981.

10 Other ways of deconstructing *Don Quixote* are readily conceivable. See,
for example, Paul Julian Smith's provocative and stimulating book
Writing in the Margin: Spanish Literature of the Golden Age, Oxford,
1988, which adopts a broadly deconstructive approach to various aspects
of the period, including the picaresque novel.

11 This aspect of *Don Quixote* is taken by the Russian Formalist theorist
Mikhail Bakhtin as an illustration of this thesis concerning the genre of
the novel, regarded as a systematically subversive interplay of languages,
dialogues and world-views, and as an expression of a carnivalesque,
popular and anti-establishment spirit in human culture. See Bakhtin's
The Dialogic Imagination, Austin, 1981, which, though not a work of
deconstructive theory, is capable of being implemented in that sense.
Originally written in Stalinist Russia, and obviously reacting against that
oppressive environment, it had a radical influence on the thought of Julia
Kristeva: e.g. her *Le Texte du roman*, The Hague, 1970.

12 There is no standard response to this difficulty, which, for reasons indi-
cated in my final paragraph, exposes the limitations of deconstruction as
an interpretative approach. The Yale critics tend to assume that since the
Crisis of the Sign is endemic to Western culture, all its literary texts,
particularly the canonical ones, must hinge upon it, whether or not their
creators were conscious of it. See J. Hillis Miller, 'Deconstructing the
deconstructors', *Diacritics*, V, 1975: 24–31, p. 31. By contrast, Barthes
and Kristeva assume that texts written in epochs heavily gripped by
theocentrism are pitifully vitiated by theocentric assumptions about the
univocal reference of the Sign, and are therefore capable of a merely limited
degree of polysemia. This assumption is central to Kristeva's *Le texte du
roman* and Barthes's *S/Z*, Paris, 1970.

13 I have used the edition of *Don Quixote* by Luis Andrés Murillo, 2 vols.
plus bibliographical appendix, Madrid, 1978. Quotations from the text
are identified by references to the appropriate volume number and page
of this edition (e.g. I, p. 100). Such references should not be confused with

mentions of a Part and Chapter of *Don Quixote*, which either have the form: Part I, Chapter 9, or the form: I, 9.

14 See *S/Z*, pp. 24−9, where the five codes are posited and explained.
15 I refer to the second edition, translated by Laurence Scott, revised by Louis Wagner, Austin, 1968.
16 See the edition of the *Novelas ejemplares* by J. B. Avalle-Arce, 3 vols., 3rd edn, Madrid, 1987, II, pp. 91−100.
17 See Chapter 5, 'The Truth of the Matter', in E. C. Riley's *Cervantes's Theory of the Novel*, Oxford, 1962.

5　PAUL JULIAN SMITH

The rhetoric of allegory in
El criticón

I Introduction

Baltasar Gracián's *El criticón*, published between 1650 and 1657, has
not received the attention it deserves.[1] As an allegorical narrative,
its didacticism and lack of concern for naturalism have proved unat-
tractive to twentieth-century critics. Modern resistance to the work
derives from unexamined preconceptions still current in traditional
literary studies. The didactic text offends the New Critics, for whom
ideas are tolerated in literature only when dissolved in the textures
of 'immediate lived experience'.[2] The anti-naturalist text offends the
literary historian, who values texts in so far as they conform to a
received progression from 'primitive' forms to 'mature' mimetic
performance. The popular image of Cervantes (as benign ironist and
technical innovator) thus presents no difficulties of assimilation.
That of Gracián (tireless teacher and wilful obscurantist) remains
obstinately indigestible.[3] When set beside the achievements of the
'Father of the Modern Novel', *El criticón* seems at best a cul-de-sac
in literary history; at worst a throwback to a hopelessly archaic form.

　　One aim of this chapter is to suggest that those characteristics
which most embarrass a modern sensibility are also those which offer
the opportunity for a revaluation of the text in which they appear.
A more sympathetic reading (one which avoids both New Critical
humanism and literary historical teleology) might focus on the
question of allegory, on the exhaustive quest for meaning staged by
the text and the residues or remainders that this quest necessarily
leaves behind. For a more subtle understanding of allegory, I appeal
here, as elsewhere, to the work of Jacques Derrida. My aim is to
juxtapose Derrida's readings of Austin and Lévi-Strauss, of Hegel
and Nietzsche, with my own reading of Gracián's masterpiece. I will
suggest that the problems of language and structure, of woman
and truth, are shared by both writers. In its attempt to combine
Renaissance and poststructuralist texts, this essay may be read as a
supplement to my *Writing in the Margin* (Oxford, 1988).

92

The basic lines of my argument are as follows. Firstly, Derrida's critique of language suggests that terms often considered to be primary or positive (such as 'voice' or 'literal meaning') are often subject to a curious slippage in which they are displaced by secondary or negative terms (such as 'writing' or 'figurative language'). And his critique of structuralism suggests that the model of structure as a stable matrix founded on a fixed centre should be replaced by a more mobile system of substitutions motivated by 'play'. Secondly, Derrida's analysis of 'woman' suggests that, as guardian of the hearth and tomb, she has served as the medium through which (male) spirit achieves universalisation; and that, as the purveyor of truth, she embodies a number of contradictory values which are the precondition of man's (phallogocentric) discourse. As we shall see, the general themes of epistemology and femininity are inseparable from images or motifs shared by the two authors: writing and speech, sound and vision, decoration and nakedness, introjection and projection. For Derrida, the figure which initiates the play of difference between these terms is the membrane or diaphragm, known variously as tympan or hymen.[4] I shall argue that it is the dark veil of metaphor which inaugurates an (unacknowledged) complicity between the quest for meaning and the quest for the woman in the allegorical narrative of *El criticón*.

Critics have often appealed to the *Agudeza* to explain Gracián's use of allegory. Thus Theodore L. Kassier[5] quotes the discourse on 'Agudeza compuesta' (LIV) which treats the proper relation between unity and diversity: without 'connection and order' the parts of a narrative are mere undigested masses (*'rudis indigestaque moles'*) or 'minced up' discourses ('amorcillados'). Each individual part must be surordinate to a universal proposition which is like the 'head' ('cabeza') of the narrative (Kassier, p. 4). In the following *discurso* (on allegory itself) Gracián treats 'the various ways in which Truth must be adorned and even disguised in order to be successfully communicated' (p. 4). He claims that there is no dish so bitter to the taste than naked truth. Just as direct light tortures the eyes even of the eagle, so the doctors of the spirit, weak-stomached, were obliged to invent the art of gilding truth, sugaring disillusionment. Truth must dress or disguise itself in the style of Deception and only then will it remedy its rival's harmful effect.

While the overt message of the passage is clear enough and the motifs conventional, the implications they suggest are revealing.

It is clearly ironic that the praise of unity and coherence should provoke a stream of disconnected and often incompatible metaphors: the chaotic forms which the body cannot absorb give way to (external) parts safely subordinate to the mastery of the head; the culinary metaphor of the bitter morsel leads into the visual motifs of the 'naked truth' and the wounded eyes of the eagle. And the medical metaphor which follows seems to 'contaminate' the final visual reference to dress and disguise, when the 'trappings' of Deceit are held to be the 'remedy' of their own effects. Hence the discourse on allegory becomes an allegorisation of discourse: Gracián can only explain the efficacy of allegory by appealing to those very techniques he is attempting to describe; and the plain language of 'naked Truth' stands revealed as a shibboleth, a figure always already embedded in the field it claims, nonetheless, to define. This is not merely to suggest that the flagrant metaphoricity of the *Agudeza* prevents it from being used as a neutral metalanguage, a tool for the dissection of the literary text.[6] It is also to argue that the disseminating character of writing (its refusal to remain anchored to a single origin or referent) is a structural rather than an incidental factor in all literary language. However much Gracián may stress the superiority of the whole to be part and of the composite to the aggregate, any stable integration of meaning into form will remain illusory. The movement from 'macro' to 'micro' structure in which 'each of these [structural elements] ... is potentially of allegorical significance' (Kassier, p. 6) is fraught with danger. For at some (unspecified) point the reader must retreat from the quest for meaning before the text disintegrates into atoms. As Kassier notes, in *El criticón*, even the smallest unit (the single syllable) can be made to bear an allegorical load.

The rhetorical definition of allegory is that it occurs when 'one thing is said and another meant'.[7] But this is only the first of the binaries associated with the trope. Thus allegory is said to require two levels: a superficial or literal level and a deeper, thematic level. And it serves 'two almost antithetical functions', namely those of facilitating communication by rendering exposition more vivid and of 'impeding or controlling communication ... [through] restrictions, concealment' (p. 9). For Kassier the two functions merge in the 'aesthetic' dimension which is the result of the variable relation between the two 'levels' (p. 9). This is a welcome advance on fixed or static conceptions of the trope, as it suggests a definition of allegory as a fluctuating, differential term, a space between linguistic categories.

But the antithetical notions of revelation and concealment elude any facile synthesis by appeal to Art. And in a footnote on the same page Kassier cites two well-known definitions of allegory in which the same problematic recurs: Dante's 'a truth hidden under the beautiful lie' and Boccaccio's contention that '[allegory] veils truth in a fair and fitting garment of fiction'. I shall suggest that it is this veil or diaphragm (which at once joins and separates plain language and figuration, truth and falsehood, woman and man) that inaugurates the allegorical process.

II Language and structure

Most modern critics admit to little difficulty in identifying the nature of Gracián's literary language. Thus when Alain Milhou[8] begins a very recent article by assuming the 'perfect coherence' of the novel's allegorical form, he is supported by a long-standing critical consensus. For Klaus Heger,[9] the cogency of Gracián's style is guaranteed by a coherent 'allegorical vision of the world', which is itself underwritten by a transcendent goal: the pilgrims' quest for Felisinda, the ideal woman (p. 34). For Marcia L. Welles,[10] 'idea and image are fused into a significant and dynamic unity' (p. 18). Ricardo Senabre's[11] more technical study includes an 'analysis of the coherence of a passage' [II, 1] (p. 69) which attempts to prove the 'unitary' and 'homogeneous' nature of the text (p. 99). He even includes a formula which claims to show how Gracián's metaphorical language works to render discrete elements equivalent: '$(x, y) \rightarrow (x = y)$' (p. 91). More recently Santos Alonso[12] has sought to show how the multiple levels of Gracián's text are reduced to a basic unity (p. 7), and how even the redundant figures of Gracián's rhetorical style serve to intensify not the signifier but the signified (p. 158). Most critics take it for granted, with Jorge Checa,[13] that the 'aim' of Gracián's allegory is to lend coherence to the artistic representation of a reality which is itself confused and disorganised (p. 137). Nonetheless, some dissonant voices are heard. For example, Kassier claims that 'in its totality, Gracián's encyclopaedic representation of man's existence ... eschews any notion of a transcendent meaning or purpose to life' (p. 48). In this last case, however, negativity does not displace but merely reverses the positive terms proposed by the other critics as keys to the text: Gracián's supposed cosmic pessimism is the new universal which is used once more to integrate a fragmented text.

If we consider the responses of readers of *El criticón* closer to Gracián's own time we discover that the modern critical consensus is by no means to be taken for granted. Gracián's English translator, the diplomat and orientalist Paul Rycaut, complains that after the opening chapters the style of the novel is 'harsh and crabbed'.[14] As he struggles 'to understand the sence [*sic*] and humour of the Author' Rycaut finds himself obliged to retrace the peregrinations of Gracián's characters, 'fancying ... that I was entred [*sic*] into those steep and thorny ways of Vertue, which Critilo teaches ...'. Rycaut stresses the supposed oriental influences on Spanish prose style, and claims that the latter's value lies in its divergence from English norms: 'their way of writing is much after that [oriental] manner, and is as well pleasant and diverting in itself as it is curious to us, who follow another form ...'. The French translator Jacques Collombat also stresses the national peculiarity of Gracián's style.[15] In his preface he advises his readers constantly to remind themselves that they are reading a Spanish book: the excess of metaphors and allegories; the curious mixture of different registers; the passing off of a mere 'pensée brillante' as a 'raison solide'; all these characteristics suggest Gracián is little concerned with verisimilitude or even truth itself (fol. A4r). Giovanni Pietro Cattaneo[16] is more sympathetic to Gracián's richness of 'invention' (fol. a3r). But he claims he has been obliged to omit tedious passages of 'Spagnuolate' and to replace Gracián's parochial references by figures better known abroad. All three translators agree on the impossibility of their task, which forces them to add to or substract from the host text. Roycaut compares his English wording to a garment inappropriate for the original body of text: it is like 'when we see Men of Years and Gravity dressed in the Fashion of the Youthful' (fol. A2v). Collombat goes further and conserves the original Spanish title as a sign of the novel's irreducible foreignness; and he also claims that he is obliged to leave Spanish idioms in the original, reproduced in italic face in his text (fols. A4r, A5r). Cattaneo also laments Gracián's use of untranslatable puns (fol. a4r). But as a 'uomo di coscienza' he has added 'curious' material of his own, gathered from other sources. He cites a Latin tag as justification for his borrowed insertions: *nihil dictum, quod prius non fuerit dictum.*

How, then, do these readers differ from their twentieth-century counterparts? First of all, they fail to recognise the supposed coherence and unity of Gracián's style. On the contrary, the linguistic opacity and diversity of the text is taken for granted and held to be a unique marker of its Spanish provenance. Collombat complains that it is not easy to understand *Gracián* where he has wished to be obscure (fol. A4v). But the translators are hardly aware of authorial intention: they do not conceive of the work as an act of communication between author and reader. What is more, they have little respect for the unity or integrity of the text: the latter is conceived as a body of fragments (puns, anecdotes, apothegms) determined in part by the language in which it is written and subject to continuing deletions or additions by third parties. The practice of seventeenth-century translators thus foregrounds a number of the necessary conditions of literary language which twentieth-century critics seek to repress: the infinite number of contexts to which any piece of writing is open; the problematic status of literal or proper meaning; the displacement of authorial presence by the proliferating webs of intertextuality.

These points are treated at length by Derrida in one of the best known of his early essays.[17] For Derrida 'communication' is never univocal and is better understood as a kind of *écriture* in the extended sense, a chain of differential marks which precludes the possibility of the pure presence of meaning or author in the text (pp. 367, 378). All writing is iterable, that is, subject to repetition and alienation. And this citationality gives rise to an inevitable duplication and duplicity which cannot be erased by appeal to the common-sense notion of a stable meaning safely anchored to a fixed centre point (pp. 375, 381). For Derrida, Austin's speech act theory has exploded the traditional concept of communication: the performative act (by which the speaker declares a meeting open or pronounces a couple man and wife) calls into question the conventional definition of communication as the transfer of a pre-existent semantic content, guaranteed by reference to an independent truth. That is, it is not an unveiling ('dévoilement') of a meaning assumed to be already there. However, the fact that Austin identifies the intention of the speaker as the origin of the speech act leads to a devaluation of citationality in his theory: if the performative is spoken by an actor or introduced into a poem it will, for Austin, become 'abnormal' or 'parasitic', no longer 'ordinary' language (pp. 383, 386). For Derrida, however, it is the exclusion of this 'secondary' term (iteration, citation, fiction) which is the very condition of possibility of Austin's system. Derrida gives a commonplace example which speech act theory cannot account for: the signature. Ostensibly (like the performative speech act) the unambiguous sign of the unique presence-to-self of its originator, the signature can function only because it is reproducible; that is, subject to repetition, iteration, and imitation (pp. 387, 392). In its very sameness, the signature is split. By closing the essay with (what appears to be) a reproduction of his own signature, Derrida playfully repeats the question of the impossible distinction between duplication and duplicity: is this mark on the page genuine or false, 'fait' or 'contrefait'? (p. 393)

Derrida's understanding of citational or fictional language offers a more flexible model for the complex diction of *El criticón* than that of Gracián's modern critics. It reverses (and thus displaces) the traditional bias towards the communication of a single stable meaning. And it suggests the possibility of a disseminating play of value which cannot be reduced to polysemy (p. 392). Let us see how this new model can suggest a new reading of a particular passage, the opening chapter of *El criticón*. The setting of the first *crisi* is the island of St Helena, a location whose status is problematic from the very beginning. The island is initially placed in a contemporary political setting: it is at the centre of the crown of Philip IV which joins the two hemispheres, and is a safe haven for Spanish shipping. Positioned between the Old and the New Worlds, St Helena exists to serve a 'portátil Europa', a twin reference to the historical continent which spreads its arms across the ocean and the mythological figure, borne over the sea by Jupiter. This first image condenses and anticipates the continuous alternation between history and myth which will occur throughout the novel, and makes the distinction between literal and figurative problematic indeed. On the next page the shipwrecked Critilo is introduced. He is compared to a swan in a second example of linguistic play: he is both 'cano' and 'canoro', white-haired and sweetly vocal when confronted with death. Once more figurative language precedes the literal object it purports to represent: the image is the first we know of Critilo. It is significant that we are offered neither physical description nor psychological motivation when Critilo is first introduced. Rather, the character is called into being by the arbitrary play of phonetic difference ('cano'/'canoro'): he has neither presence nor stable origin. In a rather similar way, Andrenio and Critilo are said to 'fill' well ('llenar') names which seem, logically, to precede them (p. 69). As Welles says, '[Andrenio's] name indicates established contents which the subsequent behaviour of the character "fills"'' (p. 97). In so far as their names refer back to an etymological origin 'Andrenio' and 'Critilo' are overtly citational: borrowed from one linguistic context (the classical), and applicable to an indefinite number of others.

This stress on citationality, then, at once institutes and undermines St Helena as centre and origin of the narrative, unfixes it from the historical and geographical context in which it is placed in the opening lines. Like the signature, Critilo and Andrenio's non-naturalistic names are at once the sign of their unique particularity and an acknowledgement that that particularity is reproducible, and thus different from itself. The citational register continues in Critilo's highly rhetorical and scandalously anti-naturalistic speech, made as he battles against the ocean. Critilo offers a version of a well-worn topic, the polemic against seafaring (p. 66); he invokes exempla of fortitude in which myth and history mingle once more (Hercules, Caesar, Charles V). The narrator compares Critilo to Tantalus, caught between water he cannot drink and land which offers no greater hope of salvation (p. 67). But the tone of the narrator's comparison is no different to that of the character's speech which precedes it: the distribution of discourse is random. It responds to no imperative in the character and thus raises the possibility that any fragment of the text can be a citation, at once duplicated and duplicitous.

Andrenio at first seems to represent an unambiguous nature which is in opposition to Critilo's self-conscious culture. For Welles (as for most critics) the pair embody the dichotomies of rational/irrational, literal/figurative, personal/general (pp. 99, 103). Exiled from language as he is at first, Andrenio's status is contradictory, not quite human: he is both angelic in looks and deeds, and as persistent as a compass in his resolve (p. 67). Yet in spite of these opening images, which locate him somewhere between the extremes of the supernatural and the blindly material, the (as yet unnamed) Andrenio is by no means purely natural. The narrator tells us that his face is 'overwritten' ('sobreescrito') by European features; and that he is dressed only in his innocence (i.e. he is naked) (p. 68). Hence, even before he acquires the power of speech, Andrenio is determined by his relation to *écriture*. He is marked by the differential codes of genealogy ('race') and cultural convention (dress), in spite of his ignorance of these systems. Even the naked body is not innocent of inscription; and nor is the desert island untouched by culture. The figure of Andrenio thus inadvertently reveals the repressed characteristics of writing: namely that it is predicated on absence, repetition, and alienation. It is significant that although Andrenio has never seen another human being, he sees in Critilo an image of himself which confirms his own sense of self-division. The narrator comments sagely that without the mediation of artifice, nature is perverted from its intended course (p. 68). But a few lines later he invokes the 'natural' and self-sufficient prestige of speech, which evolved for the purpose of communication: two children abandoned on a desert island evolved a language of their own in which to communicate (p. 69). It is nature which has cunningly brought together pleasure and necessity in speech. Likewise, Andrenio's speech is prefaced by the narrator's statement that the latter will bring to light a (pre-existing) truth, sentiments which preceded words which serve merely as vehicles for them (p. 70). Gracián thus seems to reconfirm the common-sense notion of a univocal communication between subjects which serves to unveil the semantic content it conveys. However, as we shall see, in Andrenio's actual account of himself, the terms repressed by such a model of communication (the citational, parasitic, and theatrical) stage an unexpected return.

Welles claims that Andrenio's speech reveals 'enthusiasm' and 'passionate spontaneity' (p. 192). Yet she also acknowledges its use of 'exclamatory sentences' and 'gradation to climax'. It is, in fact, thick with rhetorical patterning. More important, however, is the general point it confirms; namely that 'spontaneity' and 'naturalness' are the effect of citationality and, indeed, could not be recognised without the cultural codes to which they refer back. One linguistic feature stands out in this context, what Welles calls Andrenio's 'excessive use of adjectives' (p. 102); for in contemporary poetics the status of the epithet is much debated, at once praised and feared for its efficacy in communicating emotion.[18] It is also significant that the narrator prefaces Andrenio's (nominally oral) discourse with a textual metaphor: Andrenio tells his story 'a centones y a remiendos' (p. 71). The *cento* is of course a poem composed from borrowed fragments. According to *Autoridades*, the term is derived from a military blanket full of mends and patches. Andrenio's first speech, then, points to a moment it cannot acknowledge (in Derrida's phrase, 'a time before first') in which the citational clears the space for a discourse of authenticity which dare not acknowledge its precursor. What is more, subjectivity, like textuality, is differential. Andrenio arrives at a sense of self by observing his reflection in water and his similarity to Critilo (p. 70). But when he comments on the 'well-known differences' (p. 71) he had observed in his cave between human beings and the beasts among whom he was raised, the problem of allocating an origin for his discourse (the problem of who is speaking) arises once more. To whom are such opinions well known? The scene is presented as a model of inductive reasoning: even when alone and ignorant, man will glimpse his unique position in the universe. But Gracián cannot resist lending Andrenio supplementary knowledge to which he could not have had access in the deserts of St Helena. Of course, the scene does not rely for its effectiveness on a rigorously consistent naturalism: Gracián is not Zola. But by attributing to Andrenio current European commonplaces even as he lies in the impenetrable darkness of the cave, Gracián inadvertently reveals that there can be no zero degree of knowledge and experience, that the pure presence or still centre of subjectivity is always preceded and underwritten by textuality.

If we read Andrenio's speech as a performative act, then, it is not because it embodies the authentic presence of the speaker but because it calls into question the communication model of language as the vehicle of intentionality. In the 'theatre' of the universe (p. 73) even the innocent islander must play a role. But if the central point of origin is dissolved (if textuality decentres nature, authenticity, and literal meaning) then the structure of the work as a whole is undermined. I use the architectonic metaphor deliberately. For it is no accident that those critics who praise the coherence of Gracián's allegorical language also stress the formal unity of its construction. Welles and Kassier provide two of the more sophisticated accounts, which (once more) happen to contradict each other. Welles claims that the circular pattern of man's relation to cosmic time is supplemented by a 'directional line' from birth to death and the linear descending pattern of human history (pp. 74–5). Kassier is more critical. The proliferating detail of *El criticón* makes 'comprehensive structure difficult to perceive' from the outset (p. 10); and 'despite the orientation towards a specific goal implicit in the pilgrimage ... the constantly frustrated search for Felisinda endlessly prolongs the protagonists' journey, rendering it no more than the succession of experiences that comprise it' (p. 23). Even those techniques whose function is to knit together the disparate threads are unsuccessful: the final recapitulation of adventures at the end 'eschews any notion of progression ... [and] does not subdivide into parts or present its components in the order in which they appear in the work' (p. 25). Most critics, however, while paying lip service to the (unexamined) notion of a 'dynamic' structure, end up reconfirming a notion of text as closed, aesthetic artefact even as they claim that Gracián has managed to avoid this in his text (see, e.g., Santos, p. 50). Some critics simply reduce the antithesis thought to be embodied in the two main characters to stable equilibrium and/or transcendent synthesis (Santos, pp. 23, 26). Thus even Alain Milhou, who seeks to reread the structures of time and space in the novel in the light of an ecclesiastical context which is rarely named in *El criticón* itself, finishes by reiterating the propositions voiced in the text's conclusion: only Rome, centre of centres and theatre of truth, can provide that final and stable synthesis of opposites sought by the characters (p. 226).

However the question of structure (like that of dialectic) is more complex than most critics have supposed. In another early essay Derrida offers a critique of 'structure' in the light of signs and play.[19] An account of this essay will help to suggest what is at stake in critics' fondness for architectonic 'order' and will also facilitate a new account of the form of *El criticón*. Derrida suggests that the dynamic 'structurality' of structure (i.e. its capacity for rupture, transformation, and substitutability) is generally neutralised by a gesture which consists of lending it a centre, 'tracing it back to a point of presence, to a fixed origin'. The centre is that place in which substitution cannot occur (pp. 409, 410). Whether it is conceived as end or origin, its function is the same: to regulate the play of the text. However, if this 'transcendent signified' were to disappear, then structure would be decentred, opened up to an infinite play of meaning in which presence cedes to a purely differential system. Derrida gives the example of ethnology. Born at a moment of decentring, when European culture was no longer the unchallenged standard reference point, ethnology re-established, nonetheless, the premisses of Eurocentrism at the centre of its discipline. For example, in Lévi-Strauss the guiding thread of ethnology is a familiar dichotomy, that between nature and culture (pp. 414, 415). The former is taken to be universal and the second variable. However, by placing this distinction at the heart of his system Lévi-Strauss predetermines the field which is the object of his investigation. Any term which is conceived as 'scandalous' or anomalous (such as the prohibition of incest, which is at once cultural and universal) is only so when considered inside that system which cannot account for it (p. 416). Derrida proposes two kinds of 'interpretation of interpretation' (hermeneutic models): the first seeks to decipher a truth or origin 'beyond' play and signification, and which experiences the necessity for interpretation as an exile; the second turns away from the origin, affirms the potential of play, and tries to think beyond the transcendent centre and signified of Man and Humanism (p. 427).

The first model is that favoured by modern critics of Gracián. Confronted by a text of inexhaustible proliferation and potentially infinite substitutability, in which the play of the signifier is often irreducible to a single signified, they have sought to anchor the text to a central dichotomy (Andrenio's nature and Critilo's culture) which is thought to be initiated at the start of the text and triumphantly resolved at its close. The exile of the characters is thus also that of the critics, who struggle to reduce plurality to unity and proliferation to order. The only problem with this approach is that the achievement of perfect synthesis and true humanity (the external criterion by which the text is judged) is also the object of the text's narrative. Critics are thus condemned to repeat the propositions of the original text and to repress its tendencies towards (unmotivated) play and (supplementary) signification. As these qualities are those by which literary language is defined (in counterdistinction to a neutral language of plain speech) the loss is considerable. If we could learn to read the centre as a differential function, instead of a transcendent signified, then the potential of play would be properly addressed. This must surely be a priority in a satirical work. But such an attempt would have to take great care not to smuggle back the original hierarchy in reversed form, with 'play' now a fixed centre, and 'signification' the guarantor of stable meaning.

What, then, is the 'scandalous' term in *El criticón*, that which cannot be accounted for by the system and which threatens the stability of its operation? Klaus Heger speaks for many critics when he writes: 'The search for Felisinda ... is the supporting principle of the action, both with reference to the structure of the Byzantine novel and to the allegorical vision of the world' (p. 34). Language and structure are thus bound up with the quest for the woman. I shall suggest that as the vehicle of truth, she must be excluded from a text which can neither account for her nor exist without her.

III Women and truth

Jacques Collombat's translation of *El criticón* includes a helpful 'table des matières' at the end. The entries under *Femme* include: to be feared infinitely; they fear age; blind; omnipotent, but lose all they have; incapable of value and advice; source of quarrels; diabolical spirit; harmful to men. Woman is a blind spot for most critics of *El criticón*. At best, it seems to be understood that Gracián's misogyny (like Quevedo's anti-Semitism) is shared by so many other writers in the period that it merits no comment. Many modern readings aim to be gender-blind: thus Hilary Dansey Smith[20] ends her article on 'The Ages of Man' by claiming that the topos is an 'appropriate image for a Task that Mankind has barely embarked on: becoming fully human' (p. 47). She chooses to ignore the fact that in *El criticón* 'Mankind' is exclusively male. In this last section of my chapter I shall suggest that man's self-realisation is at the expense of woman's submission. What is more, the images of women in *El criticón* (like Collombat's list of supposed 'feminine' characteristics) reveal curious contradictions which provide the key to the (male) allegorical discourse which has produced them.

Some critics have indeed commented on the role of women in *El criticón*. It is perhaps no accident that it is in a Nietzschean study that Francisco Maldonado[21] notes the complete absence of women in the final Island of Immortality (p. 19). Kassier goes further in reading the ideological implications of Gracián's misogyny. Thus the idealised Felisinda represents the 'unattainable embodiment of the only two legitimate secular female roles, wifehood and motherhood .... With this unreachable figure Gracián clearly represents woman's total exclusion from the worthy individual's sphere of action .... It is with woman as the meretricious seductress Falsirena, Felisinda's would-be sister [*sic*] ... that man must contend' (pp. 12–13). Kassier just falls short of suggesting that there is a structural complicity between the idealisation and denigration of woman by man. I would argue myself, however, that such a complicity does exist, and that it is inextricable from a patriarchal conception of truth.

In his readings of Hegel and Nietzsche, Derrida explores the relation of woman and truth. Derrida claims that in Hegel the passage from consciousness to spirit is based on an asymmetrical opposition between singular and universal (female and male).[22] While the male

sphere of human law is public and visible, the female sphere of divine
law is private and nocturnal. The family's job is the cult of the dead
and the organisation of the tomb. The extinct (male) body has lost
its empirical existence and relies on the woman to guide it to ideal
universality: the home thus becomes a theatre in which woman
'assures representation' by abstracting masculinity from the chaotic
threat of organic nature (pp. 161, 162). Here Hegel cites the legend
of Antigone, the sister whose loyalty to her brother's corpse led to
her own death. For Derrida, the sister is the indigestible, inassimilable
remainder of Hegel's system which (as so often) enables that system
to function by virtue of its very exclusion. While wife and mother
achieve universality only through the mediation of the husband or
son, the sister possesses a 'singular singularity'. Antigone at once
overturns the male system and supports it from outside and beneath.
In a rather similar way, the crypt or tomb to which she is confined
organises the ground to which it does not itself belong (pp. 184, 187).

　　In Hegelian terms, the allegorical journey of Gracián's pilgrims
from *hombre* to *persona* is the passage from consciousness to spirit,
from singularity to universality. And it is not difficult to find examples
of the way in which women are consistently associated with the
negative side of this paradigm: the dark, enclosed space of a chaotic
nature is a leitmotif of *El criticón*, and one often gendered as feminine.
The Cave of Nothingness (III, 8) is an obvious example. Even when
the woman's role is positive it is always subordinate. Thus Felisinda
undergoes an apparent progression as the novel continues, from empirical woman (mother to Andrenio, wife to Critilo) to ideal essence
(divine spirit of Rome). But that progression is merely the motive
for the universalisation of the male pilgrims: it is the continuing
displacement of the woman and the continuing deferral of an encounter with her that facilitate a narrative process from which the
woman herself is excluded. However, the role of the sister or niece
is more difficult to account for than that of the mother. Falsirena
claims to be the daughter of Felisinda's sister (I, 12; 249) and her
misdeeds serve almost as a parody of the female duty towards the
(male) dead. The victims of the lust she provokes are kept in suspended
animation in a 'horrible cave' (p. 261). Instead of protecting them
from chaotic physicality and material decay, she condemns her victims
to that same fate: they lack even a sheet to serve as a shroud. I would
suggest, then, that Falsirena does not simply embody the demonic
qualities attributed to women by male mythology. She also disrupts

that same system, intermittently at least, by refusing to perform the labour it requires of women in order to reproduce itself. Falsirena's subterranean cave thus both supports and undermines the ground of masculinity from which it is excluded. It is a theatre in which representation is at once assured and deferred through the (temporary) internment of the male body.

It seems clear, then, that in *El criticón* woman has no identity. As the object of a male text she is best understood as a sign, a term which stands in for (represents) something else. Throughout the book she diverges not just from man, but from herself. Thus as the pilgrims enter the world, they witness two women: one is leading children to their death at the mercy of wild animals; the other attempts to save them from their fate. They represent 'Evil Inclination' and 'Reason', respectively (I, 5). But these are qualities which belong not to the women themselves but to the differing characters of the children who are setting off on life's journey. Similarly, as the pilgrims leave the world, they are confronted by Death represented as a woman in motley costume: to Critilo she is an attractive young lady; to Andrenio a disgusting crone (III, 9). Once more, the woman exists only as a vehicle for differing male values. For Derrida this lack of identity in the figure of woman is related to the way she is placed at a distance from man.[23] In the text of Nietzsche, distance both protects man from feminine charm and enables him to experience it (p. 48). The allegorical figure of truth as a woman is associated with the movement of the feminine veil, which serves the purposes of both modesty and seduction (p. 50). Thus truth, just as much as dissimulation, is an 'effect of the veil', a sense of depth or interiority called into being only when the veil has fallen (p. 58). However, if the veil is suspended, absolute truth will cease to exist. This process gives rise to three contradictory attitudes to woman in Nietzsche: first she is seen as falsehood from the viewpoint of (male) truth; second, she is viewed as truth from the perspective of the male artist; third, she affirms herself as a dionysiac, dissimulating force (p. 96). The three images are inextricable, functions of the 'rhythmic' blindness of the male writer and the action of the hymen: the veil or membrane which both joins and separates woman to man (p. 100).

El criticón insists on the distance of woman (from man and from herself) even as that distance undermines its own narrative impetus and consistency. Felisinda is, of course, constantly retreating. Even while they are courting, she addresses Critilo from a balcony

(I, 4; 107). By the time the pilgrims reach Aragón, she has moved on to Germany (I, 12; 148). Even when Critilo attempts to meet the minor character Sofisbella (Wisdom) face to face, he is told that all that remains of her in this world are 'sketches' in wise books (II, 6; 401). This is in spite of the fact that the reader has been treated to a long account of her literary judgements earlier in the chapter. It is no surprise that the chapter entitled 'Felisinda discovered' (III, 9) fails to live up to its name. It takes 'El cortesano' only a few lines to inform the pilgrims that their long-sought wife and mother has died and can now be found only in heaven (p. 737). All we are told of the men's reaction is that they are 'disabused' ('desengañados'). 'El cortesano' goes on, anticlimactically, to give them a guided tour of the city of Rome. If, as many critics believe, the quest for the woman is the structural principle which binds the novel together, that principle is summarily dismissed before the novel ends.

But the very transparency of Gracián's manoeuvres calls attention to the role of woman as figure or sign in the text. The reference to 'discovery' suggests once more a connection with the allegorical veil, which must be stripped away to reveal the authentic truth beneath: for Gracián, truth is *aletheia* (that which is drawn into light).[24] And throughout the text woman is implicated in an image repertoire which includes the face, mask, and veil. Thus Artemia claims that the human face is the image of its owner's good or evil deeds; while the deceitful Falimundo's followers all hide their faces in masks (I, 8; 176, 178). Or again, Virtelia's face is the 'living portrait of the Celestial Father' (II, 10; 479); while those who dwell in Hipocrinda's convent are disguised in the 'cloak of sanctity' and praise the efficacy of appearances (II, 7; 424, 433). But these oppositions cannot be reduced to the simple dichotomy of *ser* and *parecer*. For, unlike man, woman's very condition is deceit. Thus when asked by God what they most desire, man requested intelligence ('head'), woman beauty ('face') (II, 4; 400–1). In old age, woman's beauty inevitably becomes a mask, whatever her moral status (cited by Ramos Foster, p. 109). Even Virtelia, the personification of virtue, is not original or self-sufficient: she is said to 'copy' the perfections of the Lord (II, 10; 479). Woman thus destabilises the confident dualities on which both truth and allegory are based.

Hence if woman is non-identity and distance, she is also the veil. Like the allegorical garment, she must be ripped away to reveal the truth beneath. But this illusion of depth is itself created by the falling of the veil, the act of modesty or dissimulation. Woman can thus be presented, indifferently, as either truth or falsehood (Felisinda or Falsirena), since the figure in the text need correspond to no 'extrinsic' reality. But what of Nietzsche's third possibility, in which woman affirms herself as dionysiac force? In *El criticón* there are moments, at least, when the veil does not fall, but is suspended. Thus Falsirena's park is a 'hanging garden' ('pensil') because it 'suspends' all those who take pleasure in it (I, 12; 248). And in the Cave of Nothingness (as in that of Falsirena) Venus 'freezes' men, turning them into marble (III, 8; 718). The rhythmic blindness of the male author thus produces certain moments of suspension, in which woman is neither truth nor untruth, but undecision, undecidability: the virtuous Artemia's garden is also 'pensil' (I, 8; 173).

In his foreword to Part III of *El criticón* Gracián says that he will omit the marginal notes he had provided for the earlier parts: the margins will thus be 'left clear' ('desembaraçadas') (p. 539). He adds that if readers wish, they can fill in what the author himself has omitted. This invitation, which is clearly a version of the modesty topos traditional in such prologues, might also be seen as an invitation to the kind of 'overreading'[25] I have attempted here. As we have seen, Gracián's contemporaries outside Spain did not hesitate to adapt the text to changing circumstance. But if my reading has a moral, it is that the exclusion of printed notes will not clear the margins of a text which is dense with intertextual resonance and with structural omissions and deletions. Thus the privileging of voice and literal meaning in Gracián's literary language is bought at the cost of the repression of writing and figuration; and critics' praise of the unity and coherence of *El criticón* is at the expense of a model of structure which would account for substitution and play. What is more, the achievement of male universalisation is only made possible by (un-acknowledged) female mediation; and the quest for phallogocentric truth leads to the fragmentation of the figure of the woman. Each of the subordinate terms is marginalised. My Derridean reading of the text has thus attempted to shift the focus of attention from the centre to the periphery or margin. But it has also proposed that the rhetoric of allegory in *El criticón* is not merely a linguistic or semantic affair, but rather a question of interpretation in the broadest sense: of gender, nationality, and alterity.

Notes

1 I refer to the edition by Santos Alonso, Madrid, 1984. I have also consulted the summaries of the text in Virginia Ramos Foster, *Baltasar Gracián*, Boston, 1975.
2 See Terry Eagleton, *The Rape of Clarissa*, Oxford, 1982, p. 92.
3 For a comparison of Cervantes and Gracián see Miguel Batllori, *Gracián y el barroco*, Rome, 1958, p. 89.
4 'Tympan', in *Marges de la philosophie*, Paris, 1972, pp. i–xxv; *La Dissémination*, Paris, 1972, pp. 237–45.
5 *The Truth Disguised: Allegorical Structure and Technique in Gracián's 'Criticón'*, London, 1976.
6 Compare *Writing in the Margin*, pp. 27–9.
7 For classical definitions of allegory see Heinrich Lausberg, *Manual de retórica literaria*, Madrid, 1966–68, paras 895–901.
8 'Le Temps et l'espace dans le *Criticón*', *Bulletin Hispanique*, LXXXIX, 1987: 153–226.
9 *Estilo lingüístico y doctrina de valores*, Zaragoza, 1960.
10 *Style and Structure in Gracián's 'El Criticón'*, Chapel Hill, 1976.
11 *Gracián y 'El Criticón'*, Salamanca, 1979.
12 *Tensión semántica (lenguaje y estilo) de Gracián*, Zaragoza, 1981.
13 *Gracián y la imaginación arquitectónica*, Potomac, 1987.
14 *The Critick*, London, 1681, unnumbered.
15 *L'Homme détrompé ou Le criticón*, Paris, 1696.
16 *Il Criticon*, Venice, 1709.
17 'Signature événement contexte', in *Marges de la philosophie*, Paris, 1972, pp. 365–93.
18 See *Writing in the Margin*, pp. 61–2.
19 'La Structure, le signe, et le jeu dans le discours des sciences humaines', in *L'Ecriture et la différence*, Paris, 1967, pp. 409–28.
20 'The ages of man in Baltasar Gracián's *Criticón*', *Hispanófila*, XCII, 1988: 35–47.
21 *El ocaso de los héroes en 'El criticón'*, Zaragoza, 1945. See also Victor Bouillier, *Baltasar Gracián et Nietzsche*, Paris, 1926. When Lacan cites Gracián it is also with reference to Nietzsche. See *Ecrits*, Paris, 1969, p. 407.
22 *Glas*, Paris, 1974.
23 *Spurs/Eperons*, Chicago, 1979.
24 For truth as *aletheia* see my *The Body Hispanic: Gender and Sexuality in Spanish and Spanish American Literature*, Oxford, 1989, p. 82.
25 I borrow the term from Nancy K. Miller. As a reading of the repressed term (woman) back into the text, overreading is associated with 'arachnology': 'the interpretation and reappropriation of a story … that deploys the interwoven structures of power, gender, and identity inherent in the production of mimetic art'. See 'Arachnologies: the woman, the text, and the critic', in *Subject to Change: Reading Feminist Writing*, New York, 1988, pp. 77–101 (p. 81).

6 PETER W. EVANS

Civilisation and its discontents in *Fuenteovejuna*

As one of Lope's most universally admired plays, *Fuenteovejuna* has been subjected to an almost relentless process of critical attention.[1] A wide variety of approaches has been taken towards explicating the compelling narrative, loosely based on historical events, of a community's revenge against a cruel Lothario of a *comendador*, an action finally left unpunished if not necessarily condoned by the Reyes Católicos. But while these approaches have uniformly adopted an inflexible author-based position, unreservedly accepting the notion of authorial control and coherence, some concentrating on aesthetic, others on moral or political questions, arguing for a conservative or a radical Lope, what follows here is a project of reading against the grain, an attempt to allow the text to speak for itself, to place the author in crisis, caught between the unconscious drives of ideology and the conscious aims of private obsessions. What emerges is still the brilliant dramatist revered by tradition, but someone nevertheless to a certain extent inevitably victimised by contemporary assumptions and *creencias*, an ambivalent figure of simultaneously radical and conservative views.[2]

The process of opening up the text to its own inescapable ambivalence will ultimately focus on the rhetoric of form and content, but it must begin with the contexts of history. Set in 1476, against the background of Moorish and internecine wars between the Christian kings, the play reworks material borrowed from historical chronicles and an earlier dramatic version. Lope's use of this material has been clearly summarised in J. B. Hall's recent critical guide, and it is sufficient here to recall that, very much in keeping with Lope's characteristic taste for historical genres, the play clearly attempts to create a plausible image of life in a fifteenth-century village community.[3] We are meant to imagine the realities, both regional and national, of a period of historical turbulence, a time when the

110

nation was struggling, often against what it considered to be the various threats of Islam, Judaism, Christian rivalries and Protestantism, to create its distinctive identity, something finally achieved, even if only in propaganda terms, through the unification of Castile and Aragon in 1474. But the play succeeds in representing more than purely historical realities. The contemporary seventeenth-century relevance of the play could in any case hardly be avoided since in some walks of life, in some customs, rituals and traditions, the Spain of Philip III differed very little, of course, from the Spain of 1476. So, for all its interest in the past — serious enough, in keeping with the aims of all genuine historical drama, to avoid gross anachronisms — and for all Lope's repeated dependence on Spanish history as source material for plays of different genres, *Fuenteovejuna* is very much simultaneously a stylised version of history and a complicated aestheticised formulation, both conscious and unconscious, of contemporary political and sociological realities.

On the one hand, it is a cry for strong leadership; on the other, an exploration of the instincts and desires that sometimes turn men into monsters, women into victims and communities into thoughtless, bloodthirsty herds. In so far as it is a cry for strong leadership, the play invokes the political theories of well-known writers on kingship and tyranny, some mentioned (Plato and Aristotle), others not (Aquinas, Machiaveli, Molina, among them). But as Robin Carter sensibly warns, *Fuenteovejuna* cannot be read as a dramatic version of a carefully worked-out political argument on conflicting types of rulership and justifiable or unjustifiable forms of rebellion any more than, say, *El condenado por desconfiado* can be taken as Tirso's final position on the theology of free will.[4] The play dramatises a complex and horrific situation in which tyranny is avenged by savagery. In the process questions are raised about the motivation and consequence of human behaviour; and, as Lope develops his characters and situations, he reveals as much unconsciously about contemporary attitudes and ideological constraints as consciously about the pre-Darwinian convictions associated with irrational, barbarous instincts buried beneath the veneer of civilised society in the seventeenth century.

Never deployed purely in the interests of sensationalism, the play's images of savagery, from the sadistic excesses of the *Comendador* to the frenzied behaviour of the villagers (and not forgetting the barbarity of the Maestre or the representatives of the king), reformulate Christian teaching on the control or renunciation of instinct. These, from the Gospels themselves through to the patristic texts, merge with ancient Classical discourses and cosmological accounts of the chain of being linking humans with inanimate matter, animals and angels. Caught in the middle, humans use reason to escape from animality and to approach the angelic. The half-human, half-bestial creatures in Bosch paintings like the *Garden of Delights*, or the medieval bestiaries, are only two examples of an all too human fear of regression, through denial of reason, to pre-civilised modes of living to which artists like Lope frequently returned. His dramatisation of regression to the savage state is a feature of many plays: the brutalities inflicted on the Indians in *Arauco Domado*, the bloodthirstiness of Moors and Christians in *El bastardo Mudarra*, of honour-crazed noblemen in *Los siete comendadores de Córdoba* and *El mayordomo de la duquesa de Amalfi* are only some of the plays where he explores the darker recesses of the human psyche. In this he develops the Senecan tradition of shock horror, also inherited by Juan de la Cueva and passed on to later dramatists like Rojas Zorrilla. In all of these plays atrocities and bloodthirstiness, as the stage is littered with dismembered limbs, characters unwittingly feast off relatives and so on, have their gory justification. They allow audiences to feel suspense, horror, revulsion, but much more importantly, they hyberbolise the conviction that the civilising process never manages to make the barbarous extinct. In two other examples of Lope's interest in this topic, *El entremés del degollado* and *Arauco domado*, the first a light-hearted treatment of the subject, the second a much more serious and extended analysis, attention is drawn to the widespread evidence of savagery, even in routinely domestic situations, even when individuals in foreign lands are freed from the claustrophobia that may sometimes be said to lead them to acts of barbarism at home.

The *entremés* narrative involves a barber, a *Sacristán*, a *Regidor* and a woman, all of whom conspire to teach a gluttonous *Alcalde* a lesson by pretending to cut his throat and drenching him with blood while he is having a shave, hoping to persuade him that as his throat has been cut and is therefore incapable now of swallowing any food there is no point in his going to the banquet to which, in any case, he has not been given an invitation. Even here, in a minor farce, Lope explores simultaneously the lurking sadism of even our most trivial acts and the extent to which we are all prey to the brutality of others. In *Arauco domado*, on the other hand, he considers the paradox of a society's attempts to control the instinctual excesses of a primitive people, defined primarily in terms of their identification with nature, by the identically savage methods from which they seek to distance themselves. The brutality of the Spaniards had already been graphically recorded by, among others, Ercilla in *La Araucana* (Canto XXIV, verse 27), and Lope reproduces these horrors on stage as a climax to a play that also includes the appearances of ghosts and devils, the severing of hands, the drinking of human blood, a mother throwing her son over a cliff, and other acts of atrocity. The *non plus ultra* of many savageries, though, is perhaps the attempted exorcism of the perceived demonic threat imagined to be embodied in the Indians through the impaling of Caupolicán. The stage direction reads: 'ábranse dos puertas y véase a Caupolicán en un palo' ('two doors open revealing the impaled Caupolicán').[5]

The American wilderness here is a heightened version of the horrors at the heart of the civilised society of the old world. Here the *Conquistador*, with official licence, purges the wilderness of an excess of instinct and sexuality, but in the process releases his own latent savagery. In all of these plays, as in *Fuenteovejuna*, we are given something short of the romanticism of a Garcilaso Inca or the sympathy of a Montaigne ('Their [i.e. the cannibals'] fighting is entirely noble and disinterested'), but even so, quite clearly, an image is projected of the darker side of Christian civilisation, of the crusading *Conquistador* enterprise, which for all its celebration of *brío* leads eventually to the revelation of the beast in man.[6]

Fuenteovejuna, especially, with its closely knit community, almost nightmarish action and structure, and its claustrophobic setting gesturing at once to fifteenth-century history and contemporary historical realities – the lawless past and leaderless present, as Philip III's reign stumbles from one crisis to another – invites comparison with Freud's remarks in *Civilisation and Its Discontents* on the survival of primitive modes of being, instinct and agressiveness in patterns of behaviour attempting consciously to overcome them.[7] At one point in the discussion of the clash between the rival forces of Eros and Thanatos, Freud takes Rome as a useful analogy for the processes of civilisation, eternally evolving towards newer, better social systems, yet never entirely breaking free of outmoded, primitive models. Twentieth-century Rome carries with it, beneath its modern foundations, the relics of its own history:

> Now let us, by a flight of imagination, suppose that Rome is not a
> human habitation but a psychical entity with a similarly long and
> copious past – an entity, that is to say in which nothing that has once
> come into existence will have passed away and all the earlier phases
> of development continue to exist alongside the latest ones. This would
> mean that in Rome the palaces of the Caesars and the Septizonium
> of Septimus Severus would still be rising to their old height on the
> Palatine and the castle of S. Angelo would still be carrying on its bat-
> tlements the beautiful statues which graced it until the siege of the
> Goths, and so on.[8]

So too with *Fuenteovejuna*: the village is a psychic entity as well as
a physical structure, representing various layers and stages of human
development, drives and instincts: at one level there is a progressive
affirmation of beauty, order, love and community; at another, a
regressive embrace of power, greed, status and egocentricity. The first
tendency is ultimately represented by the villagers, the second largely
by the *Comendador*. But as others have noted (especially Robin
Carter), the division, much more complex than the image of a pastoral
Utopia projected by Antonio de Guevara, between the country-
defined villagers and city-aligned *Comendador*, never becomes
simplistic, for even before the villagers succumb to their baser instincts
in the service of what most have seen as an understandable if not
ultimately pardonable act of violence, some of their members have
already been associated with regression, and Lope is careful to point
out that the infection of the villagers by less than pastoral values is
not restricted to the purely obvious instances. The community's
integrity and achievements, its attempts to reflect through love and
justice the divine harmonies of the universe (the topic of Spitzer's
famous essay), are constantly threatened through insidious as well
as through more blatant forms of discontent.[9] *Fuenteovejuna*, a
symbolically psychic entity, remains constantly vulnerable, following
the Freudian model, to the havoc of conscious and unconscious
discontent. What Freud defined as 'discontent', Juan Huarte de San
Juan, following earlier 'psychologists', the pioneers of psychoanalysis, had already described as disease: 'en este argumento se
fundó aquel gran filósofo Demócrito Abderita cuando le probó a
Hipocrates que el hombre, dende que nace hasta que se muere, no
es otra cosa más que una perpétua enfermedad según las obras
racionales' ('the great philosopher Democritus based himself on this
argument when he proved to Hippocrates that man, from birth until

death, is nothing more than a perpetual infirmity as far as rational deeds are concerned').[10]

The greatest threat to the community in *Fuenteovejuna* is, of course, the *Comendador*, the hyperbolised symbol of primeval chaos and mirror of the villagers' darker selves. He is the devil of extreme narcissism and egocentricity, a regression to the terrible, all-powerful leader of the primal horde, an affirmation of instinct and aggressiveness ruled by sadistic desires and an urge for omnipotence. He represents all that menaces civilisation, and yet in a play so crucially attracted to powerful leadership − given the actual circumstances of weak rule, with its history of ineffectual sovereign leadership, meddling favourites and members of the Royal Family − he remains an ambivalent creation of dominant masculinity, whose full complexity can only be finally understood in terms of the patriarchal order that Lope reproduces and to a large extent accepts.

Fadrique is one of the play's several patriarchs. While he clearly embodies the nightmare of a return to primordial, pre-civilised, diabolical, id-dominated, self-centred leadership, the epitome of the Bad Father (significantly, the Maestre says he will acknowledge the *Comendador* as a 'padre' [p. 43]), the king, Fernando, represents the Good Father. He is the strong leader the play nostalgically yearns for at a time of incompetent rule, a ruler, moreover, in touch with the 'grass roots', representing the people: 'Y la villa es bien se quede/ en mí; pues de mí se vale' ('And the village shall be represented by me since it has been loyal to me') (p. 128). This is the coded political sense of the play: the king must listen to the voice of the people, not to the cynical or self-motivated flattery of the corrupt and privileged at court.

While Fadrique's henchmen, so mesmerised by the power and aggressiveness of their leader, behave like a herd in blindly following his every whim and command, the king's retinue make respected comments and suggestions. The herd instinct that characterises Fadrique's followers calls to mind Freud's remarks on group psychology:

> the lack of independence and initiative in their members, the similarity in the reactions of all of them, their reduction, so to speak, to the level of group individuals ... the weakness of intellectual ability, the lack of emotional restraint, the incapacity for moderation and delay, the inclination to exceed every limit in the expression of emotion and to work it off completely in the form of action ... these ... show an

unmistakable picture of a regression of mental activity to an earlier stage such as we are not surprised to find among savages or children.[11]

In Freud's view, human beings are basically herd animals, easily led by powerful leaders, but the process of civilisation exists, of course, precisely to curb such instincts, to combat egocentricity by promoting a feeling for community. For all his veneer of civilisation and courtly manners, Fadrique becomes, on this reading, the primordial, fittest survivor of the savage fathers, the Big Bad Wolf, both ruthless victimiser of available prey and symbol of rampant sexuality (following Bruno Bettelheim's analysis of wolves in fairy stories).[12] He is supported by a herd, the entourage of sycophants and servants in his assault on the flock of sheep in the sheepwell, *Fuenteovejuna*, the villagers trying to march to the different drum of a Catholic, largely patriarchal civilisation represented by the king and his ideological stand-ins, the other Good Fathers in the rural community, Esteban and, in embryonic form, Frondoso. Significantly, too, when the villagers opt for abandoning the principles of their civilisation — whatever the finer points about the legitimacy or otherwise in moral or legal terms of their rebellion — they betray the same herd instinct as the *Comendador's* followers, led as they are on this occasion by an outraged woman who appeals to their more primitive natures. 'Fuenteovejuna', as their battle-cry and as the only reply they are prepared to give those who question them on the responsibility for the murder, becomes not just the positive symbol for collective radical action, of the kind that has made Marxists interpret the play as an early plea for collective political awareness, and moralists as an essay in individual responsibility, but a vivid dramatisation of the herd instinct in action, refusing independence of thought and action, controlled by the hypnotic power of a strong leader, here imaged as the Amazon Laurencia.

The eventual desire of Laurencia and her followers to distance themselves ultimately from the transgressive nature of her own and the collective behaviour of the community is signposted by her refusal to become an outlaw. On the contrary, she joins the others in giving herself up, confessing collectively, and asking the Good Father for forgiveness. This action has at least three levels of significance. The most obvious is the political, namely that law-abiding citizens, content with the ideals of their civilisation, largely conservative and hierarchical as it is, having no wish to sabotage these ideals, having taken the law against their will into their own hands, surrender together in the hope of being readmitted to the social order. The second level is religious. While the wolf/lamb imagery has other implications, one of its primary meanings arises from figurative parallels with sacred texts. Matthew 10:16, 'Behold, I send you forth as sheep in the midst of wolves: be ye therefore wise as serpents, and harmless ad doves' ('mirad que Yo os envío como ovejas en medio de lobos'). Lope was far from being along among Golden Age writers to fuse religious and secular narratives and imagery. It is a platitude still worthy of emphasis that religion was an inevitable part of the fabric of almost every aspect of daily life in Golden Age society, and to a writer steeped in the traditions of the Old and New Testaments, reworking the literary resources of the Bible would have seemed like second nature. When Laurencia and Frondoso, and through them the whole community, seek the pardon of the king while owning up to their guilt, that action takes on the specifically Christian significance of the sacrificial lamb. Their action not only reinforces the legitimacy of the secular law and hierarchical social structures of government; it reinforces the Christian foundations upon which this society is based. To be a Christian, though, entails following in the footsteps of Christ, becoming a little Christ, in other words a sacrificial lamb, taking upon oneself the sins of the world, the guilt of humanity, in this case following a period of transgression, of rejecting the Christian law of cheek-turning and passive endurance, reverting to their more usual roles as lambs, as guilt-bearing martyrs to the Christian cause, eternally threatened by *Comendador/* devil figures. The momentary upsurge of pre-Christian instincts is finally subdued as the lambs return to their accepted roles in Christian society, until another set of circumstances provokes them into regressing to primordial modes of behaviour, once again providing Freud's point about the precariousness of civilised standards.

The reaffirmation by the villagers of their roles as sacrificial lambs has the force of highlighting a third sexual/political level of significance associated with their collective confession of guilt. The killing of the *Comendador* is an action motivated as much by revolt against a rampant male libido as against an overlord neglecting his obligations to the community in his care. The devil imagery associated with Fadrique points as much to his representation of uncontrolled licentiousness as to other acts of moral transgression. He epitomises carnal excess; he is a throwback to Freud's father of the primal horde in terms of his desire for all women. In this respect, as in all others, Fadrique is lost to his own narcissism, heedless of the rights of others, absolutely masterful and committed to the gratification, as a kind of pre-Nietzschean Superman of the libido, to his every sexual desire. Additionally, his quick-tempered response to female or any other kind of resistance recalls Huarte de San Juan's comments on the choleric man with his characteristic weakness for womanising: 'el colérico, según la potencia generativa se pierde por mujeres' ('in his generative capacity, the choleric man is susceptible to women').[13]

Although, admittedly, as many have observed, one of the main issues of the play arises out of the contrast between the sometimes dehumanising, debasing urges of desire and the contrary tendencies of love, the dramatisation of the *Comendador* as an easy target of moral outrage against a rampant libido raises interesting side issues. Like Tirso's *Burlador* and Calderón's more brilliant Satans, his personification of rebellion against the moral and social order, his utter contempt for the norms of sexual behaviour, all projected through a persona characterised by undoubted energy and vigour (he is the scourge of the Moors, a soldier of recognised bravery), and a taste for fine courtly language, all create a *frisson* of allure despite the havoc caused by his megalomania in the community. As the return of the villagers' depressed — sadistic, libidinal, primordial — he appeals to the id of all domesticated, civilised, obedient citizens both on and off stage. He embodies, in anticipation of Sade and Bataille, the notion of sexual desire as inseparable from danger, cruelty and, ultimately, death. The spectre of the id-driven monster within each of us is exorcised by the assault on the *Comendador*, but his destruction represents simultaneously a restraint upon instinct, a guilt-inducing act of parricide against the Bad Father, and a bloodthirsty attack on the symbol of female victimisation by Lope's spokeswoman in this play for all exploited women, Laurencia.[14]

The positioning of women in the patriarchal order as represented by the social structures of *Fuenteovejuna* has yet to be fully explored, though some scholars like Melveena McKendrick have already noted the ambivalence of Lope's feelings on the subject: 'although Lope was intellectually and emotionally more intensely concerned with the question of woman's life and rights than any other dramatist, he was at the same time woman's sternest judge in these matters ... he deplored any attempt on woman's part to deny her essential femininity. He, above all the dramatists, saw her as a sexual being.'[15]

Through Lope's play the voices of writers like Fray Luis de León and
Luis Vives speak:

> Entendiendo que el quebrar la fe a su marido, es perder las estrellas
> su luz, y caerse los cielos, y quebrantar sus leyes la naturaleza, y
> volverse todo en aquella confusión antigua y primera.[16]

> Breaking one's trust to one's husband is tantamant to the stars losing
> their light, nature its laws, and for everything to return to primal chaos.

or

> Debe la doncella estar retraída y no curarse mucho de salir a vistas,
> y sepa que es harto mala seña de su honra ser ella conocida de muchos
> y su nombre contado por la ciudad.

> A maiden must be withdrawn, curing herself of an excessive taste for
> socialising, and she should know that it's bad for her honour to be
> known by too many people and to have her name bandied about in
> the city.[17]

Prompted by developments in feminism, much writing on audience
reception theory has in recent years explored questions about reader
or spectator identification. In Hispanism scholars like T. E. May and
L. J. Woodward have already touched on this issue in stimulating
essays on Cervantes, the picaresque novel and the drama, but on the
whole without considering notions of gender that have, of course,
been the priorities of feminist theorists.[18] With these priorities in
mind, the questions now to be asked of Golden Age texts are: how
did women in the audience respond to narratives like *Fuenteovejuna*
and those like the Calderón wife-murder plays, and so on, where the
action is structured around the persecution and sometimes the rape
and killing of women? Did women identify themselves as much with
male as with female characters? Are these narratives irredeemably
patriarchal, incapable of positioning women in ways other than as
ideological stereotypes serving the interests of the male? Are sources
of pleasure available to female spectators only through masochism,
since in so many instances the thrust of the narrative springs from
the desire to castrate the phallic woman? What did women spectators
feel when faced, as in most cases − and *Fuenteovejuna* is a vivid
example − with dramatic conclusions restoring women characters,
after periods of liberation in the middle parts of these texts, to their
patriarchal roles? While these questions ultimately remain unanswer-
able, textual ambiguities and contradictory rhetoric do at least point

to the mixed responses by men as well as by women they must surely have provoked. When theologians and politicians of the day perio-dically closed down the theatres they plainly recognised the subversive potential of issues raising questions with implications stretching far beyond the constraints of their formal structures.

Undeniably, the narrative project of *Fuenteovejuna* seeks to re-establish the patriarchal order. To that extent the play conforms to ideology, refusing to contemplate a radical restructuring both in political and sexual political terms. The king's position is never threatened, the hierarchical system further endorsed, and men and women revert to their customary roles and duties. Nevertheless, the disruption of the middle part of the play, what J. E. Varey has seen as its 'al revés' moments, create resonances that live on in the con-sciousness of the spectators once they have left the theatre.[19] At the very least, through the play's depiction above all of Laurencia, but also of the other women in the play, absolute categories of sexual difference have been placed in question once the normally domesti-cated women become fearsome Amazons, in their fury and active pursuit of their aims differing little from the stereotype of the all-action male. For a while in this play, as in many other Golden Age dramas, especially those with cross-dressing motifs, women through Laurencia reclaim their pre-Oedipal, phallic heritage. In 'Female Sexuality' Freud writes: 'there can be no doubt that the bisexuality, which is present, as we believe, in the innate disposition of human beings, comes to the fore much more clearly in women than in men.... Their (women's) sexual life is regularly divided into two phases, of which the first has a masculine character, while only the second is specifically feminine.'[20]

There is a residuum of masculine phenomena in the female psyche constantly threatening to resurface in the ordinary 'female' life of a woman. Without the help of psychoanalysis, Golden Age writers seem to have understood this principle, something they in-herited from earlier writers, especially the Greeks. But the ideological implications of this knowledge are potentially extremely disruptive to a patriarchal order predicated on the assumption of sexual dif-ference. Consequently, just as the ideological project for the wholly ideologised male in the literature of this period is, at the purest level, to assert his masculinity and, if possible (though this proves very difficult, as the bulk of Lope's plays demonstrate), to distance him-self from the society of women for fear of releasing through excess of contact with them his own repressed femaleness, so women who usurp male prerogatives by appropriating qualities of character socially attached to men — activity, rationality, physical bravery — must in the end become re-feminised, their residual masculinity suppressed so as to avoid altering the balance of the patriarchal order.[21] The texts where women persecute men, such as in Lope's *La villana de Getafe* or Tirso's many comedies like *Don Gil de las calzas verdes* or *La villana de Vallecas*, and so on, and even the poetry of San Juan de la Cruz, are all examples of female acts of transgression against fixed categories of sexual difference, dramatisations of male fears of women activating their discontent with gender-based definitions of the social system. Lope's own problematic, well-documented relations with women must obviously have played an important part in his repeated explorations of this issue — and there are few plays (*La estrella de Sevilla* is one) that show an exceptional hero distancing himself from designing women — but the sheer volume of plays in the period on the topic of the female's threat to the male suggests the phenomenon is seventeenth-century ideology's most efficient way of defusing through drama the twin threats of female virility and the impairment of male masculinity. From this point of view, therefore, the closure of *Fuenteovejuna* is not just a restoration of the socio-political *status quo* but also a reaffirmation of sexual difference. Laurencia's usurpation of male prerogative in forcing the men to live up to the demands of their gender by attacking the *Comendador* and his followers, and by founding a squadron of Amazons to go into battle alongside the men, serves a worthy cause in uprooting a despised overlord, but as it threatens established concepts of sexual difference it must ultimately be disowned. Women have crossed over from the private into the public domain, their spaces, or places of definition, the house (domesticity), the river (sex, laundry), have become the battleground and the law court. Conformist society cannot tolerate the unleashed fury of women who, under the banner of action against tyranny, are actually also raising a cry against their eternal victimisation as objects of male desire. For, with all its acquiescence in accepted social norms, the play constantly dramatises the tensions, both conscious and unconscious, between drives to accept socially determined notions of femininity and resistance to these very processes. In addition to identifying themselves with male characters, whose predicaments are capable of generating for women as much as for men in the audience both pleasure and instruction (in obedience to the demands of the famous phrase, *deleitar aprovechando*), women spectators are not simply condemned in Golden Age theatre to deriving masochistic pleasures from self-identification with persecuted heroines, but also allowed in the finest, most thoughtful plays, fusion with attractive women, moving well outside the limitations of stereotype to which they may be sentenced in ordinary daily life. Just as the male is taken out of himself, confronted with his own femaleness as he finds himself empathising with the Dianas, Sirenas, Villanas at the narrative centre of so many plays, so the female puts herself in the place of the Peribáñezs, Federicos or Alonsos of the great male-centred plays. But, additionally, while the spectacle of powerless, persecuted women will all too often reduce the female spectator to a victim of ideology, many plays, like *Fuenteovejuna*, will offer them the satisfactions of a character not merely fetishised, castrated, or visualised as sexual, but within the ambivalent rhetoric of a great drama caught in the crossfire of powerful conservative attitudes, of a character challenging the norms of sexual identity.

The women's revolt in *Fuenteovejuna* is sparked off, quite obviously, by the narcissistic indulgendes of Fadrique, but the attitudes of Frondoso and Laurencia's father Esteban, overwhelmingly benign and positive though they may be, nevertheless betray the ideological condescension of which Fadrique is so grotesquely guilty.

As many have already remarked, Fadrique's attitude to Laurencia specifically and women generally is vividly characterised by animal imagery. In a study of the play's animal imagery,[22] E. Michael Ferli draws attention to Lope's indebtedness to a long poetic tradition linking love with the hunt. Desire imaged as a hunt naturally lends itself to contexts like these: the lover is the hunter, the beloved the quarry. But hunting also implies, besides the thrill of the chase, the hide-and-seek patterns of courtship, and so on, the violent consequences of eventual entrapment, killing and consumption. In its identification with the *Comendador*, this imagery can clearly be seen to represent an attitude of forceful superiority, contempt and destruction: it positions the woman as powerless, a target existing solely as a means of gratifying the desire of the privileged male. Although the *Comendador* is capable of cruelty in all other spheres of life (in his dealings, for instance, with military adversaries), his brutality and sadism towards women (not just Laurencia, but also Jacinta, whom he sentences to the lewd appetites of the soldiers), suggests a need to satisfy his lust for not only Laurencia or Jacinta but also through them, through their humiliation and treatment as creatures of the hunt, all women, visualised here as 'cazadas', the prey that must be trapped and controlled, their potential threat to the hyperbolised, disturbed male psyche once and for all disarmed.

This is an issue hinted at even in scenes between Laurencia and Frondoso or Esteban. Like Tisbea in the *Burlador*, or Marcela in *Don Quijote*, Laurencia has grown weary of male desire, fearing that most men tend to look at attractive women as sex symbols with only one thing on their mind: 'después de darnos disgusto,/es anochecer con gusto/y amanecer con enfado' ('after annoying us, it's to bed with pleasure, only to rise with anger') (p. 48). When Laurencia and Frondoso first meet in the play, for instance, there are some crucial references to eye imagery, picked up and expanded later on, especially in the songs. Traditionally, of course, women are frequently positioned as the spectacle for the male. As I have been arguing, though, to reduce the textual representation of women in this way, to seek only crude ideological meanings, is to deny the pleasure the female spectacle can offer the female spectator – empathising in this case with exhilarating Amazonian exploits – but it is nevertheless equally true not only that looking is predetermined by knowledge (Don Quijote sees monsters, not windmills, because he *knows* they are his enemy), but also that in looking at women men frequently do so through the culturally created perspectives of degrading or limiting stereotype. The association of women with duplicity and sexuality is such a common stereotype, in widespread use throughot Golden Age literature, that it slips easily into the language of even the most positive characters, as when the brave *Gracioso* – who comes to the defence of women in the play – uses the term 'dimuño' to describe Laurencia. Even Frondoso, another character who leaps to the defence of women, as when he threatens to kill the *Comendador* in the scene of his attempted seduction of Laurencia, uses language associated with possession and animals which echoes the *Comendador*'s, in the process identifying himself, however benignly, with modes of perception that inevitably lead to victimisation. Both the 'palomo' (p. 66) and 'posesión' (p. 91) references have a mainly positive set of connotations: doves are symbols of peace, possession can be a sign of love. Yet in the context of the *Comendador*'s own use of animal and possessive vocabulary their negative sides also come into view. While the animal imagery once more recalls devouring, the possessive references suggest both entrapment and the diabolical. Even when Frondoso addresses Laurencia as an 'angel' (p. 65), a term that registers his veneration while simultaneously recalling patterns of medieval cosmology, the negative force of the stereotype makes itself felt. Like so many other heroines of this and countless other texts before and since, Laurencia's womanhood is in danger of being misrepresented, despite all the noble intentions of her champion, by language which, in what is admittedly a relatively trivial instance on this occasion, victimises through exaggerated eulogy. Taking offence from terms of endearment like this has been one of feminism's least persuasive lines of attack. After all, when a parent refers to a child as a 'treasure', or a male or female Geordie addresses another adult as 'pet', there is usually no hint of condescension, since the primary, positive associations of wealth and intimacy are being invoked. Nevertheless, in certain contexts, terms of endearment can become acts of condescension or victimisation. In the context of this play what distinguishes Frondoso's remarks from the *Comendador*'s is, once again, love, but given that Frondoso also forms part of the play's complex treatment of ideological infiltration of all levels of the community, the negative implications, however faint, of Frondoso's attitude cannot be totally ignored. Even so, unlike the *Comendador*'s, Frondoso's language combines the occasional inherited ideological cliché with originality, clarity and honesty, to the extent that these are capable of expression through the limitations of language. The language of true love and selflessness are on Frondoso's lips no mere 'palabras y plumas': they prefigure his valiant defence of the woman he loves, and together they persuade her that *esquivez*, distance from all men, renunciation of love, is an unnecessary privation when there are men of decency around. The play argues through its representation of honourable men like Frondoso that language and ideology pre-date subjectivity, that the civilising process, the drive to create a civilised community, cannot ultimately succeed without attention to the distortions of reality created by language.

While, like the ideologised men in *Fuenteovejuna* and like many other women in the drama of the period, Laurencia has internalised and has become absorbed by many of the dominant stereotypes of language – to the extent of referring to herself as a 'polla' (p. 48), and as a possession (p. 102), a jewel not yet handed over to her new owner who has bought her from her father, defining herself also as nothing without a man (p. 118) — she is also characterised by a self-consciousness that eventually erupts at the moment of her defilement by the *Comendador*. An early example of her sensitivity to the entrapments of language occurs when she reacts to Frondoso's use of the term 'damas' (p. 50) when addressing herself and Pascuala. (In another speech, Pascuala also resents the use of terms like 'vida', 'ser' and 'corazón' (p. 49) on the lips of men who soon replace them with less flattering equivalents following the gratification of their desire.) From one point of view, Laurencia's criticism reflects her refusal to be treated as other than is merited by her social status as a peasant woman; from another, though, it provides an early indication of a mind grown accustomed to and suspicious of the stereotypes of male flattery. Her ability to see through such stratagems — on this occasion benign ones deployed by a man of honourable intentions — is compounded by her appropriation, where possible, of the sources of power and control too often restricted to men, as when for instance she herself, sometimes forthrightly, and sometimes with ironic feeling, uses the play's complex eye imagery.

An example of the former occurs when early in the play she confides to Mengo: 'Los hombres aborrecía,/Mengo; más desde aquel día,/los miro con otra cara ('I hated men, Mengo, but since that day I look at them differently') (p. 80); of the latter, when following the assumed rape by the *Comendador*, she has the following exchange with her father:

> *Laurencia:* ... no me nombres
> tu hija.
> *Esteban:* ¿Por qué, mis *ojos*?
> ¿Por qué?
> *Laurencia:* ... Llevóme de vuestros *ojos*
> ... no se ven aquí los golpes
> de *verme* en tantos dolores? (p. 101)

Laurencia: ... don't call me your daughter. *Esteban:* Why not, my *eyes*? Why not? *Laurencia:* ... He took me away from your eyes ... are the blows not visible, seeing me so full of woe?

While the second example refers, through sight, to the loss of control of the daughter by the father, the first highlights the use of the look by the male to control the female. The female is his spectacle, theatricalised, associated in this stereotype with nature, in other words with wild creatures and instinct, available for seduction and

consumption, a marginalised sex kept beyond the inner sanctum of
male power. And that is exactly how the song represents her:

> Al val de Fuenteovejuna
> la niña en cabellos baja;
> el caballero la sigue
> de la cruz de Calatrava.
> Entre las ramas se esconde,
> de vergonzosa y turbada;
> fingiendo que no le ha visto,
> pone delante las ramas.
> '¿Para qué te escondes,
> niña gallarda?
> Que mis linces deseos
> paredes pasan.'
> Acercóse el caballero,
> y ella confusa y turbada,
> hacer quiso celosías
> de las intrincadas ramas;
> más como quien tiene amor
> los mares y las montañas
> atraviesa fácilmente,
> la dice tales palabras:
> '¿Para qué te escondes,
> niña gallarda?
> Que mis linces deseos
> paredes pasan.' (p. 95)

To the valley of Fuenteovejuna the maid with flowing hair descends;
the knight with the Cross of Calatrava follows her. She hides, in shame
and startled; pretending she has not seen him, she shields herself with
branches. 'Why do you hide sweet maiden? For my lynx-eyed desires
pierce through walls.' The knight approached and, confused, disturbed, she sought to make screens out of the intricate branches; but as
love traverses sea and mountains, he asks 'Why do you hide, sweet
maiden? For my lynx-eyed desires pierce through walls.'

The song is a vignette, a *mise-en-abyme*, condensing and self-
consciously dramatising the frame-text's preoccupation with the
theatricalisation and sexual persecution of women. The spectacle
of a threatened woman hiding in nature — one of her designated
habitats, the libido's place of definition — trying vainly to escape
the all-powerful, ideologically sanctioned male look, presupposes
here a male spectator voyeuristically enjoying the discomfort of an

imperilled woman. At this point a female spectator's pleasure would almost certainly be governed primarily by masochism. Yet what the song lacks, female rebellion and appropriation of the look, the rest of the play provides. If the spectacle here reassures the troubled, threatened male of his masculinity, as following Lacan's argument about the mirror phase, he fetishises and castrates the woman as a means of consolidating the sense of his own unity, elsewhere the spectacle – Laurencia – rebels and for a period rejects the definition of her individuality and sex constructed for her by the male.[23]

The image in the song of the persecuted girl hiding from the look of the male provokes Laurencia as much as the actual assault upon her by the *Comendador*. The analogy with the Amazons the play so deliberately makes (p. 103) is designed to recall not only the active exploits of these fabled women but also the desexualisation of their social roles through an act of self-mutilation, the removal of the left breast as a means of improving efficiency in archery. The symbolic nature of the act, the direct assault on an area of female anatomy not only associated with maternity but with male sexual gratification as well, plays into Laurencia's anger directed both against the *Comendador* and against the general attitude towards all women, in whose name she unleashes it. Through its depiction of the *Comendador* the play shows an extreme case of women's sexual objectification by a man whose behaviour is partially sanctioned by a contradictory ideology that simultaneously denounces sexual harassment while also using it as one of the yardsticks by which to judge standards of masculinity. In this play, for all its many ambivalences, and for all its own contradictions, Lope allows women an opportunity to speak for themselves, to rise up against intolerable trivialisation and victimisation by men who treat them only as the gratifiers of their libido. The peasants' revolt in this play is primarily a women's revolt, women here identified with the peasant class so that the inferior status allotted them by ideology and dishonourable men prepared to abide by its male-enhancing priorities can all the more vividly and poignantly dramatise their exploitation. It is entirely fitting, therefore, that when the *Comendador* is finally killed his execution should take the form of a beheading. As the women and the other villagers parade his head on a lance around Fuenteovejuna, the sight inescapably suggests symbolic castration. Later artists, like Buñuel in *Tristana*, unfettered by the strict seventeenth-century laws of censorship, unambiguously identified decapitation with castration, though even before Lope's day, as Freud argues citing the Old Testament instance of Judith and Holofernes, beheading was already well known as a 'symbolic substitute for castrating'.[24] The would-be female castrator, the man who would repress women, restricting them to the safe, male-subservient roles of stereotype, is himself the victim of symbolic castration. Women, dreaded by men as harbingers of death, turn out in this play to fulfil that threat, though not in the way their oppressors had ever imagined.[25]

Notes

1 All page references are to the edition of the text prepared by W. S. Mitchell, London, 1948, reprinted 1956.
2 For a summary of traditional approaches to the play see J. B. Hall, *Lope de Vega, Fuenteovejuna*, London, 1985.
3 See Hall, *Lope de Vega*.
4 See Robin Carter, '*Fuenteovejuna* and tyranny. Some problems of linking drama with political theory', *Forum for Modern Language Studies*, XIII, 1977: 313–35.
5 See the Biblioteca de Autores Españoles volume of Marcelino Menéndez Pelayo (ed.), *Obras de Lope de Vega*, Madrid, 1969, p. 287.
6 See Montaigne, *Essays*, transl. J. M. Cohen, London, 1958, p. 114.
7 On the 'failure of leadership' of Philip III's reign, see J. H. Elliot, *Imperial Spain 1469–1716*, Harmondsworth, 1970, pp. 300–8.
8 In Sigmund Freud, *Civilization, Society and Religion: 'Group Psychology', 'Civilization and its Discontents' and other Works*, trans. James Strachey, ed. Albert Dickson, Harmondsworth, 1985, pp. 257–8.
9 Leo Spitzer, 'Un tema central y su equivalente estructural in *Fuenteove-juna*', in José Francisco Gatti (ed.), *El teatro de Lope de Vega, artículos y estudios*, 2nd edn, Buenos Aires, 1967, pp. 124–47.
10 See Juan Huarte de San Juan, *Examen de ingenios*, Buenos Aires, 1946, p. 52.
11 *Civilization and its Discontents*, p. 148.
12 See Bruno Bettelheim, *The Uses of Enchantment. The Meaning and Importance of Fairy Tales*, Harmondsworth, 1976, p. 172: 'The wolf is not just the male seducer, he also represents all the asocial, animalistic tendencies within ourselves.'
13 Huarte de San Juan, *Examen de ingenios*, p. 51.
14 See Melveena McKendrick, *Women and Society in the Golden Age*, London, 1974, p. 330.
15 See *Civilization and its Discontents*, p. 324: 'We cannot get away from the assumption that man's sense of guilt springs from the oedipus complex and was acquired at the killing of the father by the brothers banded together.'
16 See *La perfecta casada*, Madrid, 1963, p. 32.

17 See *Instrucción de la mujer cristiana*, Buenos Aires, 1944, p. 95.

18 See, for instance, L. J. Woodward, '*El casamiento engañoso y el coloquio de los perros*', *Bulletin of Hispanic Studies*, XXXVI, 1959: 80–7, and T. E. May, '*El condenado por desconfiado: 1. The Enigmas. 2. Anareto*', *Bulletin of Hispanic Studies*, XXXV, 1958: 138–56. On feminist approaches to the female subject and audience reception theory, see Teresa de Lauretis, *Alice Doesn't: Feminism, Semiotics, Cinema*, Bloomington, trans. Catherine Porter and Luce Irigaray, Ithaca, 1985, and *Speculum of the Other Woman*, trans. Gillian C. Gill, Ithaca, 1985.

19 See J. E. Varey, 'La inversión de valores en *Fuenteovejuna*', *Lectiones*, 5, Santander: Universidad Internacional Menéndez Pelayo. 1976.

20 See Sigmund Freud, *On Sexuality. Three Essays on the Theory of Sexuality and other works*, trans. James Strachey, ed. Angela Richards, Harmondsworth, 1977, p. 374. Golden Age specialists interested in applying psychoanalysis to the drama of the period include Everett W. Hesse. See, especially, *The Comedia and Points of View*, Potomac, 1984.

21 On feminine stereotypes, see Mary Ellman, *Thinking about Women*, London, 1969, pp. 56–145.

22 In 'The hunt of love: the literalization of a metaphor in *Fuenteovejuna*', *Neophilologus*, LXIII, 1979: 54–8.

23 See Jacques Lacan, *Ecrits: A Selection*, trans. Alan Sheridan, London, 1988, pp. 1–7.

24 See *On Sexuality*, p. 281.

25 Much has been written on the female threat to man. A lively and relatively recent study is by Hélène Cixous, 'Castration or decapitation?', trans. Annette Kuhn, *Signs*, VII (1), 1981: 41–55, but the pioneering study is, of course, Simone de Beauvoir's *Le Deuxième Sexe*, Paris, 1949.

I am extremely grateful to Robin Fiddian for having read a previous version of this chapter, and for making many helpful suggestions.

7 HENRY W. SULLIVAN

The political murder of the king's other body: 1562–1649

The purpose of this chapter is to look at some aspects of regicide and tyrannicide in Golden Age Spain, during the period frequently referred to as the Counter-Reformation (1563–1648) (Sullivan, 1976, pp. 13–18). This might well seem like an exercise in futility when we remind ourselves that no actual assassination of a Spanish monarch ever occurred during the Golden Age in question. But this absence of any regicide in Spain, given the contemporary history of the rest of Europe, is itself a significant fact which invites comment. Moreover, in the serious, theological literature (Mariana, Suárez) and the popular literature of the time (notably the *comedia*), great attention was paid to the issue of tyrants and the legitimacy of tyrannicide. The status and role of the king, indeed, was the most debated focus of all writing on political theology during the period. In this respect, it offers a parallel to the issue of grace and free will (the *De auxiliis* controversy) as the most debated issue in the realm of theology proper. These two questions – the neo-feudal subject's relationship to the ruler, and the sinner's relationship to God – have much in common, indeed, since both questions frame the larger issue of the relationship, in that epoch, of the human subject to the signifier in general. I am using the terms 'human subject' and 'signifier' here in the Lacanian sense and I will return to the matter of their definition presently. As for the dates in my title, I have stretched the admittedly hazy boundaries of the Counter-Reformation by a year or two for the sake of the theme of regicide. Rather than take the end of the Council of Trent (1563) as the *incipit*, I have preferred the year of the outbreak of the French Wars of Religion (1562); and for the *terminus ad quem*, I have preferred the date of King Charles I's beheading by Parliament (1649) over the year of the Treaty of Westphalia (1648).

But talk of 'king' and 'kings' immediately raises the canard of the signifying distinction implied by the person of the monarch –

the historical personage who was Philip II, for example – and the position he occupied as head of state in the Spanish Empire. The latter category is really the office of the king of Spain *per se*, as against the king who actually held the office at a particular moment in history. This kind of ontological duality is neatly expressed in the French proclamation 'le roi est mort, vive le roi!' and points to a kind of immortal, or continuous, existence of the king in a body other than his natural, or mortal, one.

The best-known work dedicated to exploring this distinction of political theology is doubtless Ernst Kantorowicz's *The King's Two Bodies* (1957). He cites the formulation of crown lawyers working at the behest of Elizabeth I in sixteenth-century England as one of the first clear elaborations of this doctrine:

> For the King has in him two Bodies, viz., a Body natural and a Body politic. His Body natural (if it be considered in itself) is a body mortal, subject to all Infirmities that come by Nature or Accident, to the Imbecility of Infancy or old Age, and to the like Defects that happen to the natural Bodies of other People. But his Body politic is a Body that cannot be seen or handled, consisting of Policy and Government, and constituted for the Direction of the People, and the Management of the public weal, and this Body is utterly void of Infancy, and old Age, and other natural defects and Imbecilities. (Kantorowicz, 1957, p. 7)

Although Kantorowicz variously terms the duality that forms the substance of his inquiry an 'absurdity' (p. 3), or 'ludicrous' and 'awkward' (p. 5), I believe that the Elizabethan formula cited points to a greater difficulty inherent in the signifying distinction between the king actually holding office and the office of king itself. We can say that the king in his 'Body natural' ('if it be considered in itself') is a fallible mortal, like anyone else; whereas in his 'Body politic' or mystical body, he is a transcendental entity: the incorporation and fountainhead of law in the nation–state. As such, he is a person who is omnipresent in the courts, assizes and the crown agents acting in his name; he is 'eternal' in the perpetuity of his legitimate succession, as well as in the efficacy, across the passage of generations, of royal statutes issuing from his mandate.

Although Lacan very rarely addressed political issues, his teaching is highly suggestive for probing further the ontological duality of the king's two Bodies. Considered in the flight of Lacan's three Orders – the Symbolic, the Imaginary and the Real – it is easy enough to see that the King's 'Body politic' is really the monarch's incorporation in the Symbolic Order, i.e. that he is a key signifier for the public structure, or Symbolic Order, of society itself. The theoretics of his 'Body natural' in terms of the Imaginary and the Real, however, presents greater problems. As happens so often in Lacanian theory, it may occur that a two-part, a binary distinction, rooted in popular parlance or conventional wisdom, actually masks over (by virtue of its intellectual neatness) an elided or suppressed element, a 'third term' (Ragland-Sullivan, 1989, pp. 40–64), which the application of Lacanian concepts will then bring to the surface. For while it is meaningful to talk of the king's Imaginary and Real Bodies as some kind of equivalent for the 'Body natural', it is important to note that the king's 'Real Body' is not the same thing as the biological organism, for example, that you can stick daggers in (as in the case, say, of Ravaillac and Henry IV of Navarre in 1610).

Though the distinction of the three Orders already predates the beginning of Lacan's official teaching in 1953, and pervades it thereafter, it is roughly correct to say that he concentrated on the elaboration of the Symbolic in the 1950s, on the Imaginary in the 1960s, and on the Real in the 1970s. In 1975, he introduced the fourth Order of the Symptom. For his own conception of the Symbolic, Lacan owed a certain intellectual debt to his friend, Claude Lévi-Strauss, and the French anthropologist's idea of 'symbolic' exchange in societies, especially in such matters as gifts, dowry, bride-price, and so on, as associated with the marriage exchange of women between men; a practice which lay at the heart of the structure of kinship in Lévi-Strauss's view and, hence, of the foundations of culture itself. But Lacan greatly extended this concept, particularly in its pertinence for language which, in Lacan's view, is the Symbolic Order *par excellence*, and not only the vehicle for every kind of exchange vital to culture, but even for the genesis of the human subject in the first place. The 'exchange', so to speak, or the 'otherness' of the cultural ethos that pre-exists the *speechless* infant, and which is actually placed as a symbol system in the mind of that same infant as a *speaking* subject later on, is fundamental to Lacan's theory of the origins of mentality. These early messages and images from others, after undergoing primary and secondary phases of repression (Freud's *Urverdraengung* and *Unterdrueckung*), form the locus of the Other and the unconscious in the child and, later still, in the mature adult.

Lacan's Symbolic Order is neutral, athematic, one might say, content-free in itself. The telephone systems that cover the globe, and even function via satellite in space, would provide a convenient analogy, and telephones actually contribute one system among many to the criss-cross of Symbolic networks in society. But the dishes, lines and cables of the GPO or AT&T send no good or evil messages as such; the users do. However, the existence of the network already implies a structure and a set of rules for its use; and in order to send a message, the user must be both familiar with these rules and prepared to submit to them. He or she must also be prepared to pay a price (a telephone bill) for the privilege of being part of the communicative, or signifying, network. Finally, the relationship of user to system is characterised by a differential, or 'rational' logic, which most people can learn; this lends the network its 'universal' dimension.

Lacan's Imaginary Order, on the other hand, functions by an identificatory, non-differential logic of merger and fantasy. On the vectors of Lacan's Schema L (*Seminar II*, p. 284; Ragland-Sullivan, 1986; p. 2), the Imaginary relation operates from the unconscious place of the ideal ego (*moi*) and is triggered by others in the here and now. Imaginary relations are marked by aggressiveness and narcissism; indeed, aggressiveness commonly arises out of the subject's 'wounded' narcissism. Ideally, the Lacanian ego seeks love and recognition above all things. The posture of the ideal ego is to send this question in implicit inversion to others, a *demande d'amour*, in order to elicit the desired recognition. What people commonly call feelings of love and hate, or 'irrational' passions, are the everyday stuff of the Imaginary Order. In the realm of politics, be it within an organisation or family or at the level of national politics, most decisions are reached at the level of the Imaginary, and then corroborated (some would say 'rationalised') at the level of the Symbolic. Hitler pitched his speeches to the German people at the Imaginary place of national identity, narcissistic pride, and grandiose fantasies of Aryan racial superiority; it was not really a Symbolic Order discourse. But this is not unusual; Churchill, *mutatis mutandis*, did the same thing in England.

So when we talk of the subject's Imaginary relation to the king, we are speaking of a crucial dimension in politics. We are also closer to the issue of regicide (and its Symbolic Order justification, tyrannicide) once we enter the Imaginary realm. It is when the aggressiveness in a given subject is excited to an intolerable degree around the issue of the king's competence or right to rule, that he may emerge as a political assassin. The assassin usually does not know the king as such; he kills a stranger. But the assassin is linked already to the 'Body natural' of the king – really a dimension of his 'Body cultural' – by the process of Imaginary identification. The degree of negative transference inspired by the 'evil king' is so great, that the assassin as subject places its annulment (through immolation) on a higher plane than the value of his own life. Behaviour such as this encourages us to classify such persons as 'fanatics'.

But we have said that the Order of the Real is also implicated in the king's Body natural. Lacan's concept of the Real, rivalled only perhaps by the complex notion of the Other, is probably the hardest single idea in all his thought. It falls outside the competence of this chapter, therefore, to even approach doing justice to it (Ragland-Sullivan, 1986, pp. 183–95). But the Real is the hole in the Other, the place of the impossible, the unsayable and the ineffable, beyond human representation. And even if the Real cannot be said, it continues to emit its effects into the other two Orders, even to show up in the Symptom. Lacan listed eight objects, certain of them detachable body parts (*objets petit a*), as both the objects of desire and the causes of desire in the circuit of the drives: the mamella or breast, the faeces, the urinary flow, the (Imaginary) phallus, the voice, the phoneme, the gaze and the void (*le rien*) (cf. *Seminar XI*, 1973). These *objets a*, though not articulable as such, open up on the hole in the Other, causing anxiety and intensifying the lack that underlies desire. The Real is that which the sleeper encounters at 'the navel of the dream' (Freud), when even unconscious representation falters and fails. The sleeper next awakes, in a cold sweat and a state of palpitation, only able to recall the nightmare as far as that point of 'fading' (aphanisis) where the Real levels of anxiety grew too intense to be tolerated.

The relevance of this for our theme lies in the overlap between the Real aspects of the king's Body natural and the Lacanian concept of the Real father. The Real father, in this view, as unconsciously and obscenely desiring, occupies a place of impossibility and, in so doing, infers chaos and confusion into the other two Orders. In the Oedipal drama, he lays two equally forceful injunctions on the son: be like me, but don't be like me. With respect to his possession of a/the mother and as guarantor of the incest taboo, the father enjoins his son to grow up and become a man (i.e. like him). At the same time and by the same token, however, although the son aspires to obey his father's wish, he cannot take his father's place as possessor of his own mother (i.e. cannot be like him). The father's double wish/command is, therefore, impossible to fulfil and partakes, by definition, of the Real. This insoluble crux around the Real father also underlines the basic impossibility of masculinity as such.

In a neo-feudal monarchy of the Counter-Reformation Spanish type, the king represents the highest absolute value after God Himself. But in the pattern of dominance and submission inherited from the medieval lord—vassal relationship, we can discern the potential for the same kind of difficulty we have described above. Although the king does not say to his vassal, 'become a man like me', he does say to him implicitly (for the sake of the organising principles of the state), 'make your desire to please me be the main focus of your desire'. At the same time and by the same token, however, he enjoins the vassal not to take, not to usurp, the monarch's place. As the first rule of feudal obedience, therefore, the vassal is also enjoined to make his main desire be *not to become like his lord*. The monarch, therefore, serves as the paragon of the desired one who, simultaneously and at all costs, is not to be desired to the point of his crown's possession by another.

It follows, then, that a motive for regicide could lie in the failure to follow the impossible injunctions of the Real father/Real king in his 'cultural' Body natural. For while we tend to fantasise all institutions as stable entities, with firmly entrenched leaders, the reality of 'life at the top' in power structures is actually precarious and life-threatening. Indeed, we have laid out convincing reasons for hostility towards the monarch in all the three Orders under discussion: Symbolic, Imaginary and Real. And so the opening question returns with all the more force than before: why did no actual assassination of a Spanish monarch ever occur during the tempestuous era of the Counter-Reformation? Even if we have subdivided the binary distinction of the Elizabethan jurists between 'Body politic' (Symbolic Order) and 'body natural' (Imaginary and Real Orders) into a ternary one, the fact remains that, while many monarchs died a violent death in Europe (Mary Stuart, William the Silent, Henry III of France, Henry IV of France, the pseudo-Dimitri of Russia, Charles I of England, and sundry reigning Queens consort), no Spanish king ever saw a dagger brandished in anger.

In the light of the preceding, therefore, it becomes pertinent to ask: 'In an act of regicide, which Body of the king is it that is being killed?' Is the intent of the assassin to end the life of what is − rather curiously and inappropriately − called the king's Body 'natural', for those cultural reasons (Imaginary, Real) we have enumerated? Or is it, rather, to strike at his Body politic and Symbolic Order signification? Is the king, in other words, being dispatched as an unworthy or undesirable office-holder, or is it the institution of monarchy itself which is being immolated? My tentative answer in this chapter is to reply that, at the beginning of the Counter-Reformation, particular kings were murdered out of circumstantial, religious motives, i.e. as heretics and/or unbelievers (Imaginary Order). But the Counter-Reformation, which started out in the early 1560s as a religious struggle, turned in the course of some eighty years into a political struggle. By the 1640s, even the absolutist Spanish monarchy had begun to crumble from revolts and internal dissension. In the outcome of the English Civil War, it seems to me, the legalised execution of Charles I in 1649 by Act of Parliament constituted a repudiation not of an incompetent monarch or a tyrant in himself, but of the concept of monarchy itself (Symbolic Order). Cromwell, for example, refused the crown when it was offered to him for the taking.

A concrete example of this gradual shift of events is the fate of Henry III of France. At the height of the Religious Wars, Henry caused two prominent leaders of the Catholic League, the Duke of Guise and his brother the Cardinal of Lorraine, to be assassinated (1588). Some seven months later, in 1589, Henry was himself assassinated by Jacques Clément, a young Dominican friar; killed, that is, by a Catholic acting out of fanatical religious conviction. The charges leveled by Clément and like-minded Leaguers at Henry III included personal vices, dissoluteness, heresy and injury to his vassals. Henry, then, was killed as an unworthy man in his 'Body natural' and for his heretical beliefs (Imaginary and Real Orders), not killed as the symbol of the French monarchy itself. Similarly, the Protestant William the Silent of Holland was stabbed to death in 1585 by the Catholic fanatic Balthasar Gerards (acting, some said, under the orders of Philip II). But, as history ran its course and Holland won its independence from Spain in 1648, Holland − like England − had moved from the traditional concept of monarchy. Although the Orange succession was maintained in the Dutch royal house, the descendants of William were styled 'Stadholders of the Netherlands' and constrained by the Calvinist Regents and mercantile aristocracy of Holland, so that the country emerged from the Treaty of Westphalia as the *Republic* of Holland. Cromwell's interim Commonwealth, also inspired by Calvinist or Puritan concepts of state organisation, bore many similarities to a republic.

At first glance, Spain seems to stand outside the general trend in Europe towards regicide and tyrannicide, or the political execution of rivals for the crown (such as the beheading of Mary, Queen of Scots in 1586 by order of Elizabeth I). Philip II was an exceedingly cautious man, whose first chain of command was a pair of secretaries chosen precisely for their inability to get along with one another, i.e. for the unlikelihood of their finding common political cause in any conspiracy against him. The most famous of them, Antonio Pérez, did finally defect to the Protestant factions abroad, but Philip was never accosted by any assassin. Philip III and Philip IV turned effective political power over to their favourites or *privados*, but neither they nor their favourites came close to serious attempts on their life. On the other hand, Charles I's favourite,, the Duke of Buckingham, was murdered by one John Felton in 1628.

In his comprehensive treatment of this whole question entitled *Tyrannicide and Drama* (1987), however, Robert Lauer has shown that the controversial issue of royal power and royal abuse was very much alive in Spain throughout the Counter-Reformation period. He sees evidence of a tyrannicide drama among neo-Senecan dramatists such as Juan de la Cueva and Cristóbal de Virués from as early as 1579 onwards. There are many seventeenth-century *comedias* that deal with the theme of tyrannicide, even if the theme is broached in indirect fashion by placing the story abroad, for example, or in the time of the Roman Empire (as Calderón does in *La gran Cenobia*). The theme was also taken up in theological tracts by figures such as Soto and Báñez, or the Jesuits Bellarmine, Molina and Suárez. The most sensational book by a Spanish Jesuit on the topic, Juan de Mariana's *De rege et institutione regis* of 1599, not only preached resistance to the abuse of royal power, but proclaimed that, in such cases, insurrection by offended vassals, and even tyrannicide, was justified. Another indication of Spanish public interest in the theocratic theory of monarchy was Quevedo's popularising work, *La política de Dios y el gobierno de Cristo* of 1626, a work that went through no less than nine editions in the year of its first appearance.

If it were possible to step back from the events in Europe during the latter half of the sixteenth century and the first half of the seventeenth, as though these were narrated on some huge tapestry, then a few clear patterns emerge. In Northern Europe, there is some parallelism between the spread of Protestantism and the shifting away from the notion of a divinely ordained monarchy towards the beginnings of government by legislative bodies (England, Holland, the Hanseatic League). Further south, in France, the religious civil war of Europe was fought at its hardest; but eventually an absolutist monarchical system arose that re-established the Catholic religion. In Spain, the Catholic religion was never seriously questioned and absolutism also became the system adopted by the Habsburgs.

But, in the earlier sixteenth century, Spain had undergone religious and spiritual upheavals ñot dissimilar from the rest of Europe, such as the demand for ecclesiastical reform, the spread of Erasmianism, the influence of Humanism, the appearance of deviant sects such as the *alumbrados* or, more controversially, the Spanish mystics, and so on. But, after the ferment of the 1520s and 1530s, a distinct reaction is palpable around 1540, as the revival of Scholasticism began to close out these novel directions. Spain, so to say, was at one point ready to move in a broad European trend, but then hesitated and drew back into a trenchant reaffirmation of traditional positions. Northern Europe, however, proceeded to move further and further away from this traditional paradigm.

The two major signifiers around which Spanish thinking defined itself were God and king, and this is faithfully reflected in the *comedia*. By signifier, following Lacan, I here mean a letter transmitted by the Symbolic Order, whose effect has a structuring or organising influence on the constitution of any given subjectivity. From this definition, it follows that one cannot really grasp the Lacanian signifier by saying what it *is*, but rather what it *does*. Taking a cue from C. S. Peirce's semiotic definition of the sign, Lacan said in the *Ecrits* that a sign represents something for someone, but 'a signifier represents the subject for another signifier' (1966, 819). This enigmatic definition underlines the fundamental Lacanian claim that there is a source of knowledge and power outside us that predates the genesis of any given human subject. This source we could call, in the first place, the sum of all signifiers in the Symbolic Order which, in their transmission, have actually determined the structure and discourse of a new speaking subject in his or her native language. This language has come from an other place; but the otherness of the cultural ethos becomes, as we have said above, the unconscious locus of the Other.

What the Spanish signifiers for God and king particularly have in common is precisely their suggestions for the relationship of the subject to power as something outside itself. In this neo-medievalising Catholic world-view, we may discern a characteristically triadic arrangement: (1) the signifier, (2) the subject, and (3) their relationship, in which the latter is eclipsed by the former. In the Catholic Church, this relationship is substantivised through the mediation of a sacramentally ordained clergy and six other grace-bestowing sacraments. There is, so to say, (1) God, (2) a subject or sinner, and (3) their relationship via grace, which last it is the sinner's place to hope for, but not demand. In the case of kinship, there is (1) a consecrated sovereign, (2) a subject or vassal, and (3) their relationship as a bond of feudal obligation between them. The authority and majesty of both signifiers – God and Spanish sovereign – is reciprocally sustaining: God consecrates the king's Body politic and his mystic authority, while the king acts as God's viceroy, His vassal, on earth.

One of the achievements of Counter-Reformation Spanish Catholicism was to reaffirm the essence of this triadic relationship in the face of the threat from late medieval nominalism. The long debate between medieval realists, who maintained that the essence of verbal terms or *nomina* was real, and nominalists, who maintained that nouns were merely conventional references without real essence, resulted in a kind of 'deconstruction' of Christian mysteries and the magic of the word. This is especially clear in the furious sixteenth-century controversy around the 'real presence' in the Host of Communion, and the myriad interpretations of Christ's words of institution: 'Hoc est corpus meum.' To what did the pronoun *hoc* actually refer? But, in the sixteenth century, to quote Diego Marín: 'Spanish theological thought, generally speaking, was a neo-Scholasticism that sought to regenerate the verbalist logic of the Middle Ages with the aid of Renaissance rationalism' (Marín, 1969, p. 142; my translation). The magic sense of the word was not lost in Spain, then, but the shimmer of the transcendent signifying relationship retained and held in public view.

An interesting contrast to this world-view can be seen in the opinion of one John Selden, a seventeenth-century English constitutionalist. He stripped the monarch of all fantastic pretensions, saying:

'A king is a thing men have made for their own sakes, for quietness's sake. Just as in one family one man is appointed to buy the meat ...' As for the mystery surrounding the king, 'Prerogative is something that can be told what it is,' said Selden, 'not something that has no name' (Lewis, 1957, p. 80). And, indeed, a salient feature of Protestantism is this stripping away of essences and any 'supernatural' claims of language in favour of naming. There is in Protestantism too a thrust towards the *autonomy* of the subject and the dissolution of the invisible bond in the structuring of subjectivity and (un)consciousness: viz., a dissolution of the relationship of subject to signifier. What is substituted is a rationalist relationship of subject to object, but with *repression* of the perceptual relationship between them. The nominalist draining off of supernatural or mystic essences left an apparently neutral object of contemplation. This quickly assumed the form of a relationship between science and matter, i.e. human science in the modern sense, and the matter of the natural universe considered as object of that human science.

The practical consequences of this radical divergence in European world-view may be seen in the kind of theological debate regarding God and sovereign that took place in Spain during the Counter-Reformation. In the neo-Scholastic literature, there is an enormous amount of thinking on the nature of the theocratic monarchy, the nature of the ideal king, the Christian case against Machiavellianism, the question of law in general, and even the law between nations. In the notorious *De auxiliis* debate concerning divine grace and free will, which ranged the Dominican and Jesuit Orders against each other in the bitterest of struggles, we can discern an exploration of the relationship of the subject to the signifier God. How does 'efficient' grace operate if human liberty is to be safeguarded? What is the meaning of human liberty if it is not to annul the 'efficacy' of grace? What does give a special Spanish stamp to the thinking on the power relations between subject and signifier is the cautious manner in which the fundamentals of this relationship are not really placed in doubt, but the room for manoeuvre within these constraints is then exploited with every kind of rationalist ingenuity. The Spanish divines, so to speak, succeeded in drawing blood from a stone.

So this, in my view, is why the murder of Spanish monarchs was never seriously contemplated by any Spaniard. Such action fitted with no Spanish subject's neo-medieval, neo-feudal preconception about the nature of the universe, divine and human order, or his own place in it. On the other hand, in an ingenious and indirect way, the theoretical possibilities that remained within the theoretical scheme were exploited to the maximum, including in the popular imaginative literature. A good example of this is the equivocal action of Rojas Zorrilla's tragedy *Del rey abajo, ninguno*, where the confusion over the identity of King Alfonso and/or the abuser of a loyal vassal's honour permits a theoretical contemplaten of regicide, but forces on the hero García a less than theoretical contemplation of the immolation of his wife and himself as the solution. When the true identity of the offender — an ordinary mortal — is revealed to García, he takes his bloody revenge on Don Mendo without hesitation.

Perhaps the most convenient and familiar example in the *comedia* of a regicide that might have been is the political theme of *La vida es sueño*. This play is, of course, immensely rich in interpretative possibilities and probably has the most complex and contradictory reception history of any of Calderón's drama (Sullivan, 1983, pp. 427–8, 440–1, 494). The basic storyline of Segismundo's destiny, for example, has many lineaments of the career of the mythical hero as schematised by Otto Rank, Joseph Campbell and others. And, from a Freudo-Lacanian point of view, the storm and stress within this Polish royal family cannot be separated from the Oedipal conflict that marks all families in greater or lesser degree. But, in the specifics of the action of *La vida es sueño*, the themes of the forceful removel of a king, usurpation by a tyrant, and the threat of popular revolt all combine to make the play a highly political tragedy with a providential or happy ending (a 'tragedia morata', in the phrase of José M. Ruano).

The action of *La vida es sueño* depends on the fundamental irony of the horoscope cast by Basilio prior to the birth of Segismundo. It seems to foretell that the son, though the legitimate heir to the throne, will usurp his father's place by force and trample him underfoot. Basilio sees in the horoscope's prophecies, therefore, the spectre of a violent uprising instigated by his own son and — assuming the prophecies to be valid — takes a series of counter-measures (keeping Segismundo's birth a secret, keeping him imprisoned in a remote tower, impoverishing his intellectual formation through the tutelage of the goaler/preceptor Clotaldo) in order to forestall their fulfilment. The irony lies in the fact that the horoscope is merely the Symbolic Order rationalisation by a learned astrologer king of the hysterical nightmares reported by his Queen, Clorilene, according to which she bore a monstruous serpent within her womb, the birth of whom would be the death of her. Inasmuch as Basilio lends substance to these fantasies, apparently validated by Clorilene's demise in giving birth to the little prince, he constructs his own doom in a *self-fulfilling* prophecy. His actions – especially if the drug experiment to test Segismundo's fitness for rule is deliberately rigged to make the prophecy come true yet again – actually precipitate the feared event.

But, however we slant the interpretation of the origins of the conflict, the fact remains that a popular revolt does take place in Poland. The exposure of the prince, incompetent to rule or not, reveals a material fact to the Polish people which Basilio has withheld from them: that they have a legitimate heir to the throne. The claims of Astolfo, Duke of Muscovy, and Estrella are seen to be fabrications of Basilio's policy, and popular sympathy swings to Segismundo. Given the appalling treatment Segismundo has received at his father's hands and the inhumanity of the drug experiment, as well as the duplicity with which Basilio has compromised Poland's national security and her political future, there might seem to be sufficient cause, or at least comprehensible motivation, for Segismundo's execution of his own father and assumption of personal power. Though Calderón, of course, thwarts this tragic, Oedipal resolution, it is worth noting that Hugo von Hofmannsthal drew substantially on this ending from the Calderonian material in the second, stage version of his political tragedy *Der Turm* ('The Tower') (1927). Here, the rebel soldier of Calderón's Act III has been transformed into Olivier, the leader of a lawless mob. Olivier has King Basilius beheaded in order to bring Segismundo to power and exploit the latter as a puppet monarch (Sullivan, 1983, pp. 351–3).

So one might say, therefore, that Segismundo's overthrow of an incompetent ruler and abuser of his vassals' loyalty, and the regicide of Basilio, constitute a future contingent ending of the play, which Calderón eschewed. He eschewed it for many reasons, but not least among them was the theocratic view of kingship which we have advanced at the heart of this chapter. For while there are numerous plays of Calderón where regicide and tyrannicide occur (Lauer, 1987), the example of contemporary Poland came too close to the mark for comfort. This was the phase of the Counter-Reformation (1635) when the Jesuits were successfully drawing the

Polish nation away from their sixteenth-century experiment with Protestantism and back to the Catholic fold (Sullivan, 1976, pp. 13–14). The last thing Calderón would have wished to suggest was the political murder of the king's 'other Body' as the Catholic solution to a constitutional dilemma.

There is, therefore, a matching of historical reality and the Spanish theory of the universe in the Peninsular nations's eschewal of regicide as any kind of solution to the political vicissitudes of the seventeenth century. To recall the distinction singled out for study by Kantorowicz, we may say that the Spaniards never seriously entertained the immolation of the king's other Body, his mystic or Symbolic Order 'Body politic', certainly not that of a Spanish monarch. As regards the king's Imaginary and Real 'Body natural', the Jesuits certainly entertained the murder of a ruler morally unfitted for sovereignty, especially in the case of heresy and religious advantage, where vassals might throw off the tyrant's yoke in a desire to return to the Church of Rome — the perpetual Spanish dream concerning Protestant England. In the Spanish popular drama, as noted, there is abundant discussion of morally unfitted sovereigns and emperors, of usurpers, and those displaying excessive ambition, lust, deceitfulness, and so on. Indeed, criticism of the king on moral and ethical grounds is a feature that grows throughout the seventeenth century, not only in the *comedias* of Calderón, for example, but also indirectly in the *autos* and in his late mythological plays, as Frederick de Armas and Margaret Greer have recently shown (de Armas, 1986; Greer, 1986). By the time of Francisco Bances Candamo, in the 1690s, criticism of the king had become patent and commonplace (in his *El esclavo de los grillos de oro*, for instance). But, still today, the Spanish drama's exploration of room for manoeuvre within the lawfully consecrated framework of authority remains one of its most tantalising attractions.

Works consulted

Armas, Frederick A. de, *The Return of Astraea: An Astral-Imperial Myth in Calderón*, Lexington, 1986.

Fishkin, James S., *Tyranny and Legitimacy: A Critique of Political Theories*, Baltimore, 1979.

Franklin, Julian H., *Jean Bodin and the Rise of Absolutist Theory*, Cambridge, 1973.

Gallegos Rocafull, José M., *La doctrina política del P. Francisco Suárez*, Mexico City, 1948.

Gómez Robledo, Ignacio, *El origen del poder político segun Francisco Suárez*, Mexico City, 1948.

Greer, Margaret Rich (ed.), Pedro Calderón de la Barca, *La estatua de Prometeo*, with a Study of the Music by Louise K. Stein, Kassel, 1986.

Jászi, Oszkár and John D. Lewis, *Against the Tyrant: the Tradition and Theory of Tyrannicide*, Glencoe, Ill., 1957.

Kantorowicz, Ernst, *The King's Two Bodies: A Study in Mediaeval Political Theology*, Princeton, 1957.

King, Preston T., *The Ideology of Order: A Comparative Analysis of Jean Bodin and Thomas Hobbes*, New York, 1974.

Lacan, Jacques, *Écrits*, Paris, 1966.

– –, *Le Séminaire, Livre XI: Les quatre concepts fondamentaux de la psychoanalyse*, Paris, 1973.

– –, *Le Séminaire, Livre II: Le moi dans la théorie de Freud et dans la technique de la psychanalyse*, Paris, 1978.

– –, *Le Séminaire, Livre VII: L'Éthique de la psychanalyse*, Paris, 1987.

Lauer, Robert, *Tyrannicide and Drama*, Stuttgart, 1987.

Lewis, John D., 1957. See Jászi and Lewis, 1957.

Marín, Diego, 1961. *La civilización española* (edición revisada, 1969). New York.

Parker, David, *The Making of French Absolutism*. New York, 1983.

Ragland-Sullivan, Ellie, *Jacques Lacan and the Philosophy of Psychoanalysis*, Urbana and Chicago, 1986.

– –, 'Seeking the Third Term: Desire, the Phallus, and the Materiality of Language', in Richard Feldstein & Judith Roof (eds.), *Feminism and Psychoanalysis*, Ithaca and London, 1989, pp. 40–64.

Reichelt, Klaus, *Barockdrama and Absolutismus: Studien zum deutschen Drama zwischen 1650 and 1700*, Frankfurt, 1981.

Sullivan, Henry W., *Tirso de Molina and the Drama of the Counter Reformation* (2nd edn, 1981). Amsterdam, 1976.

– –, *Calderón in the German Lands and the Low Countries: His Reception and Influence, 1654–1980*, Cambridge, 1983.

– –, Review of de Armas 1986 in *Renaissance Quarterly*, XI, Autumn 1987: 563–5.

– –, Review of Greer and Stein 1986 in *Hispanic Review*, XLI (3), Winter 1989: 101–3.

8 MARGARET R. GREER

Bodies of power in Calderón: *El nuevo palacio del Retiro* and *El mayor encanto, amor*

How do human beings think themselves in society? We find ourselves encased in our own physical bodies and enmeshed in a society of other similarly constituted beings. Therefore, in conceptualising social and political organisation, the human body has for centuries provided a primary image for envisioning an organic union of heterogeneous elements.[1] Aristotle, having defined man as a social animal, compared the constitution of animals to that of a well-governed city—state, and Seneca said, 'We are all parts of one great body. Nature produced us related to one another, since she created us for the same end' (quoted in James, 1983, p. 7, n. 17). The analogy entered the Christian tradition through St Paul, in his first letter to the Corinthians (12: 12—27): 'For just as the body is one and has many members, and all the members of the body, though many, are one body, so it is with Christ. For by one Spirit we were all baptised into one body – Jews or Greeks, slaves or free .... Now you are the body of Christ and individually members of it.'

Images of the body politic in seventeenth-century Spain obviously named the Habsburg monarch as head of the body, while commonly characterising the nobility as the arms of the body, and the people as the stomach or feet.[2] Yet the underlying tension that such imagery could not banish stemmed from the fact that each organ of that 'body' – and every 'cell' of that organ – was in itself a body, a separate entity whose interests were not necessarily identical to those of the socio-political organism as a whole. As James (1983, p. 8) puts it, 'persisting tension between whole and differentiation meant that the process of incorporation in the social body needed to be continually reaffirmed, and the body itself continually recreated'. The most crucial question in terms of political organisation is the relationship between the head and the rest of the body, and in monarchical systems, this question too has often been formulated in terms of body – the nature of the body of the head, at once akin to and very different from the other cells of the body politic.

The reaffirmation or recreation of the social body, in Habsburg Spain as in all other complex societies, was in large part 'performed' – in both the theatrical and transactional senses of the word – through ritual. Democratic societies of the twentieth century often view ritual as empty, anachronistic behaviour, but in the traditional European city, it was central to the competitive political process by which major urban groups defined the city's rationale and structure for internal and external consumption. As local autonomy declined before the growth of absolutism and the modern state, the organising focus of ritual shifted to the prince and his court, and the city turned from processions to theatre, often focused on the king (Trexler, *Public Life in Renaissance Florence*, pp. xix–xxi). Attention to the symbolic aspects of power can therefore reveal to us a good deal about its substance, for as Geertz (1983, p. 124) points out, the distinction between the trappings of rule and its nature are less clear and less important than 'the manner in which, a bit like mass and energy, they are transformed into each other'.

Felipe IV's *privado*, the Count-Duke of Olivares, clearly understood the manner in which the trappings of power can generate its substance, and in the 1630s an important part of his programme to enhance the glory of his monarch was the construction of the new Palace of the Buen Retiro. Within two years of its completion, Calderón de la Barca wrote two dramas centring on the king and his new palace, the *auto sacramental* entitled *El nuevo palacio del Retiro* (1634), and a court spectacle play, *El mayor encanto, amor* (1635), each central to an important ritual performed for the king and the court of Madrid. Calderón has generally been characterised as the dramatist of Catholic orthodoxy and political conservatism, the theatrical supporter of the dogmas of the counter-Reformation and Habsburg absolutism. Without attempting to paint him as some sort of secret revolutionary, I should like to suggest that if we examine these two works in the context of the ritualistic framework in which they were performed, we find that his attitude toward royal power was more complex than has generally been recognised. His presentation of the king before the public of Madrid reveals a dualism we do not find in poets of royal theatrical celebrations in other European courts. Representing the king as defender of the Catholic faith in the *auto*, Calderón paints the royal body in its new palatial habitat in one guise, and quite another as head of state in the court play.

Calderón was not unique, however, in maintaining a dualistic concept of the king; in medieval political theology, as Kantorowicz has demonstrated, the king came to be represented as *gemina persona*. Reflecting the idea of the duality of Christ, at once man and God, a parallel image evolved of the king in which he was seen as a human being in nature and a divine figure through consecration by Grace. The king was at once an imperfect and local individual subject to the laws of nature and a 'translocal' being, superior to human law and corporeal death as God's representative on earth. In the formulation of Ramírez de Prado, the prince 'tiene dos personas: una, hechura de la naturaleza, comunícasele un mismo ser con los demás hombres; otra, por favor del Cielo, para gobierno y amparo del bien público' ('possesses two natures: one, the product of Nature, renders to him the same being as other men; the other, as a favour of Heaven, for the government and protection of the public good') (quoted in Maravall, 1944, p. 182).

The dualistic concept of the king figure took divergent routes and served varying political ends over time in the several states of Europe. In England, the 'translocal' body of the monarch could expand to include Parliament or even be separated from the physical body of the king so that the Puritans could cry, 'We fight the king to defend the king' and execute the royal body natural of Charles I without abolishing the King's body politic (Kantorowicz, 1957, pp. 18–23). Moving in the opposite direction in France, the political sacralisation of the king's translocal body reached its maximum expression in Louis XIV's declaration, 'L'état, c'est moi', which posited the absorption of the entire body politic into the body of its head.[3]

With the dissolution of European religious unity and the development of the modern state system, the preservation of the state came in practice to constitute an end in itself, and Machiavelli voiced a vision of religion as an instrument in its conversation. Spanish theorists also recognised the importance of religious unity in the conservation of the monarchy: Saavedra Fajardo (Emblem 24) calls religion 'el alma de la república' ('the soul of the republic'), without which

El pueblo se dividirá en opiniones, la diversidad dellas desunirá los animos, de donde nacerán las sediciones, i conspiraciones, i dellas las mudanzas de Republicas, i Dominios. Mas Principes vemos despojados por las opiniones diversas de Religion, que por las armas (pp. 165–6).

Public opinion will divide, and the diversity of opinions will divide their spirit, from which will be born sedition and conspiracies, and from them, changes of Republics and Dominions. We see more Princes dispossessed by diversity of religious belief than by arms.

Therefore, he continues, 'El príncipe que sobre la piedra triangular de la Iglesia levantare su monarquía, la conservará firme y segura' ('The prince who erects his monarchy on the triangular rock of the Church will preserve it safe and strong') (p. 169). With even greater vigour, however, Saavedra and other Spanish writers condemned Machiavelli's inversion of state and religion as end and means, for the idea of the state as an end in itself was not acceptable in Spain; rather, the monarch's goal was to ensure the salvation of a maximum number of his subjects and to defend and promote the Catholic faith on a global scale.[4] Lacking a developed idea of nationality, the church and the king were the two common elements in the disparate, fragmented, and centrifugal Spanish monarchy. Felipe II had instituted the highly religious character of Spanish kingship, whose sacred character was maintained not by presence, as in the French model, but by distance and the dedication of most royal appearances to rituals of religious celebration (Elliott, 1989, pp. 143–54).[5]

In Spain, therefore, the Corpus Christi celebration offered an ideal opportunity for combining a celebration of the Habsburg monarch with a reaffirmation of the sociopolitical body of which he was the head.[6] Instituted in the thirteenth century as the culminating point of the liturgical year and a commemoration of the triumph of truth over heresy, Corpus Christi was celebrated with great popular enthusiasm in Spain, almost as a national rather than a universal observance (Wardropper, 1953, p. 53). Administration of the festivities passed from the church to the municipal government in all Spanish cities, and the brilliance of its celebration became a point of local pride. Concerns for balancing the local budget had constantly to be balanced with the desire to outdo other localities (*ibid.*, p. 69). As in other urban rituals, the recreation of the social body involved resolving tensions between rival groups, competing in this case for preferred position in the procession in which the consecrated host was carried through the streets of the city. By the time of Calderón, when theatrical performances had come to be the high point of the Corpus festivities, rivalry in Madrid focused on choice of time or place for viewing the *autos*, which were played in the streets of the city before the king, his councils and the general public (*ibid.*, pp. 66–7, Varey, 1987, pp. 340–1).[7]

In the 1634 *auto, El nuevo palacio del Retiro*, Calderón sets before the public a panegyric of the new palace and of Felipe IV based on the dogma of transubstantiation. The doctrinal centre which generates the allegory is the mystery of the transformation of the bread of the Eucharist into the body of Christ. Exploiting scenic effects made possible by stage machinery in the carts on which the *autos* were performed, Calderón dramatises the mystery, revealing the host on two columns in the tower of one càrt and then elevating the figure of the celestial King to replace the host while the King says:

> Esta blanca Forma, este
> círculo breve y pequeño,
> capaz esfera es de cuanto
> contiene hoy la tierra y cielo.
> Blanco pan fué; pero ya,
> transustanciado en sí mesmo,
> no es Pan, sus especies, sí,
> porque éste solo es mi Cuerpo. (150)

> This white Form, this small, brief circle, is today a sphere capable of containing earth and sky. It was white bread; but now, transubstantiated in itself, it is not Bread, but its appearance, because this alone is my Body.

By parallel movements, the *auto* transforms the new palace into Jerusalem, Felipe IV and his *valido* Olivares into the Heavenly King whose favourite is Man, and Felipe's Queen Isabel into the bride of Christ, the Church. The transformation is carried out principally through dialogue between the figures Man and Judaism. The latter is amazed to find in what had been an uncultivated olive grove ('inculta esfera / de unos olivares') (141) − because the site in which the gardens of the Buen Retiro was built had belonged to the Conde-Duque de Olivares − a palace which unites heaven and earth. Man explains that the Natural and Written Laws that Judaism knew have been superseded by the Law of Grace, which has wrought the transformation of original chaos into a heavenly garden where perfect order reigns and all species dwell in their appointed spheres: wild beasts on the earth – a reference to the Casa de Fieras or Leonera of the Buen Retiro gardens; birds in the air – the aviary housed in the gardens; and fish in the fountains and rivers – an evocation of the marvels of hydraulic engineering which decorated them. Man explains that as God's creation, he himself is His *privado* and *alcalde* (mayor) of the royal garden – Olivares's titles – in which 'La Ley de Gracia es la Reina / y el Sol de Justicia el Rey' ('The Law of Grace is the Queen / and the Sun of Justice is the King') (140).

This *auto* is not structured as a simple allegory, an abstract idea made visible through a metaphor having a stable correspondence between each theatrical figure and its referent on the second plane (Parker, 1968, pp. 58–109). Rather, it offers all the symbolic flexibility of a figural reading of the Bible, in which a variety of figures are read as prefigurations of Christ and of the coming triumph of his reign on earth. Thus, Noah's Ark was a prefiguration of the Palacio del Buen Retiro, which in turn is the Church that will save the faithful from the final conflagration, the Great Jerusalem of twelve gates described in Revelations. Similarly, Queen Isabel stands both for the Law of Grace and the Church as the bride of Christ:

> que en el esposo y la esposa,
> no hay duda quien puede ser,
> pues que son Cristo y la Iglesia,
> y son la Reina y el Rey. (139)

> there is no doubt who they might be, as husband and wife, for they are Christ and the Church, and they are the King and Queen.

The allegory in effect sanctifies the political structure of the Spanish monarchy, linking Felipe IV with God in his capacity as earthly defender of the faith.[8] Felipe is the

> Rey que del austro nos vino,
> de la Fe amante tan fiel,
> que está incluído en su nombre
> el de su Dama también,
> pues ninguno pronunció
> Felipe, sin decir fe. (139)

> King who comes to us from the south wind [austro], such a loyal lover of Faith that his very name includes that of his Lady too, for no one pronounces 'Felipe' without saying 'Faith' [fe].

Within his palace as a figure of the Church, Felipe is transformed into a 'human God':

> ... a esta fábrica de hoy
> no habrá tiempos que la muden,
> que es figura de la Iglesia,
> donde en rasgos y vislumbres
> el Rey es un Dios humano. (145)

> Time will not alter this present edifice, for it is a figure of the Church where in features and prefigurations, the King is a human God.

Staging a celestial audience, the *auto* celebrates the providence with which the king governs, distributing justice for all enemies of the faith. The audience takes place on Friday, the day when 'es bien que esté / la puerta abierta' ('it is right that the door is open') (141); Friday is the day the death of Christ opened to all the entrance of Heaven, and also the day Felipe met with his Consejo Real and held open his doors for petitions by his subjects (Stradling, 1988, p. 26). The first petition comes from 'la ciega Apostasia' ('blind Apostasy') reigning to the north, which asks for religious freedom in exchange for obedience. The King rejects the rebels' plea, sending the matter to his Council of War to check their arrogance, 'porque reinar sin fe no es reinar' ('because to rule without faith is not to rule') (146). Remedying the idolatry of the 'Gentiles of the East' he entrusts to Santa Cruz — the Marquis of Santa Cruz, who had commanded the naval forces in the Mediterranean and the army in Flanders (Elliott, 1988, pp. 370, 406). The heathens to the West ask for baptism, and the King dispatches missionaries to bring the light of the law to their blind ignorance. The Moors to the South ask that Africa be granted Christian seaports, and the King prescribes garrisoning Mámora and Orán.

This heavenly audience serves not only to extoll Felipe's foreign policy, but also to dramatise the centrality of the Habsburg power in the universe. As Geertz has pointed out, charisma in all societies depends on conveying a sense of being 'near the heart of things' (1983, p. 122), at the centre of the cosmos and connected to transcendent beings (pp. 125, 130). At the bequest of the Queen/Church and her ladies-in-waiting, Charity, Hope and Faith, the King in the *auto* dispatches his forces to North, East, South and West, on behalf of:

> La Fe, que se ha de ensalzar,
> cuando el orbe sea un rebaño
> con sólo un pastor no más. (146)

> Faith, which will be exalted when the world is one flock with only
> one shepherd.

Faith's words evoke the belief that when all people accepted the
Catholic faith, Christ would return to reign on earth, and she kneels
at Felipe's feet, dramatising the centrality of this Catholic king to
the achievement of the millenium.

The one petition that the King rejects completely, and which
finds no voice to plead for it, is that of Judaism. As Man/Olivares
explains the petition, Judaism wishes to conduct business within the
King's realm:

> En tus reinos asentar
> sus comercios, con que pueda
> hoy tratar, y contratar
> con las más remotas islas. (146)

> To establish his commerce in your realm, so that today he might
> trade and deal with the most remote islands.

The question of Jewish financial and commercial activity was very
much present in Madrid in 1634. Since the declaration of the first royal
bankruptcy of Felipe IV's reign, Olivares had worked to counter the
financial dominance of the Genoese bankers by increasing concessions
to Portuguese Jews or crypto-Jews, known as *marranos*. Olivares,
whose grandmother was of a *converso* or Christianised Jewish family,
was widely accused of being pro-Jewish for his relations with such
figures as Jacob Cansino, a North African Jew and interpreter for
Olivares. Cansino was reported to represent a number of Mediterranean Jews seeking to live in Spain and freely practise their religion
in exchange for generous contributions to the capital of the monarchy's savings banks. Olivares was instrumental in securing freedom
of movement and an edict of grace from the Inquisition for them,
in exchange for financial contributions.[9] In the *auto*, however, on
learning that such Jews do not plan to leave their own Law, the King
orders the petition destroyed, because:

> ... en mi reino no han de estar
> judíos, donde la Fe
> ha puesto su Tribunal,

> porque no será razón
> ni política será
> dar sagrado al reo, dando
> autoridad al fiscal. (146)

> There are to be no Jews in my realm, where Faith has set its Tribunal, because it is not reasonable nor politic to give refuge to the accused, while giving authority to the prosecutor.

The vehemence of the King's rejection of the petition did not reflect the actual practice of the moment. The Memorial Histórico Español of August 1634, two months after the appearance of the *auto*, reported:

> Valido anda que entran los judíos en España: lo cierto es que entran y salen á hablar al Rey y darle memoriales, y hoy ví uno con una toca blanca á la puerta del cuadro del Rey; pena me dió. (quoted in Pollin, 1973, pp. 586–7)

> It is spreading about as fact that Jews are entering Spain: what is certain is that they go in and out to talk to the King and give him petitions, and today I saw one with a white headdress at the door of the King's quarters; it distressed me.

and it was not until 1543, the year of Olivares's fall, that an Inquisition edict definitively prohibited their entrance in Spain. The *auto*'s solution was appropriate, however, to public reaffirmation of Catholic community, and characteristic of theatrical celebration of the monarch in other European courts, in which controversial issues of the day were often represented as already solved.

Throughout this 'celestial' audience, dispatching with the king all the petitions is the figure of Man, whom God has made *alcalde* (mayor, chief administrator) of his divine garden as Olivares was of the Buen Retiro. In the case of this figure too, the poles of allegorical reference are deliberately unstable, but the instability works in the opposite direction from that which pertains to the other figures. On the second plane, Man is God's *privado*, his creation, his favourite creature, but on the earthly plane, he represents at the same time mankind in general and Felipe's *privado* Olivares in particular. The confusion is politically astute, because Calderón thereby sets this controversial figure before the public in such a way that he represents all men. Each spectator can see himself figured on the stage with Olivares, at once subject to human frailties and enjoying a privileged relationship with the King/God.

> Al hombre, que su valido
> y que su privado es,
> hizo alcalde desde entonces
> de este divino vergel;
> del bien y del mal llegó
> en poco tiempo a saber;
> pero ¿cuál privado, cuál
> no supo del mal y el bien? (138)

> Man, who is His favourite, His prime minister, He made mayor of this divine garden; he soon came to know good and evil; but what favourite has not learned of good and evil?

In this passage Calderón associates original sin with a reference to the difficulty of the position of the *privado* by recalling his own 1628 play, *Saber del bien y del mal*, which dramatises the vicissitudes in the careers of two *privados*. Calderón plays with the two meanings of 'privanza' ('preference at court' and 'deprivation') in saying that Man suffered loss, 'padeció privanza', when expelled from God's first garden for committing a 'natural error' during the reign of Natural Law, but now that the Law of Grace is on the throne, his fall will not be repeated.

Through the operation of Grace in God's encarnation in Christ, Man is 'teamed with' ('corre parejas con') God. Calderón dramatises this union of Man with God by means of an evocation of other public festivities of 1633 on the occasion of the inauguration of the Buen Retiro, a 'juego de cañas'[10] in which Felipe IV and the Conde-Duque ran together as a team and the king took the prize. In the *auto*, the Queen chooses a red – 'encarnada' – livery for the pair, because 'Encarnado Dios es Hombre / y encarnado el Hombre es Dios' ('Incarnate God is Man / and in crimson, Man is God') (142). Thus attired, Man and the king pass from one side of the stage to the other, while Judaism exclaims that he can barely tell one from the other. The king takes the ring, the host, which disappears briefly from its display position on the columns, to be replaced by the king, who then descends while the host returns to view. As prize for his victory, he receives the cross, and then, elevated in the tower of one cart with a man and a woman working on either side, the king hands the cross to the queen, the Church, while the host appears in the other tower and the king explains:

   ... yo nunca me ausento,
que en ese breve RETIRO
del Pan constante me quedo
para siempre, en cuerpo y Alma,
de la forma que en el Cielo
estoy, ocupando iguales
dos lugares en un tiempo,
porque así la Ley de Gracia
me tenga siempre en el NUEVO
PALACIO del Buen Retiro. (151)

I never absent myself, for in this brief RETREAT in the Bread I am
constantly present, in body and Soul, in the form that I possess in
Heaven, occupying two places at the same time, so that the Law of
Grace has me always in the NEW PALACE of the Good Retreat.

In multiple layers of meaning symbolised by this stage movement
and text, Calderón merges in this climactic scene: the doctrine of
Christ's continuing presence on earth in the bread of the Eucharist
after his ascension to heaven; an equation of the king with Christ,
the King of Heaven; a characterisation of the Retiro palace as a
religious retreat, not a pleasure palace; and a response to critics who
charged that Felipe, in his 'Retiro', had unduly 'retreated' from active
attention to the affairs of state. After naming again Felipe and Isabel,
Man (Olivares), calling himself the 'most interested' in the promise
achieved in the New Palace, closes this political Eucharist.

   'Political Eucharist' because, as much as a religious celebration,
this *auto* stages a sociopolitical ritual, an act constitutive of community. James, observing this function of the Corpus Christi celebration of medieval England, argues that:

> the theme of Corpus Christi is society seen in terms of body; and ...
> the concept of body provided urban societies with a mythology and
> ritual in terms of which the opposites of social wholeness and social
> differentiation could be both affirmed, and also brought into a creative
> tension, one with the other. The final intention of the cult was, then,
> to express the social bond and to contribute to social integration.
> From this point of view, Corpus Christi expresses the creative role of
> religious rite and ideology in urban societies, in which the alternative
> symbols and ties of lordship, lineage and faithfulness, available in
> countrysides, were lacking. (1983, p. 4)

   The *loa* for a later performance of Calderón's *auto*[11] refers
twice to St John Chrysostom, whose sermon read at matins during

the Corpus Christi season clearly expresses this idea of social integration: 'Christ hath mingled himself with us, and infused his Body into our bodies, that we may be one together, as limbs of one body' (quoted in James, 1983, p. 9). Calderón dramatises this union in very graphic form in the last scene of the *auto*, revealing the host in the tower of one cart and in the other the king between representatives of the people, a man and a woman at work. The scene symbolises at once the union of the Catholic community with its king, who is a 'God on earth' and his and their union with God through the sacrament of the Eucharist.

Furthermore, throughout the work, Calderón evokes the constitutive parts of the community of Madrid, transformed into a celestial city.[12] He names the various royal councils, citing their presidents as Christ's apostles, and then the multitude which follows them, 'el Reino', whose 'procuradores', or deputies to the States General, are the angels (148). After showing God running as a team with his *privado*, Man, he names individually the great nobles of his court, the Almirante del Mar, who is Noah, the Count of Peñaranda as Moses, etc., and also the people who follow the King/Christ, whom he describes as:

> la villa, que significa
> de la república el cuerpo,
> la primera es, que le sigue;
> porque ésta es la Voz del Pueblo,
> que fué siguiendo sus pasos,
> su grandeza conociendo. (149)

The town, which signifies the body of the republic, is the first to follow him, because it is the Voice of the People, who followed his footsteps, recognising his greatness.

In the recitation of history which culminates with the construction of the new palace, Calderón underlines repeatedly the theme of the elect: the select faithful who were saved in Noah's Ark, those saved in the Passover, and the election of other Old Testament figures such as Caleb, David, Ephraim and Esther. And in an impressive evocation of the final conflagration, Man as God's *privado* warns that only the select faithful who inhabit the new palace, the New Jerusalem of the Catholic Church, will survive the horrors of the end of the world.

Calderón focuses almost all the action of the *auto* through the eyes of Judaism, an extremely effective dramatic structure, as it offers a logical reason for a description of the palace and the whole monarchic structure to a stranger. And, more importantly, the presence of this foreigner, at once sad and threatening, reinforces the social cohesion of the community, which defines itself in opposition to him. When the Jew refuses to participate in the celebration of the host, the implicit text is that he who refuses this God, this king, this social order and its constitutive ritual is the worst of all unbelievers and an outside condemned forever to wander lost and alone through the world.[13]

In *El nuevo palacio del Retiro*, then, we find a spectacular confirmation of the traditional view of a supremely Catholic and monarchical Calderón. The body of the king is transformed into God on earth, and the sociopolitical body is also affirmed as conforming to heaven's pattern.[14] But if we also read in context his court spectacle play of 1635, *El mayor encanto, amor*, we find a very different attitude toward the kind, his *privado*, and the new palace. In this Calderonian version of the myth of Ulysses' seduction by C˙ce, the enchanted palace represents not the salvation of man but his threatened perdition. When the play was performed, war with ⌐ance had just been renewed and Felipe's subjects were criticisng his dedication to sensual pleasures and the Conde-Duque's ascendance over him.

The purpose of this type of court spectacle, in Madrid as in other courts of the absolutist Europe of the sixteenth and seventeenth centuries, was that of entertaining the king while demonstrating to the world the power of a monarch who could stage and finance such an elaborate production. Calderonian mythological court plays share this purpose. Although the limits of this chapter do not permit an adequate exploration of the genre, we can say that Calderón, better than any other European poet, succeeded in integrating into powerfully coherent drama the diverse ingredients of the court spectacle — music, elaborate perspective scenery and stage machinery, dance, and poetic text.[15] At the same time, he achieved a form which allowed him to combine the essential explicit text of exaltation of the monarch with an implicit text that constituted a discreet criticism of certain policies or practices of the king.

Calderón inscribed the text of royal power in the framework of the fiesta, beginning with the ceremonial entry of the royal family, which focused the eyes of the assembled public on them. The display of their power was also inherent in the arrangement of the theatre, in which the stage constituted one pole of the spectacle and the royal family, seated on an elevated and well-illuminated platform, the other pole, so that spectators could always have present both visual poles of the event. The royal position occupied the ideal point for viewing the perspective scenery, and other spectators were placed in hierarchical order, with the most distinguished closest to the king. What they saw, then, was not simply the play on stage, but the more complex spectacle of watching the king see the drama (Orgel, 1975, p. 9).

We do not have a description of the curtain or prologues for *El mayor encanto*, which was performed on an island in the large lake of the Buen Retiro, but in other productions, what the spectators saw first was a curtain decorated with the names of the royal family, combined with symbols of the gods of classical mythology and other icons of royal power. The opening *loas* then exalted the king, equating him with the classical gods and proclaiming his centrality to the universe, performed in this political arena through profane, not sacred myths. Thus the ceremonial framework of the fiesta proclaimed the text of royal power, linking the king with the gods. But the central dramatic text then inverted the relation and constructed a story around the very human failings of those gods, failings which also characterised the royal spectators of the event.

El mayor encanto, amor dramatises Ulysses' relationship with Circe, in which he initially resists her magic that converts men into animals, then succumbs to love of her and finally, with great reluctance, responds to the voice of duty and leaves her island. She in fury destroys her sumptuous palace, which sinks through the stage to be replaced by a volcano throwing flames. Circe's magnificent palace and gardens are central to the play, and if the public had not immediately linked them with the Buen Retiro, in whose gardens the performance took place. Circe's words directed them towards that association when she spoke of 'el retiro / de mi Palacio' ('the retreat / [that is] my Palace') (1606).

While the *auto* explicitly associated Felipe IV with the heavenly king, in this palace play, an implicit connection is drawn between Felipe and Ulysses. The musicians sing:

Olvidado de su patria
en los palacios de Circe
vive el más valiente griego
si quien vive amando, vive. (1619)

Forgetting his country in Circe's palaces lives the most valiant Greek
— if he who lives loving [really] lives

Shortly before the performance of this play, satirical poems had been
circulating in Madrid which criticised the king for luxuriating in his
new palace while the country was at war. One poem made a sarcastic
comparison between the French king, who was 'en compaña' ('on
campaign') with the king of Spain 'en el Retiro' ('in Retreat') (Brown
and Elliott 1980, p. 196). Another employed the same word play with
'retiro/Retiro' to say that the king should be doing solitary penance
for his sins which had turned God's wrath against Spain (Deleito y
Piñuela, 1935, p. 199). Ulysses' only soldier to escape Circe's magic
laments his leader's pursuits in similar terms:

Ulises, pues, sin recelo
sólo de sus gustos trata
siempre en los brazos de Circe
y asistido de sus damas
en academias de amores,
saraos, festines y danzas. (1622)

Ulysses, heedless, cares only for his pleasure, always in Circe's arms
and accompanied by her ladies-in-waiting in debates about love,
soirées, feasts and dances.

In 1635 Felipe IV was criticised not only for his dedication to
sensual pleasures, but also for leaving the country in Olivares's hands.
It was thought that Olivares deliberately provided the king with
endless rounds of entertainments to distract him from attention to
the affairs of state; Olivares was also said to encourage the king's
weakness for women, roaming the streets of Madrid with him at night
in search of amorous adventures. The Buen Retiro was referred to
as 'el gallinero' ('the chicken coop'), not only because it contained
Olivares's aviary, but also for the quantity of non-feathered beauties
which were believed to be housed in the palace for the pleasure of
the king. Furthermore, popular opinion held Olivares guilty of using
magic to maintain his sway over Felipe (de Armas, 1986, pp. 143–6).
The President of the Consejo Real had in 1622 investigated a woman

named Leonorilla who maintained that the potions she sold were 'los mismos que el conde de Olivares daba al rey para conservar su privanza' ('the same as those the count of Olivares gave to the king to preserve his favour') (Marañon, 1965, p. 196). Others said that Olivares needed no potions because his magic powers emanated from the spirit in the cane he always carried for his gout. Olivares's use of black magic is featured in at least two other plays and Quevedo linked the Conde-Duque with Circe in *La hora de todos* (de Armas, 1986, p. 144). In that context, we can presume that the public would have seen the parallel between Circe and Ulysses and Olivares and the king when an enemy invasion is announced in *El mayor encanto, amor* and Circe's first concern is that the news should not reach Ulysses:

> Calla, calla, no prosigas
> ni lleguen ecos marciales
> a los oídos de Ulises:
> Aquí tengo de dejarle
> sepultado en blando sueño
> porque el belicoso alarde
> no pueda de mi amor nunca
> dividirle ne olvidarle. (1627)

> Be quiet, don't go on or let such martial echoes reach Ulysses' ears; I shall leave him buried here in gentle sleep, so that no call to arms can ever take him away from me or make him forget my love.

In an insistently repeated comic parallel, Calderón connects Circe's domain over Clarín with Ulysses' enslavement. She converts the *gracioso* into a monkey, and in the last line of the scene, Clarín predicts: '¡Hombres monas! Presto habrá / otro más de vuestra especie' ('Monkey-men! There will soon be another of your species') (1617). Clarín exits and Ulysses enters, to follow Circe's command that he feign love for her only to find shortly to his dismay that he really is enamoured of her. Clarín invents a word for his own state, calling himself 'enmonado' ('made a monkey'). Only two letters separate his condition from that of Ulysses, who is 'enamorado' ('in love'). Calderón underscores the parallel through repeated juxtaposition of scenes of the 'enmonado' and the 'enamorado' and seals it with an interchange between Ulysses and two friends of Clarín, Antistes and Lebrel:

Antistes: Dime Lebrel, ¿dónde está? ...
Lebrel: ¿La mona? No sé: ¡ay de mí!
Antistes: Ulises, te digo. (1629)

Antistes: Tell me, Lebrel, where is he? [16]
Lebrel: The monkey? I don't know, alas!
Antistes: Ulysses, I mean.

Clarín recovers his human form when he sees himself in a mirror, the instrument which symbolises self-knowledge in many Calderonian mythological plays. The mirror which awakens Ulysses to his bestial enslavement to passion is the sight of Achilles' arms, accompanied by Achilles' command that Ulysses remember his duty.

Where was the mirror to demonstrate to Felipe the degradation of his dignity and the need for him to resume active control of the affairs of state? In the play itself, which clearly dramatises popular criticism of the king's conduct, but does so in an attractive form, sweetening the message with a good dose of humour and spectacular brilliance.

In contrasting these two works, then, we find a Calderonian variant of the figuration of the king as *gemina persona*. In the *auto sacramental*, performed before a diverse mass audience in the streets of Madrid, Calderón transformed the king into a God on earth in his capacity as defender of the Catholic faith. But in his court spectaculars, beside the text celebrating royal power, Calderón tactfully inserted a critical text directed to the king as political leader in which he treats the monarch as a body subject to very human weaknesses.

The standard classification of Calderón as the conservative upholder of Habsburg monarchy is therefore at the same time fundamentally true and, as it has generally been applied, a simplistic formulation of his attitude toward royal power. The unqualified glorification of the monarch characteristic of other European court spectacles in the age of absolutism is in Calderón restricted to the *auto sacramental*. This is in accord with the concept of the divine right of kings that prevailed in Spain, which envisioned the monarch as both supported and controlled by divine law. Political writers such as Pedro de Rivadeneira held that kings were appointed by God as his vice-regents on earth, but were not morally or politically absolute, and an amoral abuse of power would lead to the withdrawal of God's patronage and the overthrow of a tyrant (Stradling, 1988, p. 14).

Under this concept, Calderón speaks as a loyal supporter of Felipe IV in both treatments of the king's body, each appropriately designed for the arena of its presentation and its primary audience. In the *auto*, Calderón dramatised the divine mandate of Felipe IV and the correspondence between his rule over the Spanish Empire and God's reign in heaven. The primary spectator of the court play was the king himself, and for him, within the celebratory framework, Calderón inserted a reminder of the limitations of royal autonomy, bordered by moral law and duty to his subjects.

Notes

1 Whereas rational thought has classically been characterised as abstract, transcendental manipulation of symbols independent of the processing organism, a new school of cognitive science which Lakoff calls 'experientialism' holds that even abstract thought is 'embodied' and 'imaginative', that it is shaped by bodily experience and functions through the manipulation of mental imagery similarly rooted.

2 Olivares employed the same image to formulate the relationship between Felipe IV and his royal councils: 'Your majesty has several councils .... They represent the king, and he is their head: your majesty and these ministers making between them one body.' Quoted in Stradling, 1988, p. 23.

3 Marin proposes that the full representation of the ideal of absolute power could only be effected in the royal portrait, which would efface the distance between the imperfect historical, natural body, and the idealised, sacramental and symbolic power of the political body as represented in its icons.

4 See Elliott, 1989, pp. 165–73. As Stradling (1988, p. 5) points out, these goals were inscribed in the names given Felipe at his baptism: Domingo, for the founder of the Dominican Order, guardians of religious purity through the Inquisition, and Victor de la Cruz – 'a collection which perfectly encapsulated how his parents and all the court imagined his future – as a champion of Monarchy and church in battle'.

5 However, this sacralisation did not assume form of divine kingship posited elsewhere in Europe; Spanish kings were never considered to have healing powers as was the French king, nor was there any coronation ceremony in Castile after the fourteenth century (Elliott, 1989, p. 166).

6 Significantly, Pope Pius had chosen the same occasion to assert through ritual his temporal claims in the papal states: '[in] the procession of Corpus Domini of 17 June 1462 ... Pius II played the role of the director of a monarchy's truly disconcerting stage set. Paraphrasing the arrival of God in psalm 23, verse 7 ... actors pretending to prevent his entry demand, "Who is this King Pius?" while others dressed as angels reply, "The lord of the world", playing on the fact that the pope carried the sacrament

in the procession' (Poldi, pp. 42–3). Poldi believes that the popes, adding temporal to spiritual claims, contributed to the definition of sovereignty and the early formation of the European state system.

7   The first performances were always for the king; problems of precedence are evident in documents detailing number and disposition of subsequent performances. See, e.g., Shergold and Varey, pp. 223–5, 250–1, 289–94.

8   Other Calderonian *autos* also stress the spiritual purpose of the king. For example, in *El gran teatro del mundo*, the King is saved only because he has lent a hand to Religion. Religion stumbles and he supports her, saying, 'Llegaré a tenerla yo' ('I will come to support her'), to which Discreción responds, 'Es fuerza; que nadie puede / sostenerla como vos' ('It is necessary, for no one can support her like you.'). *La segunda esposa y triunfar muriendo* dramatises the symbiotic support system between church and state and shows the King (Christ/Felipe IV) as weak Man's only refuge against death.

9   (Elliott, 1988, pp. 301–4; Pollin,. 1973, pp. 584–5; Stradling, 1988, p. 224–30.) Other prominent, and controversial *marrano* merchant financiers included Manuel López Pereira and Manuel Cortizos. The former, named 'contador de asiento' of the Consejo de Hacienda in 1636, and one of Olivares's principal financial advisers, was called by Jewish writers 'valido del valido'. Cortizos, a royal supplier, ('asentista del rey') enjoyed prominent posts in the government and spent more than 1,500 ducats entertaining the king with a play and *merienda* in the Buen Retiro.

10 Stradling (1988, p. 157) describes this event as a 'mock-battle of expensively accountred squadrons, held in the Plaza Mayor or the main arena of the Buen Retiro, to celebrate the major *fiestas* and the visits of foreign dignitaries'.

11 This *loa*, included with the Valbuena Prat edition, is from a later performance, in the reign of Carlos II. It was not written by Calderón, but he does name St John Crysostom in several other *autos*. See Brown & Elliott, 1980, p. 278, n. 47.

12 In another striking example of this function, Calderón cites the physical spaces of the social body in the *loa* of his *auto Las órdenes militares*, naming a great number of the streets of Madrid in reference to biblical occurrences.

13 A number of Calderonian *autos* are refused through the gaze of nonbelievers, and they commonly terminate with the expulsion of the heretic or Jew hidden among the community of the faithful. In *La protestación de la fe*, the figure Brazo Eclesiástico explains that 'el hereje es un nervio / cancerado, que se aparta / porque el cuerpo no inficione' ('the heretic is a cancerous nerve which is removed so that the body will not be infected') (p. 746). On the one hand, the ceremony of exorcism offers a collective release of tension which seems to answer a deep-seated psychological need in many cultures (see Greenblatt, 1988, and Muchembled, 1979). It also dramatises the disciplinary power at the centre of society, a power which displayed itself theatrically in public executions of criminals and in *autos da fe* (Maravall, 1986). Both the *auto da fe* and the *auto sacramental* are,

164 Conflicts of discourse

by definition, 'acts', which in differing degrees are acts of theatre and acts of definition and delimitation of the legitimate social body.

14 The *auto* would also serve as an ideal demonstration of Maravall's thesis (*Cultura del barroco*) that Golden Age theatre served a manipulatory, conservative function designed to uphold the hierarchical status quo.

15 See my book, *The Play of Power: Court Spectacle Plays of Calderón de la Barca*, forthcoming, Princeton.

16 Since the Spanish verb does not require a gender-specific pronoun here, the exchange works even though Clarín has been transformed into a female monkey.

Works cited

Armas, Frederick de, *The Return of Astrea: An Astral-Imperial Myth in Calderón*, Lexington, 1986.

Brown, Jonathan, and J. H. Elliott, 1980. *A Palace for a King: The Buen Retiro and the Court of Philip IV*, New Haven.

Calderón de la Barca, Pedro, *El gran teatro del mundo*, in Angel Valbuena Prat (ed.), *Obras completas*, Vol. 3, Madrid, 1959, pp. 199–222.

– –, *El mayor encanto, amor*, in Angel Valbuena Briones (ed.), *Obras completas*, Vol. 1, 1959, pp. 1595–1633.

– –, *El nuevo palacio del Retiro*, in *Obras*, 3, pp. 131–52.

– –, *Las órdenes militares*, in *Obras*, 3, pp. 1011–40.

– –, *La protestación de la fe*, in *Obras*, 3, pp. 723–48.

– –, *La segunda esposa y triunfar muriendo*, in *Obras*, 3, pp. 423–48.

Deleito y Piñuela, José, *El rey se divierte*, Madrid, 1935.

Elliott, J. H., *The Count-Duke of Olivares: The Statesman in an Age of Decline*, New Haven, 1988.

– –, *Spain and Its World., 1500–1700*, New Haven, 1989.

Geertz, Clifford, 'Centers, Kings, and Charisma: Reflections on the Symbolic of Power', in Geertz, *Local Knowledge: Further Essays in Interpretive Anthropology*, New York, 1983, pp. 121–46.

Greenblatt, Stephen, 'Shakespeare and the Exorcists', in Greenblatt, *Shakespearean Negotiations*, Berkeley, 1988, pp. 129–63.

James, Mervyn, 'Ritual drama and social body in the late medieval English town', *Past and Present*, XCVIII, 1983: 3–29.

Kantorowicz, Ernest H., *The King's Two Bodies: A Study in Medieval Political Theology*, Princeton, 1957.

Lakoff, George, *Women, Fire, and Dangerous Things: What Categories Reveal about the Mind*, Chicago, 1987.

Marañon, Gregorio, *El Conde-Duque de Olivares*, 5th edn, Madrid, 1965.

Maravall, José Antonio, *La teoría española del estado en el siglo XVII*, Madrid, 1944.

– –, *La cultura del Barroco*, Barcelona, 1979.

– –, 'Teatro, fiesta e ideología en el Barroco', in José Maria Díez Borque (comp.), *Teatro y fiesta en el Barroco. España e Iberoamérica*, Madrid, 1986, pp. 71–95.

Marin, Louis, *Le Portrait du roi*, Paris, 1981.

Muchembled, Robert, 'The Witches of the Cambrésis', in James Obelkevich (ed.), *Religion and the People, 800–1700*, Chapel Hill, 1979, pp. 221–76.

Orgel, Stephen, *The Illusion of Power: Political Theatre in the English Renaissance*. Berkeley, 1975.

Parker, A. A., *The Allegorical Drama of Calderón*, Oxford, 1968.

Poldi, Paolo, *The Papal Prince. One body and two souls: the Papal Monarchy in Early Modern Europe*, trans. Susan Haskins, Cambridge, 1987.

Pollin, Alice M., 'El Judaísmo: figura dramática del auto "El nuevo palacio del Retiro", de Calderón de la Barca', *Cuadernos hispanoamericanos*, 276: 579–88.

Saavedra Fajardo, Diego, *La idea de un príncipe político-cristiano representada en cien empresas*, Murcia, 1985.

Sánchez García, Encarnación, 'A propósito del auto *El nuevo palacio del Retiro*', in *Colloquium Calderonianum Internationale, L'Aquila 16–19 settembre 1981. Atti*, L'Aquila, 1983, pp. 445–56.

Shergold, N. D. and J. E. Varey, 'Documentos sobre los autos sacramentales en Madrid hasta 1636', *Revista de la Biblioteca, Archivo y Museo* (Madrid), 24, 1955: 203–313.

Stradling, R. A., *Philip IV and the Government of Spain 1621–1655*, Cambridge, 1988.

Trexler, Richard, *Public Life in Renaissance Florence*, New York, Academic Press, 1980.

Varey, John, *Cosmovisión y escenografía: El teatro español en el Siglo de Oro*, Madrid, 1987.

Wardropper, Bruce, *Introducción al teatro religioso del Siglo de Oro. La evolución del auto sacramental: 1500–1648*, Madrid, 1953.

9   COLIN P. THOMPSON

San Juan de la Cruz, Freud, and the human soul

My own reading of San Juan de la Cruz has recently been refreshed from an unexpected source. As I read Bruno Bettelheim's passionate plea for an account of Freud's thought which is truer to the meaning of the German original, I was struck by the surprising points of contact between two writers I had assumed to belong to different worlds.[1] Bettelheim claims that Freud has been substantially mistranslated and therefore misread. His account of Freud's view of the soul led me to reconsider San Juan's understanding of the inner workings of human personality, especially in his most systematic treatise, the *Subida del Monte Carmelo* and the *Noche oscura del alma*.[2]

San Juan is a disconcerting writer. His mystical experience and the terminology he uses to analyse it are strange to most modern readers. Freud, on the other hand, has profoundly influenced twentieth-century thought, and is popularly believed to have explained away mysticism as a form of sexual sublimation. It is easy to see why. Mystics are drawn largely from celibate communities and characteristically (but not at all self-consciously) use the language of erotic love to express the indescribable bliss of union with God. San Juan's 'Noche oscura' poem, for example, depicts in a mysterious and sensuous way a young woman leaving her house at the dead of night to be joined with her lover in the place where he awaits her. He tells us in the *Subida-Noche* that the poem is about the soul's quest for God. In a post-Freudian age, we cannot help but wonder.

I shall outline Bettelheim's case for the re-reading of Freud, then argue that the *Subida-Noche* is not nearly as dogmatic and objective as it seems. I shall look at the concept of the soul and the way of introspection in Freud and San Juan, to establish some common ground. My conclusions are only tentative: I do not mean to claim that San Juan and Freud raise the same problems in the same way, and I do not propose some kind of grand synthesis, because sharp differences remain between them. I want instead to suggest that to regard San Juan's prose as fixed in a vanished world, without attempting to interpret his difficult language in terms our own age can more readily appreciate, is to make the same kind of mistake Bettelheim ascribes to Freud's English translators: the substitution of theological or scientific dogma for an intensely human and personal quest for wholeness.

Whatever reservations people have about him, Freud's place in twentieth-century thought remains secure. Yet Bettelheim claims that he has been subject to fundamental misinterpretation. Problems of translation can, of course, prove extremely significant: Bettelheim himself refers to Jerome's remark that some translations of the Bible were not versions but perversions of the original (p. 103) as an indication of the damage he believes Freud to have suffered, while San Juan's own century was marked by fierce disputes about the meaning of Scripture.[3]

Bettelheim writes as one of the last survivors of the cultural climate in which Freud worked and as one who discovered when he had to leave Germany how differently Freud read in English. He makes one simple point in a number of ways, with considerable repercussions: 'In his work and in his writings, Freud often spoke of the soul — of its nature and structure, its developments, its attributes, how it reveals itself in all we do and dream. Unfortunately, nobody who reads him in English could guess this, because nearly all his many references to the soul ... have been excised in translation' (p. 4). He continues: 'Freud's direct and always deeply personal appeals to our common humanity appear to readers of English as abstract, depersonalized, highly theoretical, erudite, and mechanized — in short, "scientific" — statements about the strange and very complex workings of our mind' (p. 5). Psychoanalysis has become in the English-speaking world 'something that refers and applies to others as a system of intellectual constructs ... a clever, exciting game — rather than the acquisition of insights into oneself' (pp. 6–7). He explains this by 'the universal wish to remain unaware of one's own unconscious' (p. 7); in other words, Freud's interpreters have found a way of distancing themselves from the very task of self-analysis which was at the heart of Freud's teaching, by preferring objective, behavioural study to introspective analysis, which involves the individual observing others as participant, not as detached being.[4]

Bettelheim gives many persuasive examples of this process. Freud's 'Seele' is translated in the official English standard edition as 'mind'; but if Freud had meant 'mind' he would have written 'Geist': 'In German the word *Seele* has retained its full meaning as man's essence, as that which is most spiritual and worthy in man. *Seele* ought to have been translated in this sense.' 'Geist' refers primarily to the rational and conscious part of the human being; 'the idea of the soul, by contrast, definitely includes much of which we are not consciously aware' (p. 77). *Psyche*, the soul, is 'a term full of the richest meaning, endowed with emotion, comprehensively human and unscientific' (pp. 11–12).

Bettelheim further argues that the ordinary and familiar words Freud, like his German readers, used all his life – 'das Ich', 'das Es' and 'das Über-Ich' ('the I', 'the It" and 'above- (or 'over-, upper-) I') – have been turned into technical terms – the ego, the id and the super-ego, respectively. He comments: 'To mistranslate *Ich* as "ego" is to transform it into jargon that no longer conveys the personal commitment we make when we say "I" or "me" – not to mention our subconscious memories of the deep emotional experience we had when, in infancy, we discovered ourselves as we learned to say "I"' (pp. 53–4). He continues: 'Where Freud selected a word that, used in daily parlance, makes us feel vibrantly alive, the translations present us with a term from a dead language that reeks of erudition precisely when it should emanate vitality' (p. 55). Bettelheim finds the same process at work in the translations of Freud's metaphors and allusions, including the famous Oedipus complex (pp. 20–30). Freud's language produced a literature or richness, subtlety, complexity and ambiguity, and should not be misrepresented to support mechanistic or deterministic views of the human being. For Freud, the soul is part of our common humanity, the place where our emotional and intellectual lives are rooted, and where the past accumulates to haunt us. Bettelheim concludes: 'Freud never faltered in his conviction that it was important to think in terms of the soul when trying to comprehend his system, because no other concept could make equally clear what he meant.'

Bettelheim claims that English readers of Freud are faced with the presuppositions of translators which stand in the way of a proper appreciation of Freud's work; and that part of this problem is the translators' attempts to make objective and scientific what was never intended to be so. Readers of San Juan may be tempted in the same direction but for different reasons. His analytical language is as technical as Freud's appears to be in English translation, but more inaccessible. Ego, id, superego and Oedipus complex are all familiar terms today, whereas we do not speak of the sensitive and spiritual parts of the soul or its three faculties. Faced with the jargon of a past tradition and insensitive to the tensions in San Juan's purpose and method, readers may experience him as if he were in his own way as objective and dogmatic as Freud is thought to be, but about beliefs and experiences they do not share. They will find his prose cold and distant, in contrast to the passion and mystery of his poems.

San Juan is clear about his aims and equally clear that he cannot fulfil them. Like all mystical writers, he acknowledges that the experiences he intends to describe are beyond description and can only be understood by sharing them. Failure and inadequacy are thus written into the text in ways its author cheerfully confesses (e.g. N2.17), for experience of God cannot be neatly captured and reduced to comprehensible categories. San Juan even allows the reader freedom to depart from his own expositions: 'no hay para qué atarse a la declaración' ('you do not have to be bound to the exposition'), he announces in the prologue to the *Cántico*. Mystical knowledge cannot distinctly be grasped except in faith, where we love before we understand; other readers, with other such experiences, may bring their own perspectives to bear on his text. It is therefore fitting that when he announces the purpose and the structure of the *Subida-Noche*, he should find himself unable to adhere to them rigidly.

San Juan tells us he is writing for a restricted readership: not even for nuns and friars in general, but for Discalced Carmelites, who followed the reform of the Order begun by Santa Teresa and San Juan for those who found the relaxed Rule a barrier to spiritual progress: 'Ni aun mi principal intento es hablar con todos, sino con algunas personas de nuestra sagrada Religión de los primitivos del Monte Carmelo, así frailes como monjas' ('Nor is my main purpose to speak to everybody, but to some of those of our holy Order of the primitives of Mount Carmel, friars as well as nuns') (*Subida*, prologue 9). As his analysis proceeds, he makes it clear that even they may only reach a certain point on the journey: 'Que no todos los que se exercitan de propósito en el camino del espíritu lleva Dios a contemplación, ni aun a la mitad (el porqué El se lo sabe)' ('God does not bring all those who deliberately exercise themselves on the spiritual road to contemplation, not even half of them (the reason he himself knows)'

(N1.9.9). In other words, some of the already highly-restricted readership will find parts of the treatise beyond their reach.

But by no means everything he writes can refer only to Discalced Carmelites, most of whom will have passed through the purgation and mortification of the active night of the senses. They can be little tempted by 'riquezas, estados, oficios... hijos, parientes, casamientos' ('riches, positions, jobs ... children, relatives, marriages') (S3.18.1), yet he devotes two chapters (S3.18–19) to the damage pleasure in temporal goods can do to the spirit. These early states need to be described for the sake of the completeness of the system, yet they open the commentary out to other, less advanced readers. Other important elements in the text are the common patrimony of all Christians: San Juan uses the Bible to provide authority for his teaching and he expounds principles of scholastic philosophy and Christian theology which belong to a more general frame of reference than the road to union with God which only a very few may reach. And for all that he is writing for people well practised in the art of loving God, he uses a whole range of similes and analogies to illustrate his teaching, as if it needed to be lightened or sweetened for those who could not easily take it neat. Although it is true that the nuns for whom he wrote were excluded as women from biblical and theological education, all these elements of the *Subida-Noche* question his own stated purpose and imply a wider potential readership.

Similar lapses mark the work's structure. He begins his commentary by stating that all its teaching is contained within the 'Noche oscura' poem, which he quotes in full:

> Y porque tengo de ir fundando sobre ellas lo que dijere, las he querido poner aquí juntas para que se entienda y vea junta toda la sustancia de lo que se ha de escribir; aunque al tiempo de la declaración convendrá poner cada canción de por sí, y ni más ni menos los versos de cada una, según lo pidiera la materia y declaración. (*Subida*, Argumento)

> And because I shall be basing what I say on them [the verses], I have placed them here together so that the whole substance of what is to be written can be seen and understood together; although when it comes to the explanation it will be more appropriate to give each verse by itself, and indeed each line of each verse, as the subject matter and the explanation may require.

There is nothing surprising about the statement, except that San Juan pays scant attention to it thereafter. The commentary on the poem is unfinished; few chapters offer the kind of poetic commentary he promises (S1.4; 1.14−15; 2.1; N1.1; 1.11; 1.13−14; 2.4; 2.11; 2.14−15; 2.22−25), and most of these are brief in comparison with the doctrinal chapters. Their bunching towards the end of the *Noche* indicates both haste and a late attempt to comply with his original intention. Although he manages to reach the end of the third verse, the great majority of the commentary derives from the first line of the poem, to which he returns several times (N1.1, 1.8, 2.5). For long chapters of the *Subida-Noche*, therefore, the poem remains in the background or is ignored.

The doctrinal plan is not always followed, either, and the exposition remains incomplete. The beginning of the commentary proper is a masterpiece of confusions. The first chapter of the *Subida* announces the general plan. There are two main kinds of night: of the sensual and spiritual parts of the soul. Each has an active and a passive aspect. This gives us the following fourfold scheme: active night of the senses (S1), and of the spirit (S2−3); passive night of the senses (N1) and of the spirit (N2). Having just announced it, he at once divides the night into three parts (S1.2) and applies this new scheme to the journey of the soul, giving three reasons why the metaphor is appropriate for the journey. It is night at the point of departure, the mortification of the human senses; night by virtue of the journey itself, the road of faith, which is darkness to the understanding; and night by virtue of the end of the journey, God, who is darkness to the soul in this life. These reasons are connected through a wonderfully complex and imaginative exegesis from the Book of Tobit with the three parts of natural night − after twilight, when light fades; midnight, which is total darkness; and before dawn, as the darkness is ending. Though the fourfold division governs the work, the introduction of another pattern foreshadows a tension which runs through the *Subida-Noche* between the structure San Juan has in mind and other possible structures suggested by the poem or by questions occuring in the course of the exposition and needing their own treatment.

In a systematic exposition, many things will be treated sequentially, for the sake of clarity of analysis, which are experienced in more complex ways. San Juan is clear, for example, that there is no simple progression from the purging of the senses to that of the spirit, since the first is only completed by the second (N2.1). Such chronologies of inner experience are simply ways of clarifying its muddled realms. Like Aquinas's *Summa*, San Juan's system is more helpfully seen as a journey than as a rigid structure.

   The fact that even in so apparently ordered a treatise as the *Subida-Noche* San Juan does not adhere to his own system suggests that he understood its limits and knew that the same journey might be charted differently from other points of view. Though he frequently pauses to remind us where we are, where we have come from and where we are going (e.g. S2.8.1; 2.28.1; 3.33.1), he is also aware of his tendency to digress, especially where he expounds biblical passages more or less connected to the exposition but usually related to 'dudas', or questions arising in a scholastic manner from his argument (e.g. (S2.7.−19−22). Twice he uses a quite different structural analysis: the traditional scheme of the seven deadly sins (N1.2−7) is used to expound the passive night of the senses, and the ten degrees of love, based on St Bernard and St Thomas (N2.19−20) form an alternative account of the whole journey.

   That different schemes and structures collide confirms San Juan's own sense that the spiritual journey is not capable of the neat packaging that too dominant a structure would impose. A remark in CB14−15.2 helps us to understand his attitude towards his own systematic discourse:

> No se ha de entender que a todas las [almas] que llegan a este estado se les comunica todo lo que en estas dos canciones se declara, ni en una misma manera y medida de conocimiento y sentimiento; porque a unas almas se les da más y otras menos, y a unas en una manera y a otras en otra, aunque lo uno y lo otro puede ser en este estado del desposorio espiritual. Mas pónese aquí lo más que puede ser, porque en ello se comprehende todo.

> It should not be supposed that everything which is explained in these two verses is communicated to all [souls] which reach this state, nor in the same manner or measure of knowledge or feeling; because some souls are given more and others less, and some in one way and others in another, although the one and the other can be found in this state of spiritual betrothal. But the most that can happen is stated here, since everything is included in it.

   Experience will never fit systems; at best, systems will map out sufficient varieties of experience to give the traveller orientation and permit progress towards the next landmark. The rigidity of San Juan's system is more apparent than real, and we misread him if we think it is closed. His concept of 'alma' (soul) is a case in point.

We can too readily assume that he means by it what we mean: that indefinable core of human personality which some believe survives physical death. But, like Freud, San Juan means the whole inner life of the human personality, including all those drives and desires which Freud identified as 'Ich', 'Es' and 'Über-Ich'. San Juan divides his 'alma' into two parts, the lower (or sensual) and the higher (or spiritual). It contains all human appetites and desires, good and evil, and only when the sensual appetites of the lower soul have been purged can the journey to God proceed. Once his basic understanding of the soul is grasped, the Aristotelian–scholastic distinctions he makes between other aspects of human personality become less of a barrier to twentieth-century readers. The division into the three 'potencias' (faculties), of 'entendimiento', 'memoria', and 'voluntad' (understanding, memory and will), comes to control the flow of his analysis in the *Subida-Noche*. The life of the soul is rational ('entendimiento'), volitional ('voluntad') and temporal ('memoria'). Knowing, loving and remembering are activities of the whole soul. They do not represent self-contained realities, but describe recognisable and interconnected human activities.

San Juan believes, following Aristotelian rather than Platonic tradition, that at its origin the soul is a *tabula rasa*, a blank slate. All knowledge is mediated by the senses and appropriated internally by the respective faculties. The three 'theological virtues' of faith, hope and charity are the proper objects of their attention. Once purged, they are free to be opened out to their true object of contemplation, God. Human intellect, obscured by partial or sinful knowledge, must be purged by faith: human reason must enter the darkness of unknowing before the mind can begin to glimpse the dazzling brightness of God. Human memory, full of burdens from the past, must be purged by hope, which comes from the divine purpose, not some imagined human good. Human will, the seat of sinfulness because it is turned towards love of the creatures rather than the Creator, must be purged by the love which comes from God and is God, so that all other motivations are left behind or consumed in its burning flame. The process of purgation is long, arduous and painful. It has two related aspects, which San Juan calls active and passive. The active part is what lies within our competence to do, but the passive only God can work, when all our efforts are exhausted. There is a limit to human activity on the journey; at a crucial stage its powers cease, and God alone acts to bring the soul to union (hence the active search of the woman in the 'Noche' poem leads to a passive experience of union with the Beloved).

'Alma' therefore includes not only our highest aspirations and the source of our best actions and noblest feelings, but also all the other desires which pull us in the opposite direction, towards self-indulgence and away from God. The 'alma' is a place of pain and conflict, which contains all that motivates us, drives us towards destructive or creative activity; a vast region, infinitely spacious, little understood. Like Freud, San Juan finds on his journey through these dark and unknown regions much that needs to be brought out into the open and faced and understood for any progress towards the goal to be possible. He discovers disabling mechanisms at work, some dressed in religious clothes, and he clarifies many of the confusions which others on the journey will meet.

According to Bettelheim, 'introspection is what psychoanalysis is all about', yet at least in America, 'psychological research and teaching ... are either behaviourally, cognitively, or physiologically oriented and concentrate almost exclusively on what can be measured or observed from the outside: introspection plays no part' (p. 19). He insists that the American practice of Freud, which located psycho-analysis in the world of medicine and restricted it to doctors, moved away from what it was intended to be, 'a call to greater humanity, and a way to achieve it' (p. 33). He examines the myth of Oedipus to restore to it the significance Freud intended, that the failure of Oedipus to know himself brought about his fate. The admonition inscribed on the temple at Corinth, *gnothi seauton* ('know thyself'), is of course a commonplace of spiritual writers through the ages. 'We must know ourselves in order to free ourselves from destructive powers' (p. 27); while part of that process means 'that we shall have to enter a world of darkness and uncertainty, a world of chaos that defies clear-cut translation and interpretation' (p. 69). Freud's psychology, claims Bettelheim, is 'an introspective psychology that tries to elucidate the darkest recesses of the soul' and is thus not subject to proofs by behaviouralistic studies: 'A good life denies neither its real and often painful difficulties nor the dark aspects of our psyche; rather, it is a life in which our hardship are not permitted to engulf us in despair, and our dark impulses are not allowed to draw us into their chaotic and often destructive orbit' (p. 110). As the journey towards self-knowledge proceeds, there will be encountered dark, painful and destructive forces which nevertheless can be confronted and overcome – very familiar ground to readers of San Juan.

San Juan does not use archetypal myths (Eros and Psyche, Narcissus, Oedipus) to illustrate his system, though it is interesting to note how much Freud looked back into the biblical and classical past in order to speak meaningfully about the individual present. San Juan's authorities are Scripture and Tradition, his analysis based on Christian teaching and a number of philosophical common-places derived from his Aristotelenian–scholastic training: the presence of God in the soul (*imago Dei*), the doctrine of contraries and of love creating likeness between lover and beloved on the other. He writes from within an orthodox Roman Catholic position, in which God is the source and the goal of every created being and object and without him nothing could exist at all. He is present in all, even in the greatest sinner. 'Y esta manera de unión siempre está hecha entre Dios y las criaturas todas, en la cual les está conservando el ser que tienen; de manera que, si [de ellas] desta manera faltase, luego se aniquilarían y dejarían de ser' ('And this kind of union ever exists between God and all the creatures, in which he is keeping them in their particular being; so that if he were to be lacking [from them] in this way, they would at once be annihilated and cease to be') (S2.5.3).

The journey begins as the soul, tied to a material body, feels exiled from its true home and in danger of being all but engulfed by the desires and demands of the bodily senses; its goal is the realisation of its full potential, which, according to San Juan, is nothing less than union with God in every part of the soul's being, participation or transformation in God. He uses bold language to describe this but always stops short of any suggestion that the soul's identity is merged into some universal divine substance.[5] His poems represent this journey in a language of symbol and allusion, which the commentaries describe and analyse in a language more abstract and technical (though not without generating its own analogies). The true fulfilment of human personality is found in the 'spiritual marriage' of union with God, known only to a few, and fleetingly, in this life, but granted to all the faithful in the beatific vision in heaven. That is the goal of the integrated personality, and on the journey every instinct, need, craving, is ruthlessly exposed and, unless entirely consistent with the goal, removed. For between the beginning and the end of the journey lies an inner country full of dangers and conflicts and traps, and terrible experiences, known as the 'dark nights of the soul'. It is in his charting of this journey that San Juan comes closest to Freud, for his treatises are, quite simply, psychoanalysis, analysis of the soul.

The route San Juan's journey takes is introspective, and for all their images of exuberant beauty drawn from the natural creation, his poems, as he sees them, are landscapes of the soul. The external world is the metaphorical mirror of the real world within. Nowhere does he express this more forcefully than in CB1.7−8, commenting on the opening lines of the poem, '¿Adónde te escondiste, / Amado...?' ('where did you hide yourself, Beloved?'):

> ¡oh, pues, alma hermosísima entre todas las criaturas, que tanto deseas saber el lugar donde está tu Amado para buscarle y unirte con él, ya se te dice que tú misma eres el aposento donde él mora y el retrete y escondrijo donde está escondido .... ¿Qué más quieres, ¡oh alma!, y qué más buscas fuera de ti, pues dentro de ti tienes tus riquezas, tus deleites, tu satisfacción, tu hartura y tu reino, que es tu Amado, a quien desea y busca tu alma? Gózate y alégrate en tu interior recogimiento con él, pues le tienes tan cerca .... Sólo hay una cosa, es a saber, que, aunque está dentro de ti, está escondido.

> Ah, soul, most beautiful among all the creatures, desiring so greatly to know the place where your Beloved is to find him and be united with him, he is telling you that you yourself are the place where he dwells and the room and the hiding-place where he is hidden .... What else do you want, oh soul, and what else do you seek outside yourself, since within you you have your riches, delights, satisfaction, fullness and kingdom, which is your Beloved, whom your soul desires and seeks? Rejoice and be glad in your inner withdrawal with him, since you have him so close .... There is but one thing, which is that although he is within you, he is hidden.

There is, in other words, no point in looking outside or beyond the soul for the ultimate answer to the question, where is God? The soul is his 'aposento... retrete y escondrijo' where he is 'escondido', and therefore very near.[6] The book of creation may be read for signs of God's existence (as indeed it is in CA4−5), but its true role is to become a source of metaphor for the inward journey: the kingdom of God is within (Luke 17:21), and you are God's temple (2 Cor. 6:16). God may be very near, but he is hidden. The journey must therefore involve a process of uncovering and discovering, and it is in finding the way towards the hidden Beloved that the soul will encounter its severest tests. San Juan continues:

Muy bien haces, ¡oh alma!, en buscarle siempre escondido, porque
mucho ensalzas a Dios y mucho te llegas a El teniéndole por más alto
y profundo que todo cuanto puedes alcanzar ... que, pues es Dios
inaccesible y escondido ... aunque más te parezca que le hallas y le
sientes y le entiendes, siempre le has de tener por escondido y le has
de servir escondido en escondido. (1.12, pp. 577–8)[7]

You do very well, oh soul, to seek him always hidden, since you greatly
exalt God and reach him more by holding him to be higher and deeper
than anything you can grasp .... For, since God is inaccessible and
hidden, however much you think you have found or experienced or
understood him, you must always hold him to be hidden and you must
serve him hidden in hiddenness.

The soul, hidden from the exterior world and the clamour of the self,
goes by introspection towards the hiddenness of God within.

Like Freud, San Juan looks inward to confront, in his own
terms, those unseen forces in the soul which prevent it from reaching
its goal. His understanding of destructive powers is theological: only
God's intervention (the passive nights) can finally break their hold
over the soul. While Freud found dreams indicative of buried desires
and fears, San Juan analyses a whole range of paranormal experiences
(visions, locutions, raptures and so on; S3.7–14), undoubtedly shared
by him and those whom he guided, and is able to distinguish the good
from the evil. Many of these areas of mystical experience are am-
biguous, coming perhaps from God, perhaps from the Devil, but
always the result of bodily weakness; hence his injunction to negate
them always, that is, not to trust them as a basis for further growth
(e.g. N2.16.10; 24.8). Darkness and uncertainty play a central part
in San Juan's journey, as synonyms for the night of the soul, though,
like all symbols, they compress together a whole range of meaning.
Uncertainty, 'not knowing' ('no saber'), is one of his most characteristic metaphors for faith. The dark nights, each more painful and
terrible than the last, become a source of ultimate good because they
lead to union: though they are experienced negatively, their effect
is positive. Like Freud, he believes that only by facing inner darkness
and pain and learning to understand its cause and its effect can the
soul find release. He does not stop till he reaches the root, an
important image in his exposition of the passive night (N2.2.1; 10.9),
for only then is purgation complete.

His analysis of inner states also enables him to assess outward
behaviour. A good example of this occurs in the chapters on the seven

deadly sins in N1.2–7, one of those alternative schemes which cut across the rhythm of the *Subida-Noche*. Out of an entirely common-place topic, he makes a penetrating analysis of the kind of religious practice which to most observers would seem to reveal a genuine devotion. He applies the seven deadly sins to the spiritual or higher part of the soul, addressing himself to those who have already made considerable progress in purgation of the senses. Spiritual sins are more insidious than the sensual variety, because they are more difficult to recognise and therefore to root out. He exposes the inadequacies of the kinds of religious devotion which such people prize, in order to uncover its true motivation, which remains harmfully attached to self. Those who fall into spiritual pride love talking about spiritual things in front of others, rather than continuing to learn from them; do not listen to spiritual directors who are critical but try to find others who will offer more palatable counsel; hide or gloss over sins; and are impatient because they are not yet saints. The cure is humility and (a nice paradox, because it is another deadly sin) 'santa envidia' ('holy envy') to serve God and others; a willingness to learn from all kinds of people; and a fundamental honesty about sins. With such attitudes, the grace of God has room to pursue its healing work. Spiritual avarice shows itself in greed for consolations from books, teaching, images, rosaries and the like, that is, for pleasurable external things. This unmasking of religiosity is most strongly marked in the chapter on spiritual greed, where excessive penitence, fasting and reception of communion are all shown to be the result of a desire to please the self rather than God, and to seek self-gratification, not the rough path of the Cross.

In the chapter on spiritual lust San Juan asks why physical lust so often interrupts moments of great devotion, such as receiving communion. His answer is that since the action takes place at the level of the senses, these easily turn to other objects of delight. He is quite straightforward about it. He identifies distinct personality types: depressives (melancholics), who are especially prone to ugly imagin-ings at moments of greatest spiritual joy, and for whom fear of such is alone sufficient to create them; and weak and impressionable types, who are easily swayed from spiritual to physical pleasure.

San Juan runs out of steam in his chapters on spiritual anger, envy and sloth, combining the last two, because he has effectively said all he wants to say. Religious devotion in itself is not a necessary sign of spiritual growth or divine favour; indeed, it may become a stumbling-block on the way to God. But he insists, in a vivid metaphor, that the work of the dark night is to cure these 'niñerías', this infantile, regressive behaviour, through temptation, aridity and travail, 'destetándolos Dios de los pechos destos gustos y sabores en puras sequedades y tinieblas interiores' ('as God detaches them from the breasts of these pleasures and delights into pure dryness and inner darkness') (7.5). His insistence that some forms of religious behaviour are infantile and that the soul must be weaned away from them, and his understanding of the dark areas within human experience and the necessity of facing them and dealing with them, make him a natural ally of Freud rather than an enemy.

Were there space, other connections between Freud and San Juan might be explored: San Juan's concept of passivity and Freud's 'das Es'; the distinction both make between what may be termed knowledge and wisdom; the roles of the spiritual director and the psychoanalyst, and the dangers which attend them. There is a final area, though, which deserves comment: their use of metaphor. Bettelheim underlines its importance in Freud's writing: 'In psychology we can describe only with the help of comparisons' (quoted in *The Question of Lay Analysis*, London, 1985, p.37). He gives three reasons for Freud's frequent use of a relatively small number of these: 'Psychoanalysis, though it is confronted with hard, objective facts, does not deal with them as such but devotes itself to the imagination and exploration of hidden causes, which can only be inferred' (p.37). Second, 'because of repression, or the influence of censorship, the unconscious reveals itself in symbols or metaphors, and psychoanalysis, in its concern with the unconscious, tries to speak about it in its own metaphoric language' (pp.37–8). Last, 'metaphors are more likely than a purely intellectual statement to touch a human chord and arouse our emotions, and thus give us a feeling for what is meant' (p.38). Freud also stressed that poets and great artists spoke in metaphors about the contents of their own unconscious and 'knew all along what he had to discover through laborious work' (p.38). Hence he often quoted Goethe, Shakespeare and others. Among his most common metaphors are those of illness, where 'the body stands for the soul' (p.39), the Oedipus myth, the midwife, who helps to give birth to another's child, and archaeology, 'unearthing the deeply buried remnants of the past' (p.42). These are metaphors and should not be treated as theoretical or factual statements.

Metaphorical language is of course essential to San Juan. It is the only language possible for mystics, since the experiences they record are literally indescribable. His great poems work in different ways. The *Noche* and the *Llama* are both like solar systems, with satellite metaphors circling the central orbs of night and flame: journey, house, staircase, breeze, touch, lilies; wounding, veil, touch, caverns, breath. The much longer *Cántico* has constellations of metaphor drawn from the whole creation and attracted to the figures of the bride and bridegroom.

In his prose commentaries, a similar distinction can be made. While the *Cantico*, as I have shown elsewhere, follows closely the imagery of the poem and attempts to elucidate each image, creating fresh ones in the process, the *Noche* is a schematic exposition of the main stages of the spiritual journey under the embracing metaphor of night.[8] 'Noche' expands to become a controlling symbol for its most important features: the place where it starts (escape by a stairway from a house at night), the journey itself (guided by an inner light through the darkness) and the destination (union in the dark). It also embraces active and passive purgation and privation, faith and God himself. Though he is teaching adepts, San Juan finds himself constantly in need of analogy to make sure that his expositions are properly grasped. He uses images of transformation and participation for describing human growth towards fulfilment, and one of his favourite analogies is that of the child weaned from its mother's breast and learning to stand on its own feet, itself of biblical provenance (Hebr. 5:12, N1.12.1; 1 John 3:2, N2.20.5). Infantile dependence on God must be left behind for a more mature relationship. The journey as he sees it is always offering new possibilities of growth.

What happens when, as it inevitably must, San Juan's treatises are read by people who are neither Discalced Carmelites nor looking for spiritual teaching, who reject his beliefs, or who, even if they do not, would hardly express them in sixteenth-century scholastic language? Can they only be read to discover how the author was trapped by his own presuppositions or unable to follow them through so that the text constantly undermines itself and witnesses to the impossibility of his self-appointed task? I have been trying to show, through Bettelheim's re-reading of Freud, how twentieth-century readers who find San Juan's experience and his attempt to communicate it alien to their cast of mind may yet find it meanfingful.

Let us, for the sake of comparison, follow briefly a different path and offer a reading of San Juan which tries to make sense of the puzzle he leaves us, that one kind of experience should produce two such apparently different kinds of literature as his poetry (mysterious, rich, exotic, sensuous) and his prose (analytical, bare, didactic). San Juan's spiritual teaching is radically negative before it can be affirmative. Everything that is not God or does not come directly from God to the soul must be negated, including, as we have seen, unhealthy religious practice. On one side of the ontological gulf are the creatures, everything that is made; on the other, God their Creator. There is no bridge across it; only God can in the end bring the soul over to himself, when it is sufficiently detached from the creaturely. Suppose this teaching is thought of as an interior analogue of the totalitarianism of post-Tridentine Spain, of the attempted silencing by the Inquisition and the Crown of all forms of dissent. San Juan's internalised version of this speaks for example of the suppression of the appetites and his controlling metaphors are 'noche', 'sequedad' and 'vacío', night, drought and emptiness. To make up for this poverty there is the promise of heaven, not in fact postponed until beyond death but to be enjoyed, if fleetingly, in mystical union with God in this life. There must always be a reward for the obedient poor so that they will not strive to overthrow the rich and the powerful. But his poetry, which came first, can be seen as a splendidly anarchic protest against any kind of repression, with its exuberant imagery, its strongly sexual language and its rapid movements across time and space.

Such an analysis will be attractive to some and it has its own kind of logic. It might therefore be thought that San Juan is easily approached by the kind of criticism which sees his work as fixed in its own time, determined by its presuppositions, yet unable in the end to contain itself and bound to fail, thereby allowing readers of other times and cultures to bring their own presuppositions with them to the interpretation of the text. I have tried to suggest instead, by looking at those elements of his work which undermine his expressed purpose, that San Juan is only too well aware of the impossibility of achieving what he sets out to do. His experience is so intense that it is not exhausted by one literary form, but goes on to create another. He is constrained to use apparently ordered forms, yet fully conscious of inevitable failure, because of the confusion of all human categories and speech which results from the direct experience of God. Those who would connect the radical negation of his teaching with the suppression of political dissent in the age of Philip II might also remember that his voice comes to us out of one of the few kinds of communism to have withstood the test of time — monasticism.

One of Freud's legacies is to tempt us to believe that there is a straightforward explanation at the human level for mystical experience. But another, if Bettelheim is to be believed, takes us in a more creative direction and reveals a continuity in European thought where most of us see a fundamental dichotomy. San Juan probes deeply into the life of the human soul, as he sets out on a journey to climb (paradoxically) the mountain of those innermost regions which remain as unexplored by most of us as they were by his contemporaries.[9] He contends that this journey is open to anyone, and that anyone may find, as long as they are not too proud to seek help, the healing of all the darkness and pain through which they must inevitably pass. For all his apparent objectivity San Juan is first and foremost subjecting himself to analysis. It is because he has made the ascent which is a descent into the soul that he can be a guide to others; and he invites those who read him to remember that it is they, not some imaginary person, who are being described and analysed in what he writes. The results of his exploration are both great art and psychological perception, living in tension with each other. The mystic and the psychoanalyst may follow different roads, but are united by their insistence on the importance of looking within. They may be exceptional in their vocation or their perceptiveness, but they are both writing about what lies within common human experience.

Once the Western Church began to neglect its own tradition of introspection, which goes back at least to St Augustine's *Confessions*, a neglect more sharply marked in Protestantism than in Catholicism, the development of another form was perhaps inevitable, given the human need for self-understanding. Freudian psychology in its 'professional' and 'scientific' guise came subsequently to fill the vacuum; the spiritual director gave way to the analyst, the confessional to the couch. Only now, with signs of a revival of interest in traditional spirituality in the West, is there some hope that inward growth and development can resume their proper place in the life of the soul, and that fruitful dialogue, of the kind I believe Bettelheim makes possible, may replace mutual incomprehension or suspicion between prayer and psychiatry.[10] The study of mystical literature will be a rich source of material for this, because once we leave behind facile assumptions about them, we begin to discover that mystics are wise and experienced guides to the fears and hopes which struggle for articulation in the uncharted deep of the human soul.

Notes

1 Bruno Bettelheim, *Freud and Man's Soul*, London, 1985.
2 San Juan never explicitly states that the *Subida* and the *Noche* are one work, but the structure of the treatise makes this clear, as do other references (e.g. S1.1.1–2; 1.13.1; *Llama de amor viva*, 1.25). All quotations and references are from *San Juan de la Cruz. Obras completas*, eleventh edn, Madrid, 1982; translations are mine.
3 Not only between Protestants and Catholics, but also among Catholics: see my *The Strife of Tongues. Fray Luis de León and the Golden Age of Spain*, Cambridge, 1988, pp. 36–85.
4 It is interesting to note that both San Juan and Freud find a threefold distinction in analysing the soul necessary, although it works differently in each case.
5 See my *The Poet and the Mystic*, Oxford, 1977, pp. 162–4.
6 A good example of the way San Juan's poetic sense informs his prose: 'escondrijo ... escondido' shows both assonance and a play on the root 'esconder' (the figure of *adnominatio* or *polyptoton*).
7 The theme of hiddenness is particularly to the fore in CA 32–4.
8 *The Poet and the Mystic*, pp. 118–45.
9 This paradox is fundamental to San Juan: ascent to God involves descent into the soul. See, for example, my piece 'The many paradoxes of the mystics', in *Homenaje a Eugenio Asensio*, Madrid, 1988, pp. 482–5.
10 One of the signs of this revival is the increasing number of texts and books being published; for example, the major series *Classics of Western Spirituality* (SPCK, London) is producing new translations of many neglected works.

The play of difference: a reading of Góngora's *Soledades*

From the date of first appearance, Góngora's *Soledades* have been perceived as uncanonical and problematic. Francisco Cascales, who found Góngora so dangerously subversive as to merit description as 'Mahoma de la poesía española' ('the Mohamet of Spanish poetry') – a revealingly expressive phrase in devoutly orthodox post-Tridentine Catholic Spain – roundly declared that Góngora's language 'no es bueno para poema heroico, ni lírico, ni trágico, ni cómico; luego es inútil' ('it will serve for neither a heroic, nor lyric, nor tragic, nor comic poem; therefore it is useless').[1] One of Góngora's defenders, though he comes to a more positive conclusion, is forced to admit the same generic indeterminacy:

> Dexando pues, varios pareceres, supuesto que no es dramático, tampoco puede ser épico, ni la fábula ni la acción es de Herae o persona ilustre, ni acomodado el verso; menos es romançe, por más que tenga del mixto, porque demás de no aiudarle el verso, ni introduce Príncipes por sujeto del Poema, ni cortes, ni guerras, ni aventuras, como el Ariosto, el Tasso Padre y el Alemani. Bucólico no es aunque en él entren Pastores ni Haliéutico, aunque pescadores, ni Cinegético, aunque caçadores; porque ninguno es sujeto adecuado y trata o a de tratar juntamente de otros.[2]

> Thus leaving on one side various opinions, as it is not dramatic, neither can it be epic; neither the story nor the action concern a hero or illustrious person, nor is the verse appropriate; even less is it a romance, however mixed its style, for beside receiving no assistance from the verse, it neither introduces princes as subject of the poem, nor courts, nor wars, nor adventures, as do Ariosto, the elder Tasso and Alemani. It is not Bucolic, thought it contains shepherds, nor piscatorial, though it has fishermen, nor Venatory, though it has huntsmen; because none of these is an adequate subject and it [the poem] deals or attempts to deal also with others.

Because of the inclusiveness, the commentator somewhat lamely concludes,

> porque introduce a todos los referidos es necesario confesar que es Poema que los admite y abraza a todos; qual sea éste, es sin duda el Mélico o Lyrico llamado así por ser canto, que esto es Melos, al son de la Lyra.

> Because it includes all the aforementioned, we must acknowledge that it is a poem that admits and embraces them all; this mode is undoubtedly the Melic or Lyric, so-called because it is a song, which is Melos, accompanied by the sound of the lyre.

I think this stylistic indeterminacy is in no sense accidental, but is, as John Beverley maintains,[3] deliberate and intentional evidence of Góngora's consistent transgression, inversion and subversion of canonical patterns and structures at every level in the *Soledades*. Many of these transgressions have been the subject of extensive commentary by critics of the poem. For example, some seventeenth-century commentators found it distasteful that Góngora should have attributed to base *codicia* (greed) the voyages of heroic discoverers such as Magellan and Columbus. Modern critics, Dámaso Alonso, Robert Jammes and John Beverley, in particular,[4] have taken this, together with the absence of overt Christian reference, as evidence of Góngora's detachment from and indifference to the ideological values upheld by seventeenth-century Spain's ruling classes: ardently pious evangelistic Catholicism, hierarchic patriarchal valorisation of honour, patriotic exaltation of Spain's seafaring and military exploits. Jammes, in particular, notices the lack of specific mention of Christian ceremony and dogma in Góngora's presentation of the peasant wedding in the first *Soledad*: 'il y a ici une véritable "paganisation" des cérémonies religieuses catholiques, alors que la tendance générale de cette époque était, au contraire, de "christianiser" l'héritage culturel du paganisme' ('we have here a veritable "paganisation" of Catholic religious ceremonies, whereas, on the contrary, the general tendency of this epoch was to "Christianise" the cultural heritage of paganism') (Etudes, 599, fn. 59).

Maurice Molho, in a detailed analysis of the first four lines of the Dedication to the *Soledades*, sees in the near-homonymy of *silva*, the loose and flexible metre in which the *Soledades* are written, and *selva*, the wilderness in which the poem's protagonist wanders, a cipher of Góngora's rejection of order: 'd'une part, la *selva*, paysage naturel, indompté ... d'autre part, la *silva*, forme a-strophique, dédale de vers inégaux et de rimes enchevetrées – *forêt métrique, exubérante et indisciplinée'* (my emphasis) ('on one hand the *selva*, a natural, untamed landscape... on the other hand, the *silva*, an a-strophic form, a labyrinth of uneven verses and tangled rhymes – an exuberant and disciplined metric forest'). The verbal slippage, or *différance selva/ silva* to Molho represents a 'refus de structure' ('a rejection of structure') in terms of metre and 'substance poétique'. Thus the terms elide because of their 'fondamentale identité' ('fundamental identity').[5]

Paul Julian Smith[6] illuminatingly studies the sexual and textual transgression implicit in the generic indeterminacy of the *Soledades*.[6] Just as the *Soledades* are notoriously resistant to confinement within a specific genre, so in them, as in the *Polifemo*, Góngora inverts the gender paradigm, valorising its traditionally negative side: woman, ornament, lyric. So the wrestling match which comes towards the conclusion of the first *Soledad*, a topos which is a set-piece of epic, and, as Smith says, 'comes to Góngora saturated with the heroic value of the *Iliad* and the *Aeneid*' (*The Body Hispanic*, p. 59), is robbed of the martial, civic and patriarchal ethos of epic, and has no transcendental function in the inconsequential narrative of the *Soledades*. Moreover, Góngora insists on the public display of his near-naked wrestlers, and the spectacle is explicitly offered up for the female witness of the bride and other village girls, so appearing to propose 'an alternative perspective to that of the hegemonic male gaze' (p. 59). For Smith this and other transgressions of hierarchy 'suggests not so much a simple reversal of the paradigm, as the collapse of the economy of meaning' (p. 67).

At every point, the text of the *Soledades* resounds with the clangour of linguistic dissonance. At its most obvious level, this is evident in the lack of stylistic decorum in the use of the 'high', *culto*, sublime style applied to mundane, bucolic matter – a practice that outraged Góngora's contemporary critics, from Juan de Jáuregui, who in his *Antídoto a la pestilente poesía de las 'Soledades'* (1614), objected rather peevishly to the description of a farmyard cock as a turbaned sultan:

> y – de coral barbado – no de oro
> ciñe, sino de púrpura, turbante (*Soledad* I, 11.290–291)
>
> Bearded with coral on his head behold / A
> turban pound with purple if not gold[7]

on the grounds that (a) farmyard fowl do not wear turbans, and (b) certainly not purple ones. Even Gracián, otherwise a wholehearted admirer of Góngora, was dismayed by this penchant of his, and in *Crisi IV*, Part II of *El Criticón* lamented that in Góngora 'moral teaching did not match heroic composition, nor serious topics the refinement of style, nor yet subject-matter the proud splendour ('bizarría') of the verse, nor the subtlety of his conceits.'

Equally disconcerting, unpredictable und apparently arbitrary is the way in which incongruous humour repeatedly and anarchically disrupts the dignity of the text. This shows itself in its simplest form in an enjoyment of irreverent schoolboy puns, like that on the ram's death in *Soledades* I, I.160 which 'redimió con su muerte tantas vides' ('by killing him redeemed the threatened vine'). A pun that again turns on a near-homonymy between *vides* (vines), and *vidas* (lives), thereby making the line into a blasphemous allusion to the death of Christ redeeming lives.

More subtly, there are passages where humour arises not from verbal play, but from the discontinuity between the gravity of the language and the undignified image it projects. So, in the midst of the wedding games of *Soledad* I, with their celebration of the beauty of the agile, vigorous bodies of young *serranos* (mountain men), gracefully running and leaping, is inserted the description of an overweight young cowherd's ignominious disaster as he attempts to emulate the performance in the long jump of one of his athletic companions:

un vaquero de aquellos montes, grueso,
membrudo, fuerte roble,
que ágil a pesar de lo robusto,
alaire se arrebata, violentando
lo grave tanto, que lo precipita
– Icaro montañés – su mismo peso,
de la menuda hierba el senso blando
piélago duro hecho a su ruina. (*Soledad* I, L.1004–1011)

A peasant, a strong herdsman, sinewy / Robust
as any oak, agile as well / Despite his sturdiness,
now to rebel / Against his hugeness, and the air defy; /
who should at last descend, / A mountain Icarus,
through his own weight, / On the soft bosom of the
grass to lie, / The hard sea of his fate.

Not only does the tortuous syntax mimic the majestic, slow-motion parabola of the corpulent youth's progress through the air, but the dignity of language itself is subverted. It is not simply the physical law of gravity that is defied ('violentando lo *grave*'), it is the very *gravitas* of decorum and linguistic propriety that is violated. The gratuitousness and inconsequentiality of this burlesque episode undermines and calls into ironic question the seriousness of the pastoral/mythological artifice of the convention in which it is set.

Another example of grotesque incongruity between linguistic register and subject-matter occurs when an aged *cabrero* (goatherd) is interrupted in mid-homiletic reflection on the transience of all things — thoughts generated by the sight of once proud, now ruined towers. Suddenly a disorderly 'torrente de armas y de perros, / que si precipitados no los cerros, / las personas tras de un lobo traía ('torrent great nearby, / Hunters and arms and dogs composed its train / Carried, to hunt the wolf, the people there'). Abruptly abandoning his guest, the wandering *peregrino*, in mid-sentence, the hitherto dignified rustic is galvanised into improbably frenetic movement: 'el venatorio estruendo, / pasos dando veloces, / número crece y multiplica voces' ('with paces swift he strode / Toward the venatorial companies / To augment their number, multiply their cries'). It is not simply the puppet-like arbitrariness of the *cabrero*'s sudden change of behaviour that disturbs the reader here, but the calculated inappropriateness of the final symmetrically parallelistic phrases using terminology expressive of mathematical precision: '*número* crece y *multiplica* voces' to describe what has already been described as a tumultuous, disorderly rout ('*torrente* de armas y de perros', 'precipitados', 'venatorio *estruendo*'). The effect is to create in the reader a sense of a capricious doubleness of vision, before which terms unpredictably mutate in a void of indeterminacy, or rather in the arena of the play of textuality.

Góngora's text is one of flagrant excess, overabundance and contradiction, in scandalous defiance of stylistic decorum or the Aristolelian golden mean of discretion. It seems appropriate that in scholastic rhetoric the term for the syntactical figure most commonly used by Góngora, as it were, his stylistic signature, hyperbaton (dislocation of normal syntactical order), is *transgressio*. In the *Soledades*, distinctions are blurred, categories and norms are called into question, imagery and metaphor are caught up in a restless process of metamorphosis in a text that remains always open and labile. It is always a process, never a culmination, and in this respect, seems more appropriately considered in terms of a synergesis rather than, say, Hegelian synthesis or *discordia concors*.

Contradiction, generic indeterminacy and radical ambivalence are, as we have seen, dominant aspects of the style and thought of the *Soledades*. Spitzer commented that Góngora's play on doubling and division 'parece en verdad una exteriorización del desdoblamiento del poeta (o del protagonista que observa las cosas como él)'[8] ('seems in truth an exteriorisation of the poets's doubleness [or of the protagonist, who observes things as his author does]'). The poem is built around the spatial figure of a *soledad confusa* as a natural and psychic wilderness, where language creates a *nature* in which distinctions are capriciously — but also systematically — blurred, e.g. the constant use of 'transelemental' imagery, or the creation of a twilight zone in which light and darkness merge: the already quoted lines describing the grassy sward on which the young *serrano* comes to grief as a *piélago duro* ('hard sea'), the earlier 'Libia de ondas' ('a Libyan desert of waves') and, most expressively, lines 42–45 of *Soledad* I, which combine blurring of both light and the boundaries between sea and land:

No bien pues de su luz los horizontes
– que hacían desigual confusamente
montes de agua y piélagos de montes –
desdorados los siente.

Then the horizon from the evening light / – which made unequal and confusedly / Mountains of water, oceans of the height – / Not well distinguishing.

In this passage it is made clear that the experience of blurring is not perceived as harmonious synthesis, but as inequality and confusion (note the stress on *desigual* and *confusamente*) which is both external-ised (in the landscape) and internal to the state of consciousness of the perceiving protagonist – and by extension, of the reader plunged into the dynamic and bewildering labyrinthine confusion of the *Soledades*.

An extreme example of disjunction and doubleness of statement is to be found in the diatribe / lament of the 'político serrano, / de canas grave' ('a politic old man, with white hairs grave') in lines 366–502 of *Soledad* I. Ostensibly this lament is appropriate to the figure of the *serrano* as a wise and aged Arcadian shepherd who has suffered the misfortune of losing son and possessions in shipwreck. As such, it links up with the topos of the praise of Golden Age, innocence, unspoilt by the greed, envy, cunning and aggression of civilisation – a topos inherent in the bucolic convention, and which, in the form of *'menosprecio de corte y alabanza de aldea'* ('vituperation of court/town, praise of the country') was a contemporary topic restated at some length in earlier lines (*Soledad* I, 88–129). However, the overwhelming effect of the passage is that of panegyric, as becomes obvious when the *serrano* describes the appalling dangers and apparently insurmountable obstacles faced by discoverers such as Magellan, Columbus and Núñez de Balboa. In fact, the *serrano*'s lament is, on a smaller scale, a Spanish equivalent of Camoens's *Os Lusiadas*, with similar theme and the same heroic intent. It also offers an arena for the most magnificent display of Góngora's linguistic virtuosity, where, in restlessly metamorphosing metaphors all is clothed in rich and wonderful strangeness, becomes a source of *admiratio*. Take, for example, lines 370–8 of *Soledad* I, with their sustained succession of transelemental metaphors to describe a ship – itself a metonymy of the strangeness and treachery of the discoverers' navigations. From a 'mal nacido pino' ('ill-starred pine') – itself a metonymy – which 'furrows' the wavy fields of the sea, it is unpredictably transformed, in a beautiful image, into a gigantic floating flower – a 'vaga Clicie del viento' ('vague Clytie of the breeze'), following the wind in its sails rather than the course of the sun, as did the nymph Clytie transformed into a heliotrope. In the next two lines, the ship becomes a marine monster, covered in beechwood scales, to end, ominously, as a latter-day marine replica of the treacherous Greek gift – the wooden horse – that brought fire and destruction to Troy.

I have already mentioned the inconsequentiality of the narrative of the *Soledades*. More significantly, it is, as is notorious, an 'unfinished', incomplete poem that ends abruptly as night falls after the excitement of the hawking hunt at the end of the second *Soledad*. Further, though, as Beverley states, 'the whole poem is like a "day" ', beginning with the luminosity of the opening scenes and ending abruptly as the owl's wing eclipses the sun in the final lines of the *Soledad segunda* (*Aspects*, pp. 42–4). Within the poem, the narration floats unanchored in the no-time of the text. One of Góngora's contemporaries complained rather petulantly of the temporal inconsistencies of a text in which at one point the peasants huddle shivering over a log fire, as in winter, while at another sweat drips from their faces as in the burning heat of summer.[9] On a grander scale, we have seen the insouciance with which Góngora juxtaposes allusions to classical mythology to an account of the near-contemporary voyages of the great discoverers. If the *Soledades* are set in a pastoral Utopia or no-place, then the narrative unfolds in a kind of Uchronia where all sense of time is lost.

The text, like life itself, remains 'open', its possibilities are never closed. It starts *in medias res*, with the rescue of the shipwrecked stranger from the waves, and may thus be said to have neither a true beginning nor end, rather like Borges's *Libro de arena*, which never begins and never ends, but simply goes on unfolding, never becoming stable, finished or closed. Rather it must be seen in terms of perpetual becoming, never reaching static còmpletion, always spurring the reader on to further readings as the text is so obviously incomplete. It can thus permit itself to remain eternally open and inconclusive.

Carlos Fuentes has called Latin American literature a 'peregrinación inconclusa' ('an incomplete pilgrimage'),[10] which might serve as an apt description of the *Soledades*, with their denial of any stable meaning or definitive resolution. To sustain this open-endedness and to prevent textual closure, the *Soledades* display a vital postponement of any revelation, resolution of enigmas, stability, climax or conclusion. In the unceasing shuttle of the play of meanings, ultimately the text surrenders very little, leaving the reader in a state of suspended uncertainty. Indeed, the text becomes a process of endless referral, practising the infinite deferment of any transcendental signified truth, locus or centre. In other words, it becomes a perpetual process of *différance*, Derrida's term combining both 'differing' and 'deferring' ('différer' − 'différance').

Derrida's theory is based on Saussure's insight on the differential, 'diacritical' nature of the linguistic sign: 'Dans la langue il n'y a que des différences *sans termes positifs*' ('In language, there are only differences *without positive terms*'). Thus the 'value' of a sign is not concrete, stable or tangible − 'positif' − but is determined by its functional equivalences, differences and oppositions to other signs surrounding it in a system. So, as Derrida explains, every sign contains a 'trace' of other signs (as every text / reading contains a 'trace' of other texts and readings), never being complete in itself as its identity is disseminated. Meaning is therefore endlessly deferred from sign to sign through time and language. This process, Derrida explains, can never be arrested, as there is no escape from the sign system, nor should it be attempted, as this would be tantamount to a restoration of the 'centre', arresting and foreclosing the infinite play of meaning, 'closing' the text and its potential for further readings, its 'interlecturalité'.[11]

The most straightforward method of postponement is to thwart any quest or project, and it might be said that viewed as a process of *peregrinación* − pilgrimage − the act of postponing haunts the entire text of the *Soledades*. A kind of *décalage* and constant shifting severs any stability and subverts any clear centredness, so that the text refracts into fragmentation, a metamorphic process of perpetual becoming. As it has no centre, it must be seen in terms of a process rather than a finished, canonical end-product or entelechy.

The vital, life-giving *deférrance* becomes the 'suspense' of the text itself, always holding out the allurement of some ultimate meaning or resolution to resolve the tantalising obscurities and enigmas raised. Yet on arrival at the 'end' the hermeneutic 'promise' remains unfulfilled. It remains always deceitfully immanent, perpetually abeyant. The reader thus finds herself engaged on a pursuit of an ever-receding floating centre; the text itself becomes a sort of self-decentring play, an artistic ruse.

The mainspring of the process, then, is a lack, or absence, so that questing after fulfilment may be endlessly perpetuated, generating further meanings or readings, unending textuality. The desire for a centre/presence is a motivating force in the text, but like Freud's 'pleasure principle', were it to find its conclusion, it would cease to generate itself, freezing the play of meaning.

Much has been written about the protagonist of the *Soledades*. Molho describes him as a 'protagoniste mystérieux, spectateur neutre, dont l'intériorité échappe ('a mysterious protagonist, a neutral spectator, whose inwardness escapes us').[12] He is unnamed; when he first appears, it is as the figure of *absence* − 'náufrago y desdeñado sobre *ausente*' − ('*absent*, disdained and shipwrecked') (my emphasis), whose only defining characteristic is that of beauty (in the first of a succession of classical analogies, he is likened to Ganymede, commonest of homosexual icons). He is described variously as 'el peregrino' ('the pilgrim'), 'el forastero' ('the stranger'), 'extranjero errante' ('wandering foreigner'), 'mísero extranjero' ('unhappy foreigner'), 'inconsiderado peregrino' ('unthinking pilgrim'), 'el joven' and 'el mancebo' ('the youth'), 'el caminante' ('the wanderer') and 'el huésped' ('the guest'). Though he is designated as a 'peregrino' ('pilgrim'), no clear goal of his quest is ever specified: he appears passive and directionless, led haphazardly from incident to incident by the rustics he encounters by chance. We never discover precisely who he is, nor why nor what he is fleeing, though belatedly we learn that he is the melancholy victim of an ill-starred love-affair, – which, however, plays no part in the text of the poem. Juan de Jáuregui's judgement of him is particularly biting and dismissive:

> Pasemos luego a la traza de esta fábula o lo que se es: allí sale un mancebito, la principal figura que Vmd nos representa, y no le da nombre. Este fue al mar, y vino del mar, sin que sepáis cómo ni para qué; él no sirve más que de mirón: no dice cosa buena ni mala, ni despega su boca.[13]

> Let us move on to the story of this fable, or whatever it may be: a young spark enters, the principal figure that your Honour presents to us, but he is given no name. This youth went to sea, and came from the sea, without your knowing, either how or why; he is nothing more than a peeping Tom: He says nothing either good or bad, nor indeed opens his mouth.

Vilanova, in his erudite study of the peregrino de amor ('pilgrim of love'), finds his immediate antecedents in the allegorical/sentimental heroes of the Byzantine novel, much in vogue in early seventeenth-century Spain. For him, Góngora's *peregrino* is the representation of Everyman, the human condition, uniting in himself a feeling of yearning and disillusionment, with a desire to flee the world in search of solitude.[14] Like the *Soledades* itself, however, there is a curious incompleteness about the protagonist: he is immature, passive, impersonal and lacking in prudence. To Beverley, the pilgrim 'bears within himself a new sense of *difference* and *absence* a psychic division into opposing or perverted forms' (*Aspects*, p. 29). He is 'at *dis-ease* with his world, at the margin of accepted thought and society' (*ibid.*, p. 65).

The pilgrim is the embodiment of unsatisfied desire, of a quest after fulfilment that is perpetually deferred. I have said the *Soledades* is a text without closure; centreless, mobile, contradictory and polysemic. The inconsistency and 'unrealiability' of the protagonist contributes to this process of decentring: the 'fragmented' protagonist is constantly refracted and disprivileged as a central unity, witholding stability and transcendent meaning from the labile, constantly metamorphosing text. In his blankness, passivity and impersonality, his dubious status as subject of the poem, the *peregrino* is in every way a subversion of conventional conceptions of the hero. He becomes, in this respect, a parody of traditional protagonists.

As such, he diverges sharply from the heroes of Classical antiquity, and is perhaps appealing particularly to a curiously modern taste for the incomplete, the unfulfilled quest. Borges, in a interview with F. Dauster, made this distinction explicit:

> en los libros antiguos, las buscas eran siempre afortunadas: los argonautas conquistaron el vellocino y Galahad el Santo Grial. Ahora, en cambio, agrada misteriosamente el concepto de una busca infinita, o de la busca de una cosa que, hallada, tiene consecuencias funestas.[15]

> In ancient texts, quests were always successful: the Argonauts captured the Golden Fleece, and Galahad the Holy Grail. Nowadays, on the other hand, the concept of an endless quest, or the search for something which, when found, has fatal consequences, is mysteriously pleasing.

It is interesting that Góngora should inscribe over the figure of the *peregrino* a palimpsest of allusions to rash, ill-fated adolescents of Classical mythology: Ganymede, Arion, Icarus, Cadmus, Adonis, Acteon, Pyramus, Narcissus. He is thereby inserted within the paradigm of archetypes of disaster/death precipitated by an excess of desire.

Góngora's fondness for Classical allusion is well known: the text of the *Soledades* is encrusted with a richly-jewelled tissue of Classical reference. Yet even here, Góngora's tendency to capricious and creative subversiveness is at work. His joyous capacity for the debunking of Classical myth, evidenced by his famous burlesque *romance* on the deaths of Hero and Leander, is vigorously present in the *Soledades*, as the description of the overweight cowherd as an 'Icaro montañés' ('a mountain Icarus') demonstrates. The deflation of the dignity of Classical allusion is most frequently the function of the incongruity of the referent to the signified. The educated seventeenth-century reader must surely have winced to see the epithet typically applied to the hero of the *Aeneid, pius*, in the formula '*pius Aeneas*', reduced to bathos as the term descriptive of a mere broken plank, a 'breve tabla', which in the preceding line at the beginning of the first *Soledades* is qualified as a '*piadoso* miembro roto' i.e. the pitying (but also *pious*, with all the attendant connotations of filial piety, as in the case of Aeneas), broken branch of a pine tree. The inversion of the classical model goes further, since Aeneas received his epithet because he rescued his father by carrying him on his back from the conflagration of burning Troy, whereas the mundane broken plank has performed the function of rescuing the *peregrino* not from fire, but from *water* − the sea.

Typically, Góngora's technique is, as here, that of the inversion of terms, as in describing a ship as a 'vaga Clicie del viento' ('vague Clytie of the breeze'). Where the nymph Clytie was metamorphosed into a heliotrope, so that she might follow the course of her beloved (visible) Apollo, the sun throughout the day, the ship is like Clytie only in that it *follows* one of the natural elements, the wind (invisible, intangible) in its sails.

Sometimes the effects of such inversion are more searching and wide-reaching. The *peregrino*, snatched from death at the beginning of the *Soledades*, is haunted by its shadow throughout the poem, as his lament in lines 116−171 of the second *Soledad* makes eloquently plain. He is likened to Narcissus, and like him is in love with his own image. But Góngora does not simply recapitulate the traditional myth of the relation between Narcissus and the nymph Echo, he reinvents it. John Brenkman, in his analysis of the treatment of the Narcissus myth in Ovid's *Metamorphoses*,[15] states that 'Ovid's narrative does not ... supply a set of stable meanings that can serve to anchor another text's thematic organization ... it situates its central characters, Narcissus and Echo, in a way that allows contradictory interpretations of their relation to one another' (p. 293). The stories of Narcissus and Echo fall into a pattern of parallelism, in that each character is drawn towards death when desire is not reciprocated by another. For Echo, the other is another like herself, while for Narcissus the other is his mirror image. Associated with each character is a form of repetition or duplication: the *verbal* repetition of Echo's voice and the *visual* repetition of Narcissus's reflection. Within the parallels, however, operate a series of differences: Echo is condemned to be incapable of independent verbal articulation; she must always repeat another's speech regardless of its relation to her own thought, so that there is always the danger that she will be prevented from saying what she intends or means. In her 'dialogue' with Narcissus, by repeating only the latter part of Narcissus's phrases, she thereby changes their intended meaning. So, Narcissus's 'huc coeamus' ('here let us meet') is repeated as the much more suggestive 'coeamus' ('let us come together/copulate'). To his 'ante emoriat quam sit tibi copia nostri' ('may I die before my abundance is yours'), she returns 'sit tibi copia nostri' ('let my abundance be yours'). Now what makes Echo's words her own – *sua verba, verbis suis* – is the deception, the 'blindness' that makes Narcissus fail to recognise these words as his own.

Self-recognition is however crucial to the process of Narcissus's falling in love with his own image. The blind seer Tiresias had prophesied that the youth would live to old age 'si se no noverit' ('if he does not know himself'). Seeing his own image reflected in the water, Narcissus makes the crucial statement: 'iste ego sum' ('I am that one'), marking the moment when he not only recognises the image as image, but also *recognises himself* (as image). What is impossible in the encounter with his own reflection is dialogue (because his reflected image is of course mute), so that the experience of the moment of self-recognition becomes an ironic reversal of the encounter with Echo.

Now in Góngora's lapidary reformulation of the myth, it is the allurements of court that encourage the courtier, that modern Narcissus, to pursue Echo and disdain fountains/springs: 'ecos solicitar, desdeñar *fuentes*' (*Soledad* I, I.114, my emphasis). The traditional myth of Narcissus and Echo offers parallels that allow their stories to intersect in a way which gives meaning to their difference. In Góngora's inversion of the myth, it is plain that *his* Narcissus rejects self-recognition and self-knowledge in favour of the deceiving echoes of flattery. By so doing, he collapses and inverts the hierarchy that privileges *vox* (which in the traditional myth of Echo was immortal) over *imago* (dependent on the body, and therefore mortal). Language is plural, mobile, volatile: meanings can therefore never be stable but are relational, differential, always pregnant with the possibility of treachery and self-deception. A further change in the traditional myth reinforces the inversion. Originally, Narcissus saw his image reflected in a pool; in Góngora this becomes 'fuentes' (fountains/springs), entailing connotations of the source of both life and truth, precisely the certainty and 'truth' that is inaccessible to language.

In Góngora's *Soledades* canonical values are constantly subverted, contradiction and play between elements never stops; the text is at every moment metamorphosing, so that no one state can ever attain stable being long enough to establish itself. In the *Soledades*, nothing is immutable, all boundaries and dualities unpredictably slide into each other in the play of textuality and literary self-reflexiveness. The verbal play of the *Soledades* is an unceasing process of construction and deconstruction, alternating destruction and creation. In this respect, it recalls Nietzsche's seminal vision of the play of the artist, innocent of judgement or moral bias, impelled by an ever-renewed desire to create: 'A Becoming and a Passing, a building and destroying, without any moral bias is in this world only the play of the artist and the child.'[16]

Notes

1 Francisco Cascales, *Cartas filológicas*, Madrid, 1959, II, p. 186.

2 *Examen del Antídoto: Apología por la 'Soledad' de Don Luis de Góngora, contra el autor del Antídoto*, in M. Artigas, *Don Luis de Góngora. Biografía y Estudio crítico*, Madrid, 1925, Appendix VII, p. 424.

3 'Jáuregui's charge of inconsistent decorum in the *Soledades* is strictly correct, but also ... this dissonance was *intended* by Góngora.' *Aspects of Góngora's 'Soledades'*, Amsterdam, 1980, p. 62.

4 Robert Jammes, *Etudes sur l'oeuvre poétique de D. Luis de Góngora*, Bordeaux, 1967; Dámaso Alonso, *Estudios y ensayos gongorinos*, Madrid, 1960; John Beverley, *op. cit.* and Introduction to Luis de Góngora, *Soledades*, Madrid, 1979; 'Barroco de estado. Góngora y el gongorismo', in *Del 'Lazarillo' al Sandinismo*, Minneapolis, 1987.

5 Maurice Molho, *Sémantique et poétique. A propos des 'Soledades' de Góngora*, Bordeaux, 1969.

6 'Barthes, Góngora and non-sense', *Publications of the Modern Language Association* 1986, 102; *The Body Hispanic: Gender and Sexuality in Spanish and Spanish American Literature*, Oxford, 1989.

7 Translations of the *Soledades* are taken from Edward Meryon Wilson, *The Solitudes of D. Luis de Góngora*, Cambridge, 1965.

8 Leo Spitzer, 'La *Soledad primera* de Góngora: notas críticas y explicativas a la nueva edición de Dámaso Alonso', *Revista de Filología Hispánica*, II, 1940: 171–2.

9 Ana Martínez Arancón (ed.), *La batalla en torno a Góngora*, Madrid, 1978, p. 189.

10 *La nueva novela hispanoamericana*, Mexico, 1969, p. 67.

11 Jacques Derrida, *De la grammatologie*, Paris, 1967, Paris, 1972.

12 Molho, 1969, pp. 35–6.

13 *Antídoto contra las 'Soledades' aplicado a su autor para defenderle de sí mismo* (1614), in J. Jordán de Urriés, *Biografía y estudio crítico de Jáuregui*, Madrid, 1899, p. 150.

14 Antonio Vilanova, 'El peregrino de amor en las *Soledades* de Góngora, *Estudios dedicados a Menéndez Pidal*, III, Madrid, 1952, pp. 421–60.

15 Quoted in D. L. Shaw, *Borges: Ficciones*, London, 1976, p. 18.

16 John Brenkman, 'Narcissus in the text', *Georgia Review*, XXX, 1976: 293–327.

17 F. W. Nietzsche, *Philosophy during the Tragic Age of the Greeks* (1873), *Early Greek Philosophy and other Essays*, trans. M. Mugge, Edinburgh, 1911, p. 107.

INDEX